Speech—Interpersonal Communication

Speech—Interpersonal Communication

GORDON WISEMAN

Ohio University

LARRY BARKER

Purdue University

CHANDLER PUBLISHING COMPANY

124 Spear Street, San Francisco, California 94105

Science Research Associates, Inc., 259 East Erie Street, Chicago, Illinois 60611
A Subsidiary of IBM

Dedicated to the two J's

Judy and Jeanne

CONTENTS

vii

PREFACE

Much of the recent knowledge in the areas of communication and general semantics has brought greater understanding to students of speech and/or communication. Often this information has not been integrated into contemporary speech textbooks or has not been reduced to the practical level. The authors have a firm conviction that training students in the skills of public speaking is only one of the goals of the speech teacher. College graduates will be called upon many times to give public speeches, but an even more extensive part of their lives will involve day-to-day communication. Thus every effort must be expended to train individuals to communicate effectively on an interpersonal and intrapersonal basis. Communication is not an act which should be isolated to the classroom or the platform. It is a vital force in the everyday affairs of each individual, involving some precepts which can be taught and others which must be caught. Thus the authors view public speaking as interpersonal communication.

Basic to the entire art of communication is the individual's inherent need to understand himself and to communicate within himself. As he communicates within himself he is able to understand what he means, and from this basis he can interpret the events that occur about him. Consequently, he understands more fully the self-expressions of others, and attempts to express himself more effectively. In the study of communication it is imperative that the individual first know his own basis of operation or his life orientation. As he understands himself and begins to understand the life orientations of others, he is then able to complete the communication cycle which brings about his desired response.

All phases of the communication process must be emphasized. These phases are pictorialized in this text through two idealized communication models developed by the authors. The first describes the process of intrapersonal communication, or that which takes place within the communicator. The second describes the dynamics of interpersonal communication, or communication between two or more individuals. These models have been designed to help the student of public speaking learn how the communication process relates to his realm of personal experience.

In this book the traditional rhetorical concepts have been used as a foundation upon which to base newer communication precepts. These communication precepts are placed in perspectives suitable for the beginning speech student. The eclectic approach incorporated in this work is derived primarily from the areas of general semantics, creative problem solving, guidance, and social psychology as well as speech. With these areas in mind the authors have developed, specifically for students, a practical approach to communication.

The text has several unique features. One is a programed section on listening which has been incorporated into Chapter 11, "The Responding Communicator." This instructional program has been used extensively by the authors in their courses and has been tested and validated.[1]

Another feature is the inclusion of materials on communication evaluation. Chapter 7, on communication evaluation, is designed for conventional speech classes with an emphasis on communication. In addition, a special section on speech evaluation which incorporates a brief survey of research and writings in the area of evaluation is included. This section is designed for classes utilizing student evaluations as well as for classes emphasizing the importance of communication evaluation. The

---

[1] Larry L. Barker and Gordon Wiseman, "A Comparative Study of Recall and Recognition Produced through Programed Instruction and Lectures on Listening When Time Is Constant," *Central States Speech Journal,* Vol. XVI, No. 2 (May, 1965), pp. 140–141.

synthesis of research and suggested readings should be especially helpful to those colleges and universities utilizing peer-group instruction, since evaluation is the basis of the peer-group method.

A special unit on nonverbal communication is incorporated in Chapter 10, "Communication without Words." This area is vital to communication theory and is much broader than the use of gestures and visual aids. Theory and research in kinesics (human nonverbal communication) aids the communicator in receiving more meaningful messages and can help eliminate many breakdowns in communication.

Terminology developed in the new areas of communication has been utilized to expand and clarify traditional concepts. This terminology has been used in the sense of a new breed, spawned by old and contemporary concepts, rather than the clothing of old ideas with new words. This terminology has been established to help the individual adjust to his ever-changing world. Man is truly a dynamic process in a dynamic environment; in order for communication to occur, both the originating communicator and the responding communicator must not only be cognizant of their changing world, but must have the tools to implement their knowledge.

The material presented here is the result of actual classroom experimentation. Whenever possible, illustrations have been drawn from the classroom experience with the life orientation of college students kept foremost in mind. This text is designed to satisfy the needs of courses in the fundamentals of speech and public speaking which train students to communicate on an interpersonal level.

ACKNOWLEDGMENTS

Many friends and colleagues have aided in the creation of this book. We acknowledge gratefully the innumerable influences of teachers we have had and books we have studied. We are especially indebted to our wives, who have patiently checked the manuscript, provided new insights into the material, and supplied needed encouragement to bring the ideas to fruition.

We extend our appreciation to Philip Emmert III, who during the preliminary planning shared in some of the discussions concerning certain concepts which were later incorporated by the authors into the manuscript for the textbook and an earlier workbook. Our thanks to Richard Behnke who aided in the design of the communication models. We are grateful to Mrs. Rene Erickson and Mrs. Roy Amore, who spent hours reading earlier drafts and giving helpful suggestions. Our gratitude also goes to several people who typed the different drafts of the manuscript, including Ingrid Carlson and Mary Lou Griffin, but especially to Mrs. Roy Ambrester, who typed the final draft.

A special dedication is made to our students, who have helped us test ideas, given us many helpful suggestions, and suffered from neglect while we were completing the book. To the great host of others who must remain unnamed because we are unaware of their specific contributions to our thinking, we are deeply grateful. Of course, we take final responsibility for any errors or omissions in the manuscript.

G.W.
L.B.

Speech—Interpersonal Communication

Communication: Preview | 1

Man is a communicator. He has the desire as well as the ability to communicate. This ability includes not only the physical mechanism in terms of vocal folds, resonators, and articulators, but the distinctive capacity to symbolize. He is able to assign a symbol to an object, to recognize that object through the symbol as it has been used in the past, to identify the object in relationship to other objects, and to predict future events surrounding that object.

The ability to symbolize is at the heart of the communicative process. Symbols are the tools of the process, but man's distinct ability to interpret, manipulate, and make new symbols is the product of the process. Animals convey messages by using sound and gesture, but never by using meaningful words. Man alone is able to refine his message and to pass it along. Alfred Korzybski suggests that man's ability to symbolize makes him a *time-binder*.[1] Time-binding refers to man's ability to pass on knowledge from generation to generation and from culture to culture. Man does not have to start each generation anew. He is able to take the knowledge of the past, check it against present facts and predict the future. Time-binding is the one characteristic that clearly distinguishes man from all other forms of life. Because of this ability, he is able to control and change his environment to a greater degree than can other forms of life.

Those who have hunted rabbits are well aware of the amazing

---

[1] Alfred Korzybski, *Science and Sanity,* 4th ed. (Lakeville, Conn.: Institute of General Semantics, 1958), pp. 223–224.

way that nature protects the rabbit. When danger approaches, the rabbit freezes in his tracks and it is almost impossible to see him because of protective covering. However, when this same rabbit is on the highway and danger approaches, freezing in his tracks means his death, not his protection. A mother rabbit can watch this tragic scene but does not have the ability to interpret the incident or to pass an interpretation on to her young. Man does have this ability, and symbolization is the means at his disposal to accomplish this task. It is his most valuable tool and weapon, useful and dangerous both to himself and to others.

THE DEVELOPMENT OF COMMUNICATION

Perhaps "In the beginning was the word . . ." was true in the sense that man was not man until he spoke. Man is a dominion haver, a namer, and a predicator. Man was to have dominion over the animals and they were to be subservient to him in spite of the fact that man is one of the most defenseless of earth's creatures. The normal means by which animals protect themselves, such as claws, teeth, hoofs, and hide, are in man insufficient to protect him. How does this relatively helpless creature survive? Man survives by his ability to use his head—the brain that he has been given. This unique survival mechanism is implemented through his symbol-using capacity. With the power to manipulate words, and so to reason on many levels, he surmounts the need for fangs and armor.

Man's brain is extremely complex. There are from 10 to 15 billion nerve cells in the normal brain. A simple computer has only about 23,000 valves. The brain contains more nerve lines than all the telephone lines in the world put together. The electrical signals from your brain come from 200,000 living thermometer cells, a half-million pressure-sensing cells, and 3 or 4 million pain-sensing cells, or as responses to signals from the eyes, ears, and nose, as well as the areas sensitive to taste and touch. As an amazing example of miniaturization, the brain sorts, stores, and acts upon myriad impulses. To build a computer to equal the brain's potential would be fantastic. It would require many city blocks to house such a computer, and the waters of Niagara to cool it. Yet all that such a machine could do, and much more, goes on gently in every human head, using very little energy and generating almost no heat. The brain weighs only 50 ounces, and occupies a volume of about $1\frac{1}{2}$ quarts. The quarter inch of its cortex not only enables man to have dominion over animals, but gives him the ability to learn and enables him to symbolize the ideas that are created by the brain. Thus he is able to mediate human behavior by learned abstractions, carried on invisibly in the central nervous system. Symbolization and the formation of social groups permit the transmission of information from one generation to the next. The time-binding process is possible only because man can give a thing a name.

Man's ability to give names to things, events, and qualities and to see relationships has provided him with an objective framework and a technique for communicating. Because of this power of symbolization man is able to hold several events and conditions in consciousness and deal with them abstractly by means of their names. The ability to symbolize has its drawbacks as well as its assets; much of Chapter 5 discusses this process of symbolization. Without names, organized warfare would be virtually impossible. Much of the pain and misery of the world today can be attributed to the misinterpretation and manipulation of words. On the positive side, it is language, the highest achievement of the symbolic mind, that sets man apart from the animal kingdom. An individual's concept of the world is intimately related to the nature of his language.

If it is language that gives man his unique place in nature, then it is man's ability to predicate that allows him to function in the world. The ability to predicate makes each individual an independent, self-conscious monitor, reponsible for his own survival and welfare. Man is not only able to describe objects in the past or in faraway places, but he is able to predict certain events to come, either as a result of his own articulate knowing and thinking or through an assimilation of ideas communicated to him. At the present time, with the help of machines, man has developed this ability to the point of being able to predict 2 hours after the polls close who will win an election, or to estimate the number of automobiles which will be produced in any given year. This ability lets man live a broader kind of life in addition to the anatomical and physiological life of the body. He can conduct himself in accordance with articulate reason or logic as well as by conditioned response.

The ability to predicate makes organization possible so that man is able to provide for the present and future needs of himself and others. On the personal level man signs contracts, enters into agreements, and controls his future behavior because of this ability to predicate. Man, in the language of general semantics, makes maps of territories that do not even exist. Communication holds society together, and communication by means of language is man's distinctive activity. Others may argue about how man acquired this ability. One of the purposes of this text is to interpret man's unique ability to symbolize and to show its relationship to communication. This ability is an integral part of man's orientation to reality and results in his continuous unimpeded flow of articulate knowing, thinking, communicating, and organizing.

THE IMPORTANCE OF COMMUNICATION TO THE INDIVIDUAL

Communication is the primary means of socialization of the individual. As a person becomes increasingly active as a member of his community, communication plays a larger role not only in his social life but in his personal behavior, feelings, and thoughts. Personal interaction is the basis for growth. Communication is the means by which human beings interact. Communication is as important to social growth as food is to physical growth.

Physical, social, and mental existence depend upon communication. Each affects the other until it would be foolish to try to distinguish where one begins and the other leaves off. Communication shapes personality and personality determines the pattern of communication. Elwood Murray emphasizes this connection between speech and personality. He stresses the idea that training in communication can do much to enhance the total personality. It is not enough for a student to possess brilliance of intellect, have an understanding of the social and economic world, have an appreciation of the finer things of literature, music, and the arts, but he must understand communication if he is going to contribute to the society in which he lives. Furthermore, communication is the major means through which the total personality expresses itself in social relations. Dr. Murray continues to discuss the close interaction of communication which makes personality possible and then defines speech as "a tool of social adjustment, which reflects the efficient personality, and as a psychological and sociological technique of modifying human behavior by means of body, voice, thought, and language." [2] There is not much question but that communication and personality grow, develop, differentiate, and become refined together.

Man has not only the desire but also the need to communicate. Man is a social being, and he cannot interact without communicating. For too many years teachers of speech have emphasized "public speaking" and have not stressed other communication needs. For most individuals there are few instances in each day when there is not some desire or need to communicate. Communication varies in importance, but often a breakdown in a minor communication situation can create major problems.

An encounter with a college roommate may seem unimportant at the moment but, if there is a breakdown, seeds of bitterness can make it important later. Successful communication in a casual encounter between boy and girl may lead to a desire to know each other better and may ultimately end in a lifelong communication encounter. As you study the ideas in this text try to implement them in your everyday living. Your room, the classroom, organizations to which you belong—all are laboratories in communication if you would use them as such. Observe your own communication and that of others so that you can make corrections while you are in this training period.

Too often people think that only politicians and preachers need to know how to communicate. However, the communication needs of most individuals are just as great as those of either of these types of communicators. An individual may never en-

---

[2] Elwood Murray, *The Speech Personality* (New York: J. B. Lippincott Company, 1944), p. 10.

counter the number of people that the preacher or politican does, but the successful communicative act is just as important for the individual's survival and well-being. Communication in the home among members of the family determines not only the outlook on life but also the success of the unit. The oft repeated statement "I cannot talk to my children" does not mean the parent does not have the vocal ability but rather that he feels he can no longer communicate with the children. Very often children turn to others for help because they are not able to communicate with their parents.

No matter what phase of public life one examines, examples of the need for communication are ever present. The school board does not communicate to the people and the tax levy fails. The senator is unable to communicate with his constituency, and he fails to be re-elected, even though he might be a good senator. An applicant fails to communicate with his prospective employer, and does not get the job. Perhaps he is a better mechanic than the man who got the job, but he did not get the chance to prove this. Many interviews are for the purpose of seeing just how well the person can communicate. The employer has the records; he now wants to see which applicant is the better communicator.

No matter what the level of man's existence, he is confronted with the need to communicate. His private and public success is determined by his ability to "sell himself"—to communicate. Even the researcher who hides himself away from the world must ultimately communicate his findings or his work is in vain. Thus communication is important for man's survival regardless of the smallness or greatness of the situation, or the amount, kind, or level of communication.

COMMUNICATION DEFINED

Communication has been defined by many people in many different ways, but a look at some of the key ideas found in most of the definitions will help to form a working definition. Some of these key words are *interaction, relationship, integration, process,* and *influence. Interaction* implies that more than one element is involved and that the elements are not static but are changing and interacting. *Relationship* suggests a sorting of elements to find common concerns or likenesses. *Integration* suggests a pulling together of the common elements toward a single objective or goal. *Process* suggests growth, development, changes which move toward a central objective. *Influence* suggests an ultimate contact, an evaluation as to whether communication was successful. Thus a working definition might be that communication is a process which involves a series of interactions where relationships are discovered and integrated towards a specific objective, that of trying to influence one another. The kind of communication and the level on which it is employed will be determined by the objective of the communication.

LEVELS OF COMMUNICATION

Communication may be categorized in many ways with divisions and subdivisions. The generally accepted levels of communication include intrapersonal, interpersonal, mass, and cultural. These four levels will provide the scope needed to understand the process. However, people communicate on many levels, for many reasons, with many people, in many ways. As you look back on even a part of your day you will find many examples. Your first communication encounter probably was your alarm clock which communicated to you that it was time to get up (nonverbal communication). As you awoke, in your mind you ran through the coming events of the day (intrapersonal communication). The trip to the shower brought your first interpersonal communication as you greeted others and they greeted you. You talked about the weather, tests coming up, and other things (meta communication). As you turned on the shower and found only cold water (chemical communication), you inferred that they must be doing dishes in the cafeteria.

As you started back to your room a friend motioned to you (gestural communication) and you discussed some of the ideas that your committee is working on. Walking to your room you made the decision about what to wear. One outfit you enjoyed but it is not worn on campus (cultural communication) so you decided on something else. Turning on the radio you picked up the news (mass communication) and weather. You left a note for your roommate (written communication) and as you left your room your stomach growled (physical communication) and you decided to try to get some breakfast.

The line was long so you began to discuss with those around you how the service could be improved (group communication) and you finally decided to write a letter to the school paper (written communication) and see if you could get some action on the slow service. As you approached the serving table the smell of bacon (chemical communication) made you hungry for bacon and eggs. A short interpersonal communication encounter assured you that there was bacon but no eggs, so you settled for bacon and French toast. Breakfast finished, a quick glance at your watch (visual communication) told you that you must hurry to make your first class. Your communication day was just started. These ideas are just a few examples of the many interactions in your day that involve communication. Some of the following definitions will aid you as you interpret your actions for a normal day.

INTRAPERSONAL COMMUNICATION

Intrapersonal communication is that communication which takes place within an individual. Communication on this level forms the basis for evaluative ability and handles reactions to events, ideas, and experiences.

The subjective reality is formed on the intrapersonal level by the kind of communicating one does with oneself. Patterns for handling interpersonal communication are formed on the intrapersonal level. A great deal of attention must be given to this level if communication is to be successful. Intrapersonal communication is the base of operation for all communication—the reflection area for ideas, thoughts, and feelings, and primarily for interpersonal communication.

INTERPERSONAL COMMUNICATION

Interpersonal communication is that communication or interaction that takes place between two or more persons. This is the level of communication that takes place every day as mother and child or boyfriend and girlfriend communicate, or the communication that takes place in the family, church, classroom, or fraternity. Relationships are formed at this level and are maintained by continuing interpersonal communication. In terms of your individual happiness and welfare, the most serious breakdowns occur at this level. Communication should be kept on a level of ideas and not personalities. However, very often one's personality does become involved and when this happens it is not easy to back down because to do so would mean a "loss of face." A breakdown can come about in varying degrees of seriousness. It may be a momentary incident that will be forgotten within the hour, or it may be remembered for the lifetime of the communicators involved.

The factor that complicates the picture is that the situation may be considered a tragedy by one person and never be given a second thought by the other. This difference in feeling often brings the accusation, "You showed me no understanding. What is more, you did not even seem to care." This seeming lack of understanding makes the gulf seem more vast. If the desire to communicate is strong enough, the difference may be resolved, but if not, the irritation may remain and will often exhibit its ugly head in devious ways of getting even. A large percentage of your day is spent communicating on the interpersonal level. This is the level that you should constantly analyze if you want to be a successful communicator.

MASS COMMUNICATION

The intrapersonal and interpersonal levels of communication are basic to all communication. From these two points one can move to levels of group or mass communications or on to cultural levels of communication. Mass communication involves one speaking to many, rather than many or a mass speaking to one. When speaking of the *mass media* as communication the letter *s* is added to the word *communication* to distinguish it from communication on other levels. Most studies in this field suggest that for mass communications to be successful it must seem like interpersonal communication. Popular radio and television personalities have had the ability to make their audiences feel that they were being talked to personally and not just as masses of people. The story is told of a little boy so engrossed in a program that when he met the performer, who asked what his name was, he answered in amazement, "Why, you don't even remember me." Listeners who discuss these personalities often speak of them as friends. The instantaneous transmission of events makes this area of communication an important one for study.

CULTURAL COMMUNICATION

Cultural communication is that communication concerned with elements of the culture. It may include one culture communicating with another or the culture communicating to one individual on the intrapersonal or interpersonal level. Cultural exchanges in art, music, and dance are often encouraged so that there may be better communication among peoples of the world. This can be done on the mass communication level when a Russian ballet troupe communicates to an audience in New York City, or on the interpersonal level when a Russian family visits an American home in Portsmouth, Ohio. The common goal in cultural communication is to expedite better communication on all levels.

Your culture communicates to you what you should wear, eat, do, and so on. Most of your habits, customs, beliefs, and manners of doing things are communicated to you by your culture. A communication breakdown can come about when you associate with people of different cultures on an interpersonal level, and a breakdown on the intrapersonal level can be caused when you decide you are not going to listen to the dictates of your culture. Some of these breakdowns occur when you move from one culture to the other and do not make an adequate adjustment. The college man says, "Certainly I have a black umbrella here at school, but I would not be caught dead with one back home." As a student moves from the culture of the college campus to the culture of his home, adjustments must be made on the intrapersonal and interpersonal level. Cultural communication and mass communications are all worthy areas for study, but in the final analysis your basic concerns are on the intrapersonal and interpersonal levels. The focus of this text is placed on these two levels because through them interaction with society is made possible. Every kind of communication is filtered through your intrapersonal communication and then implemented on an interpersonal level.

The implementation of communication may be classified as verbal or as nonverbal. The basic emphasis is on verbal communication, which in its larger aspect includes writing, reading, speaking, and listening. Chapter 10 relates some important ideas concerning nonverbal communication. This area is worthy of study because it often aids in interpreting meaning, which may be unclear in verbal communication.

Communication is a process concerned with all situations involving meaning. It is the means by which you make evaluations and determine relationships. Thus communication is concerned with your attempt (1) to express yourself to others or to tell others what you mean (interpersonal communication), (2) to understand the expression of others or determine what they mean (interpersonal communication), (3) to interpret the world and events around you or to determine the meaning of things (cultural communication), and (4) to understand or to decide what you mean (intrapersonal communication).

QUESTIONS FOR DISCUSSION

1. What are some occupations in which communication plays a major role?

2. What cultural patterns are involved in communication on the campus?

3. In what ways does communication affect personality and personality affect communication?

EXERCISES

[Forms for completing the exercises marked with an asterisk are supplied in *Worksheets for Speech—Interpersonal Communication* (San Francisco: Chandler Publishing Company, 1967).]

1. In order of preference, list the five most important aspects of your life, then determine the part that communication plays in each.*

2. Find an example where a communicator failed in the purposes

intended and analyze the communication to discover reasons for the failure.*

3. Keep a list of your major interpersonal encounters during one day and estimate the part communication played in each encounter.

4. From your communication today, pick out three illustrations where your decisions determined behavior for the future.

5. Make a list of cues that a speaker would expect to receive as feedback from a responding communicator. Determine what these cues might mean. Let someone else give his interpretation of these cues.

6. Give a number of illustrations showing the "time-binding" characteristics of our language.

7. What are four ways that you carry on communication with yourself?

8. Contrast and compare the process of learning and the process of communicating.

9. Study college life and make a list of the ways this culture affects your communication.

10. Make a list of the items you spend time talking to yourself about; discuss these items with a close friend and see if he changes your point of view.

SUGGESTED READINGS

Berlo, David K., *The Process of Communication*. New York: Holt, Rinehart, and Winston, Inc., 1960. Chapter 1, "Communication: Scope and Purpose," pp. 1–21.

Cherry, Colin, "Communication Theory and Human Behavior," *Studies in Communication*. London: Martin, Secker and Warburg, 1955, pp. 45–67.

———, *On Human Communication*. New York: John Wiley and Sons, Inc., 1957.

Haney, William V., *Communication, Patterns and Incidents*. Homewood, Ill.: Richard D. Irwin, Inc., 1961. Chapter 1, "Introduction," pp. 1–4; Chapter 2, "Misevaluation and Miscommunication," pp. 5–11.

Miller, George A., *Language and Communication*. New York: McGraw-Hill Book Company, Inc., 1951. Chapter 1, "By Way of Introduction," pp. 1–9; Chapter 12, "The Social Approach," pp. 249–275.

Murray, Elwood, *The Speech Personality*. New York: J. B. Lippincott Company, 1944. Chapter 1, "How Your Speech Personality Develops," pp. 1–16.

Smith, Alfred G. (ed.), *Communication and Culture*. New York: Holt, Rinehart and Winston, Inc., 1966.

Communication: Overview | 2

Communication is a dynamic process. Because of the human variable, the relative nature of matter, and the transformations in language, change and communication go together. This dynamic concept of change is an important one for you as a student of communication to master, for unless you accept the fact that situations change, you may become enslaved in habitual channels. You may be ineffective in your communication because you fail to realize that one listener hears you differently from another or, what is more likely, you may forget that the same listener may hear you differently upon different occasions.

Not only do human biases and self-interests affect perception, but physical properties cause changes to occur within the communication setting. A large room imposes different demands upon communicators than does a small room. A well-ventilated room causes you to communicate differently than does a stuffy room. Noises outside and within the room affect the way you must transmit your messages, not only from word to word but also from moment to moment. Communicators must consider the fact that human beings and physical factors change in order to achieve successful communication. One of the best ways to understand this dynamic nature of communication is by studying models of the communication process.

COMMUNICATION MODELS

Communication models serve three main purposes: (1) They describe the process of communication, (2) they show visual relationships, and (3) they aid in finding and in correcting communication breakdowns. Thus communication models are designed to help the student of public speaking improve his own intrapersonal and interpersonal communication.

A communication model is similar in nature to other types of models with which you may be familiar. It is a representation of the process of communication in the same sense that a model car is a representation of the original car. The use of various types of models in instruction is not new. The early speech teachers in Greece required their students to study the style and delivery of the great orators of their day and to attempt to imitate their presentations. Through observing these model speakers, the students could learn the elements of successful communication and adapt the observed techniques to their own speeches.

Aristotle, the famed philosopher and rhetorician, is credited with formulating the first verbal communication model. In his *Rhetoric,* he wrote that three elements are basic to any communication: a speaker, a message, and a listener. A pictorialization of his model is shown in Fig. 1.

SPEAKER   (MESSAGE)   LISTENER

FIGURE 1.   ARISTOTLE'S COMMUNICATION MODEL

Though many communication models have been developed since this verbal one by Aristotle, they still contain the same three basic components. There must be a source for the message, a message to send, and someone to receive the message.

CONTEMPORARY MODELS

Contemporary students of communication classify models in two different ways. The first is according to type and the second is according to purpose. Smith, drawing from other authors, classified models into four general types—iconic or physical models, verbal-pictorial models, analogues, and symbolic models.[1]

---

[1] Ronald L. Smith, "General Models of Communication." Report presented at the 1962 summer conference of the National Society for the Study of Communication, pp. 1–5.

These types of models are classified in order as they progress from less abstract to more abstract representations.

Briefly, iconic models are physical representations of objects or processes.[2] Voodoo dolls are iconic models in that they are miniature replicas of the people they represent. Other iconic models may be found in books and magazines in the form of pictures, or in art galleries in the form of painting and sculpture. Iconic models are usually scaled up or down according to the dimensions of the object which the model represents.

Verbal-pictorial models are used to clarify or emphasize concepts and processes. The verbal portion of the model is amplified by a graphic or pictorial representation of the words themselves. This pictorialization helps to reinforce the words and make the process being described more meaningful. The communication models which are discussed in this chapter will be of the verbal-pictorial type.

Since it is impossible to describe all the characteristics of an event or object, the verbal-pictorial model must often be expanded. The analogue extends this model by substituting one property or characteristic of one object for another. The most common type of analogue is the map where the different colors stand for different types of terrain, roads, and towns. Graphs and charts are common types of pictorial analogues in that they represent properties in different forms. Murray states:

> Models, which are only very careful analogies, are useful for the discovery of hypotheses and not for the verification of theories. Although all analogies are "false" . . . some are less so than others. . . . Experience in related areas where the relationships are known seems to be the only basis that we have for exploring and describing some of the darker corners of the caverns of communication processes and behaviors.[3]

Another type, the symbolic model, is most commonly found in the realm of mathematics. The symbolic model is formed by

---

[2] See Irwin B. J. Bross, *Design for Decision* (New York: The Macmillan Company, 1953), pp. 162–165.

[3] Elwood Murray, "Future Directions in Communication Research: An Assessment of the Possible Use of Analogues," *The Journal of Communication,* Vol. 11 (March, 1961), p. 3.

substituting symbols for the objects they represent. For example, the equation for determining the area of a circle (πr^2) is a symbolic model. Symbolic models are used for purposes of efficiency. It is often easier to work with symbols than with the actual objects.

At this point you should recognize that language itself is a symbolic model. You use word symbols to represent objects, ideas, emotions, and events. Language is a convenient symbolic model which enables you to expand your experiences beyond that which you perceive with your senses. Additional explanations of these ideas are found in Chapter 5.

The second classification of models is according to purpose. It is beyond the scope of this text to provide a comprehensive treatment of the purposes of models but a brief discussion is presented to assist you in understanding the models presented. Most models of the communication process may be termed "idealized" in that they assert what communication should and would be if all specified and unspecified variables were operating simultaneously in the communication system. The primary value of such models is for instructional purposes; they provide an illustration of the dynamics of the communication process while permitting an examination of the visual relationships among specific variables which operate in the process.

Another purpose of communication models is to describe a process as it occurs, hopefully as a result of observation and research. These idealized models serve as reflections of theories about the communication process. For a list of the most widely known idealized communication models consult the suggested readings at the end of this chapter. Keep in mind that these models are theoretical in nature. The models presented in this section have been developed to provide a framework for understanding the processes of intrapersonal communication and interpersonal communication, and to serve as bases for further investigation of the communication process throughout the remainder of the text.

Do not try to classify or pigeonhole each communication situation into the terms of the model, but rather try to apply the knowledge of communication gained from these models to practical everyday communicating situations. Theoretical knowledge of models void of practical application is of little value.

Before proceeding with an explanation of more complex models it will be easier if you begin by studying a basic idealized model developed by Wilbur Schramm.[4]

SCHRAMM'S MODEL

Wilbur Schramm is one of the foremost authors in the field of communication theory. His model is probably one of the best known of the more than 20 developed. The Schramm model is basic and lacks complexity. Although it is not the first contemporary model, it is chosen because it is representative of the other models and includes a *field of experience* which is often neglected by other writers. Schramm's model is diagrammed in Fig. 2.

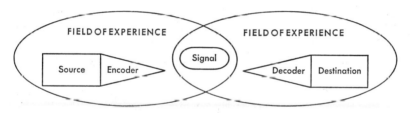

FIGURE 2. SCHRAMM'S MODEL

Perhaps you will be able to comprehend the meaning of this process more fully if it is applied to a practical communication setting. Imagine that you are sitting in a theatre and the lady in front of you has on a feathered hat which is blocking your view. You tap her on the shoulder to secure her attention, and ask, "Would you please remove your hat?" She looks surprised, hesitates, and then quickly takes off her hat.

What has actually happened in this simple communication incident? You were the *source* of the message. You felt a need to communicate and put your needs into understandable symbols or words. This process of converting thoughts into symbols is

---

[4] Wilbur Schramm, "How Communication Works," *The Process and Effects of Mass Communication* (Urbana: University of Illinois Press, 1955), p. 6.

called *encoding.* You then encoded the words and *transmitted* them through the air waves to the lady. The words themselves were the *message* or *signal.* The air waves served as a medium or channel of transmission. The lady received this signal and *decoded* these words back into thoughts which were meaningful to her. This process of decoding is the reverse of the encoding process mentioned above. The lady was the *destination* of your message. Your *field of experience* included such factors as hereditary dispositions, acquired psychological dispositions, subjective states and processes, situational phases, and ongoing stages of individual development. The greater the similarity of your field of experience with that of the lady, the more likely it would be that she would be able to comprehend your message. Since language is a prime factor in your field of experience, it plays a major role in the understanding of messages. If the lady, for example, did not understand English, this lack of overlap in your fields of experience could have caused a breakdown in communication. Schramm suggests that the fields of experience of the source and the receiver must overlap in some way in order for the communication to be successful. In summary then:

The *source* is the speaker's mind. It is the source of the idea.

The *encoding* process is that which occurs when the idea is translated into word symbols.

The *signal* is the actual message. It is transmitted through a channel or medium (such as light or air waves).

The *decoding* process involves attaching meaning to language symbols or objects.

The *destination* is the listener's mind. It is the "target" of the message.

The *field of experience* is the total makeup of the individual. It involves all of his past influences and experience up to the moment of communication.

WISEMAN-BARKER COMMUNICATION MODELS

After this brief introduction to communication models, you are ready to study the more specific factors of the communication

cycle, as represented in the Wiseman-Barker models. To learn
the more intricate parts of the communication processes study
the two models (Figs. 3 and 4). The first of these models describes the process of intrapersonal communication and the
second describes interpersonal communication. These models
complement each other and attempt to show relationships
among the different types of messages. Intrapersonal communication is diagrammed in Fig. 3.

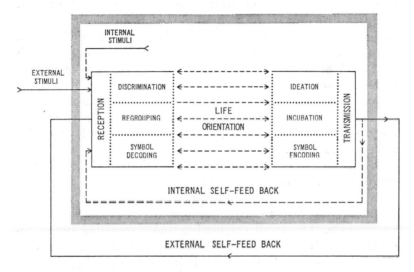

FIGURE 3.   INTRAPERSONAL COMMUNICATION MODEL

To understand the model, familiarize yourself with the term-
inologies and read the detailed description of the process of
intrapersonal communication. It will be helpful to refer back
to the diagram after reading about each part or process in order
to perceive the interactions and relationships which are present.

You will recall from Chapter 1 that intrapersonal communication refers to the creating, functioning, and evaluation of
symbolic processes which operate within the originating or responding communicator. It ranges from simply thinking, medi-
tating, and reflecting to talking to oneself or writing oneself a
memo. Ruesch and Bateson suggest certain characteristics of the
intrapersonal network which differentiate it from other levels of

communication.[5] For example, in intrapersonal communication, the self-observer (communicator) is the sole participant. Both the origin and destination of intrapersonal messages are within the life space of one organism. In addition, correction of errors is extremely difficult in intrapersonal communication. Self-feedback is much less effective than that received from an external observer. Unfortunately the symbolic codification system can never be adequately investigated in intrapersonal communication because of the amount of personal involvement present. The fact that intrapersonal communication is difficult to examine and analyze makes it even more important to understand. Intrapersonal communication is the foundation upon which interpersonal communication is based and it is necessary to understand how you communicate to yourself before you study the process of communicating with others. Remember that intrapersonal communication may take place without interpersonal communication, but interpersonal communication involves intrapersonal communication.

In the model of intrapersonal communication the entire rectangular area represents the communicator, either originating or responding. Since identical processes occur in both types of communicators it does not matter which you choose to serve as an example. The terms originating and responding communicator will be discussed when the interpersonal communication model is presented. At this point it is sufficient to recognize that the originating communicator is the person who initiates the messages to be communicated and the responding communicator is the person who receives these messages and responds to them.

The internal processes which occur in communication are set in motion by certain types of stimuli. These include stimuli both internal and external to the communicator.

INTERNAL STIMULI

The internal stimuli are nerve impulses received by the brain as a result of the psychological or physiological state of the body at a given instant. You have a stomachache, you feel tired and

---

[5] Jurgen Ruesch and Gregory Bateson, *Communication: The Social Matrix of Psychiatry* (New York: W. W. Norton and Company, Inc., 1951), p. 278.

run-down, you are thirsty. These various types of internal stimuli may cause you to communicate. The stomachache may stimulate a call to the doctor, the tiredness may result in refusing to play a round of golf, and the thirstiness may result in a request for a glass of water. These internal stimuli may be psychological as well as physiological in nature. Psychological feelings of anticipation, apprehension, tension, joy, or happiness may stimulate communication.

EXTERNAL STIMULI

External stimuli impinge upon the communicator from his immediate environment; they are received from sources outside the communicator's body. Basically, external stimuli are of two types.

Overt

Overt stimuli are those which the communicator receives at the conscious level. They are received through one of the sensory organs and transmitted to the brain. A pretty girl walking down the street may be an overt stimulus to a young man who is approaching her. He may feel a desire to communicate as a result of seeing her. A sign in a store window can be an external stimulus to a prospective buyer. Other external stimuli might be a question asked by a professor in class, the aroma of a sizzling steak, the sound of a television commercial or a song, or even the sight of clouds in the sky indicating rain. All of these overt external stimuli affect the individual in different ways.

Rarely does only one overt stimulus affect an individual at a given instant. Usually several will affect him simultaneously. The degree to which overt stimuli affect the behavior or communication of an individual depends on a complex of factors such as strength of the stimuli, the familiarity with the stimuli, and the emotional connotations which the stimuli produces. However, overt external stimuli are only one type which may reach the individual.

Covert

Covert stimuli are those external stimuli which are received by the individual at the preconscious or subconscious level. The most common example of this type of reception occurs when you read a book while thinking about something else. You cannot deny that your eyes received the stimuli in the form of words on the printed page. Your eyes were open; light waves were reflecting off of the page and were being received by the retina. What occurred, then, to keep you from remembering what you read?

Psychologists would say that you received the stimulus at the subconscious level and that the information was actually stored in your central nervous system. Some feel that through hypnosis this information can be brought to the conscious level and made useful to the individual.

The threshold of consciousness (or perception) is that point below which stimuli are not recognized at the conscious level. For example, if your threshold of perception for visual images were 1/30 of a second, you would not perceive a picture flashed on a screen for 1/60 of a second. The picture would have been below your threshold of perception. Many stimuli received below the threshold of consciousness may affect your communication without your being consciously aware of them. The actual degree to which these covert stimuli affect communication and persuasion has not been determined, but it is certain that many stimuli affect you which are not consciously recognized. Other types of covert stimuli might be background music in a motion picture, subliminal advertising,[6] unnoticed traffic noises, or a radio playing while you are studying.

RECEPTION

There are virtually hundreds of stimuli which may be reaching you at any given instant. Some will be below the threshold of perception and others will be strong enough to reach your conscious level. The process by which the stimuli are received by the body is called the process of *reception*. Reception takes place in each of the five senses. You receive stimuli of smell, taste, sound, sight, and touch. The process of reception is, then,

---

[6] For a summary and definition of subliminal research see Louis Cheskin, "Subliminal Research—Implications for Persuasion," *Today's Speech,* VII (April, 1959), pp. 19–21.

the physiological process of receiving stimuli and converting them into nerve impulses, which are transmitted to the brain.

In intrapersonal communication both internal and external receptors transmit information to the central nervous system. Internal receptors such as nerve endings relate information in the form of feelings and/or sensations which reflect the state of the individual communicator. The external receptors, located on or near the surface of the body, react to physical, mechanical, and chemical stimuli and provide information concerning relations between the communicator and his environment.

Since at a given instant countless external and internal stimuli are reaching you, there must be some process which enables you to cope with all of them. Although you receive all stimuli that are present in the physical communication setting, it is obvious that you do not communicate as a result of every stimulus you receive. What, then, determines which stimuli are allowed to reach the conscious level and stimulate thought? One factor is the relative strength of the stimulus. In terms of verbal stimuli this could mean the actual intensity or loudness of the message. In terms of visual stimuli this could be the size of a visual aid or the magnitude of a gesture or movement. Other factors besides intensity, however, help determine which stimuli reach you at the conscious level.

Discrimination

The first of these factors is called discrimination. This selection process determines what stimuli are allowed to stimulate thought. At a given moment you feel a draft around your ankles, your right shoe is too tight, there are sirens blaring outside the building, the hum of the fluorescent light is present, the wall is covered with paintings, and the speaker in the front of the room, wearing a straw hat and checkered shirt, is talking. These many stimuli as well as countless others are all reaching you simultaneously, but you cannot possibly take time to think about each one. Of those mentioned perhaps the strongest stimuli are your aching feet, the words of the speaker, and his straw hat. The discrimination process screened out all of the insignificant or weak stimuli without your ever being aware of them. This

process occurred below the conscious level. Without this discrimination process your mind would literally be cluttered with
so many thoughts that you could not devote sufficient attention
to any one of them. When the discrimination process occurs,
there must be a second process which operates almost simultaneously. This process is regrouping.

Regrouping

The regrouping process orders the stimuli. In the situation
described above, you are now vaguely aware that there are
slight pains in your right foot and that the speaker is wearing
an unusual hat, but his words are demanding most of your
conscious attention. The regrouping process has occurred, plac-
ing the strongest and most important stimuli at the conscious
level. This process puts the stimuli into a sequence which is
meaningful to the communicator and lets him act upon the
strongest and most important stimulus first, the medium stimulus next, and the weaker stimuli after that. Remember that the
stimuli are not received in a preconceived order and follow no
pattern of arrangement. Through the regrouping process, some
order is made out of the chaos of the many diverse stimuli which
are received. When the discrimination and regrouping processes
are completed, the first of two symbolic transformations occurs.

DECODING

To be meaningful to the communicator the stimuli must be
given symbols. Decoding changes the raw stimuli into thought
symbols. The symbolic process is one of giving symbols to ideas,
places, things, sounds, and smells. What these thought symbols
are no one knows for sure, but most biologists agree that you
think in terms of electrochemical impulses. The initial symbolic
process of decoding is followed by ideation and incubation.

IDEATION

Ideation is the process of thinking, planning, and organizing
your thoughts. Osborn calls this process a "free wheeling of the
mind." He defines ideation as "the part of the (communication)
process which calls for thinking up all possible tentative ideas

as tentative solutions or as leads to other ideas which in turn might lead to solutions." [7] Robert Frost described it as a "rumpling of the brain." This process may be brief in the case of normal conversation. However, in the instance where you have time to prepare a communication over an extended period, ideation becomes one of the most important processes in the communication cycle. Your past associations with the topic, including books and magazines you have read, conversations about the topic, radio programs, motion pictures, and television shows —all are included in your storehouse of knowledge and associations. The ideation process involves drawing together information and relating it to the proposed message you desire to communicate. You may even need to search for new information as a part of this procedure. This information might come from external sources when you have sufficient time to develop and research your topic, for the limits of the ideation process extend to all other sources of information you have available in the time allowed for developing the message.

INCUBATION

Incubation is the process of letting ideas "jell" in the mind and pick up the flavor of relationships buried there. The term "incubation" has come to be used for what happens when a problem or an idea is allowed to form and grow in the mind until it has had time to take useful shape and direction. Most people sense what incubation is—a period for hatching, for growing before being put forth. By setting your thoughts aside for awhile you may reconsider them later with a fresher and more original approach. Many English teachers suggest that you place a theme in a drawer and let it lie there for a few days before you revise it. During the time that you lay it aside, other associations may occur to you which were not present at the time of writing. This period of letting the ideas "jell" is in essence an incubation period. In oral communication this incubation period may be a fraction of a second or it may be lengthy. A

---

[7] Alex Osborn, *Applied Imagination* (New York: Charles Scribner's Sons, 1957), p. 146.

frequent fault of many communicators is the tendency to eliminate or abbreviate the incubation period. This practice may
cause them to speak hastily without weighing ideas.

ENCODING

The final symbolic process is one of encoding your thought
symbols into words and meaningful gestures. It is the reverse of
the decoding process described earlier. The encoding process is
the final step before transmitting the message.

TRANSMISSION

The word symbols and gestures must go through the physical
process of transmission in order to be received by the audience.
Transmission is the process of sending coded messages along a
selected medium. Usually the media are air or light waves. In
the case of intrapersonal communication the transmisson may
also be through brain cells or nerve impulses. Messages are
transmitted internally from the nervous system to the smooth
muscles in order to regulate the movements of the communicator. Transmission to external sources is made by contracting
certain muscles, adding an energy source, and providing a reso-
nator.

LIFE ORIENTATION

The process of life orientation interacts with all of the processes mentioned above. This concept is so important to communication that an entire section in Chapter 3 is devoted to it.
Briefly, your life orientation is the result of the sum total of
social, hereditary, and personal factors which have influenced
your development. The factors which have contributed to your
life orientation are unique to you as an individual. Because
everyone's life orientation is different, communication problems
often arise.

FEEDBACK

When you think of feedback you usually think of receiving
messages from the responding communicator. This type of feedback will be discussed later, but there are additional types of
feedback available to originating and responding communica-

tors. These are termed *external self-feedback* and *internal self-feedback*.

External self-feedback is that portion of the message which the communicator receives through air waves. It is that part of your message which you hear yourself. This external self-feedback can help you correct messages if you listen for your own mistakes.

Internal self-feedback is usually felt through bone conduction and muscular movement. You might feel your tongue "twisted" and know that you have formed the wrong word or perceive a gesture that was the opposite of what was intended. Both of these types of self-feedback allow you to alter your messages if you perceive yourself making a mistake or becoming unclear.

Having studied the process of intrapersonal communication, now consider this process in the larger context of interpersonal communication. The authors' model of interpersonal communication is shown in Fig. 4.

You will note that the model of intrapersonal communication,

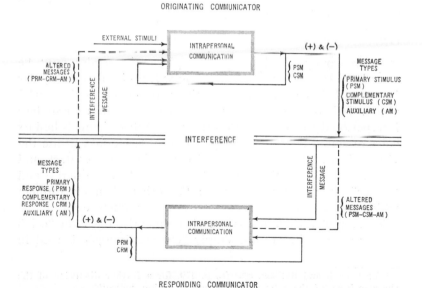

FIGURE 4. INTERPERSONAL COMMUNICATION MODEL

although described separately, is actually a part of the model of interpersonal communication. In interpersonal communication, intrapersonal communication serves an intermediary but necessary function. It is interesting to compare the characteristics of the interpersonal communication network with those of intrapersonal communication discussed earlier.[8] In interpersonal communication the possibilities of receiving, transmitting, and evaluating messages are equally divided, and, therefore, the participating individuals (originating and responding communicators) compose approximately equivalent parts of the system. Correction of errors is possible because both the source and destination of messages are known to the sender and the receiver. In addition the receiver must be both an active participator and observer in the interpersonal communication system.

Interpersonal systems differ from intrapersonal ones in three main areas: (1) participation of communicator, (2) location and destination of the message, and (3) possibilities for correcting errors. Keep these differences in mind as you study the model of interpersonal communication. First make a careful study of the model and as you learn the following new terminology, relate it to the model.

ORIGINATING COMMUNICATOR

Before communication can take place, the sender must be stimulated to produce a message. You will notice that the sender is not called the speaker, transmitter, or talker in the model above. This is because the sender of a message in a face-to-face interpersonal communication setting uses other channels besides voice or sound for communication purposes. He may utilize the visual channel for gestures, facial expressions, eye contact, and movement. Since the terms "speaker," "transmitter," and "talker" do not usually include the other channels through which messages are sent, they do not completely describe the originator of a communication. Consequently, the term "originating communicator" (or simply "communicator") is used in

---

[8] See Ruesch and Bateson, *op. cit.*, p. 279, for a further discussion of the characteristics of the interpersonal communication network.

this text to indicate that the sender initiates the process of communication with the receiver.

The originating communicator has at his disposal a number of different channels which he may utilize in the communication process. He may be a television announcer relating the events of the day to millions of eager listeners, an after-dinner speaker striving to amuse a somber audience of businessmen, a clerk in a shoe store attempting to sell a new pair of shoes, a teacher in the classroom trying to challenge his students, or a college man seeking a date for Saturday's dance. The originating communicator is more than a speaker. He uses gestures, facial expressions, movement, visual aids, and proper dress, as well as his vocal presentation to communicate his ideas. He is the originator of a message which is presented in order to receive a response. The messages of the originating communicator are the means through which he can successfully satisfy his need to communicate. This need is aroused through one of several types of stimuli which affect him.

As an originating communicator, you transmit three basic kinds of messages to the receiver.

1. Primary stimulus messages: These messages are effected by the original stimulus and are conveyed along the medium of transmission (channel) which the originating communicator selects as the most effective for the particular message.

2. Complementary stimulus messages: These messages are also effected by the original stimulus but are conveyed along media of transmission other than that of the primary stimulus message. The purpose of the complementary stimulus messages is to reinforce the primary stimulus message.

3. Auxiliary messages: These messages are not affected by the original stimulus. They are characteristics of the communicator, his voice and his appearance, which are not consciously controlled by the communicator as a result of the particular communication stimulus, but which do transmit messages to the audience.

All three types of messages may be either positive (+) or negative (−) in their effect upon the audience. They are intended, by the originating communicator, to have a positive effect but often fail to do so. A typical example would involve extraneous gestures, such as waving arms while talking, which are intended to reinforce the primary stimulus message, but which actually attract attention to themselves and detract from the important message being transmitted.

Primary Stimulus Messages

Consider a situation. You are excitedly discussing a fish you caught last summer and illustrating the size of the fish with your hands. The words you are saying are your primary stimulus message. They are the most important part of your entire communication complex because without words the message cannot be understood by the responding communicator. If he simply sees you moving your hands without hearing your words he could assume you are describing the size of a rock, a snake, or any one of a dozen other things. The primary stimulus message could have been transmitted through the visual channel if you had simply shown a picture of the fish. In that case words would not have been necessary to get the point across.

Complementary Stimulus Messages

When you are describing verbally the fish you have caught, the gestures with your hands are complementary stimulus messages. Though they are not the primary transmitter of the messages, they are serving to reinforce or amplify your primary stimulus messages. If your picture of the fish is the primary stimulus message, casual remarks about the circumstances surrounding the photograph would be your complementary stimulus message. Remember that the complementary stimulus message always intends to amplify or reinforce the primary stimulus message.

Auxiliary Messages

Because you are so involved in your narration, you have not noticed that your appearance is disheveled, but your responding communicator may have. The fact that your hair is not combed may have affected the message you are transmitting. This is an auxiliary message because it is something about you that is not a direct result of your original stimulus to communicate. Your body build and the colors of your hair, eyes, and complexion are all forms of auxiliary messages which transmit information about you to the responding communicator.

RESPONDING COMMUNICATOR

The term *listener* cannot completely describe the receiver of the communication for the same reasons that the terms *speaker* or *talker* do not completely describe the originator of a communication. Listening is only one type of message reception. You receive messages through all of the five senses—sight, sound, taste, smell, and touch—not just through the aural channel. When you perceive a gesture a speaker makes or a picture he has drawn on the blackboard, you are doing more than just listening. In addition, for the communication cycle to be completed, the receiver must respond to the originating communicator. Consequently, the receiver of the communication is called the *responding communicator*.

The responding communicator is the destination of the originating communicator's messages. He may be a person answering the phone, a student answering a question posed by his instructor, a panelist on a quiz show answering a question asked by the moderator, a debater refuting the charges of his opponent, or a friend reflecting on a comment that his roommate has just made. The term "responding communicator" implies that he receives messages from the originating communicator through all possible channels and that he reacts to them. Without a response to a message which is transmitted, the process of communication cannot be completed.

In informal conversation the responding communicator may change roles and become the originating communicator. It is not unusual for a responding communicator to respond to a communication and then add additional comments which start an entirely new cycle of communication. The communicator must be willing to adapt and exchange roles when necessary, recognizing the responsibilities and duties he must perform in each role.

The responding communicator, having gone through physical and psychological processes similar to those of the originating communicator, transmits three types of messages.

1. Primary response messages: These messages are a result of the original stimulus received from the originating communicator. They are transmitted through the medium of transmission which the responding communicator selects as most appropriate and effective.

2. Complementary response messages: These messages are a result of original stimulus received from the originating communicator but are transmitted in channels other than that used to send the primary response message. They are designed to reinforce the primary response message though there may not be any of these present in some situations.

3. Auxiliary messages: These messages are the same as those of the originating communicator and concern the responding communicator's physical and vocal characteristics.

Primary Response Messages

Having heard an inspiring speech you applaud loudly. This applause through the aural channel is a primary response message. This feedback is transmitted to the originating communicator through the channel you feel is most appropriate to express your response to his messages. In many instances primary response messages take the form of smiles, questioning expressions, or nods of the head. In these instances, the channel for the primary response message is a visual one.

Complementary Response Messages

In conversation the movement of your head accompanying the word *yes* or *no* would be a complementary response message. It would reinforce the primary response message. In the case of a formal speaking situation, complementary response messages are not always present, because the nod without any verbal counterpart would take on the role of a primary response message. Another form of complementary response message might be gestures accompanying answers to questions posed by the originating communicator.

(+) and (−)

The bracketed plus and minus symbols by each type of message indicate the different type of effects the messages may have upon the receiver. Those messages which may be controlled by the sender are generally designed to have a positive effect upon the receiver but in reality they may not. Those messages independent of the sender's control may also have either positive or negative effects upon the receiver. For example, a person's appearance (a form of auxiliary message) may enhance his communication without the communicator ever being aware of this fact. It could also detract from his message unknowingly. The bracketed symbols should remind the student of communication that even though a message is intended to procure a certain response from the receiver there is a possibility that it may not. It takes more than good intentions to become a successful communicator.

FEEDBACK

The combination of these three types of messages provide the feedback that enables the originating communicator to gauge the effectiveness of his communication. Feedback from the responding communicator may be of three types.

1. Positive feedback: This feedback shows the originating communicator that his message was understood by the responding communicator. It does not imply that the responder necessarily agrees with the originator, but it does indicate understanding of the message.

2. Negative feedback: This feedback shows the originator that his message was not understood. It does not imply disagreement, just a lack of understanding.

3. Ambiguous feedback: This feedback is unclear to the originating communicator. He must determine whether it is positive or negative and act accordingly.

INTERFERENCE

All messages are affected by interference—stimuli present in the communication setting which distort the primary, complementary, and auxiliary messages. You have often observed interference on a television set. It may have been in the form of "snow" or lines across the screen. Interference is always present in the communication system in the form of extraneous sounds or objects moving in the background. The sound of honking horns, humming fluorescent lights, speakers talking in the next room, or workmen hammering on a house next door are all common forms of interference. The interference present in the communication system tends to *alter* the previously mentioned types of messages. This alteration may not be noticeable at times, but at other times may cause confusion in receiving the message which the originating communicator intends to transmit. It is the job of the communicator to allow for interference which may be present in the system and to adjust his messages accordingly.

INTERFERENCE MESSAGES

Interference messages are similar to interference. These are messages present in the communication setting arising from sources other than the originating communicator. In addition to sounds and sights which tend to alter messages sent by the originating and responding communicators, there may be other messages present in the communication system which could attract attention from the communicator's message. Interference messages may be "No Smoking" signs on the wall, writing on the blackboard behind the originating communicator, whispering neighbors, music from a record player, or any message originating in the communication system (outside of the communicator) to which symbolic meaning may be attached. These messages are interference in the sense that they tend to detract the responding communicator from the message being transmitted. Many interference messages can be controlled by the communicator before he begins to communicate in order to lessen their effect on his communication. He can control these by erasing the blackboard, asking for all talking to be stopped, or turning off the record player.

BREAKDOWNS IN COMMUNICATION

In any complicated system, breakdowns are possible. When there is a broken wire in an electrical circuit a power failure may result. Likewise, a break in the communication cycle can result in failure to accomplish the purpose of the message. The points where breakdowns in communication may occur are numerous. Any of the processes or factors described in this chapter may be susceptible to communication breakdowns. However, there are three distinct places in the cycle where most communication breakdowns tend to occur. These are in the originating communicator's *messages,* in the *reception* of the responding communicator, and in the *feedback* which the responding communicator transmits.

The symbols which the originating communicator chooses to relay his message must be understandable by the responding communicator. If the former uses symbols which are foreign to the latter, the message cannot be understood. (See Chapter 5 for further discussion of this topic.) Also, the channel selected for the transmission of the message must be one which the responding communicator can receive. For example, if the responding communicator is looking out the window at a passing parade it would be of little value to try to diagram a process on the blackboard for him to comprehend.

Reception can cause breakdowns because of the discrimination and regrouping processes which occur. If these processes filter out the message of the originating communicator, then a breakdown is likely to occur. The originating communicator must make his messages intense and interesting enough to insure that his message reaches the conscious level of the responding communicator. Physical difficulties of the responding communicator, such as deafness or color blindness, could also produce breakdowns if the originating communicator were not aware of these conditions.

Perhaps the most frequent area in which breakdowns occur is in the transmitting and interpreting of feedback. The responding communicator has a duty to respond to the messages of the originating communicator. If he does not, he breaks the cycle of communication. Even when he does transmit feedback, breakdowns can occur in the interpretation of these messages by the originating communicator. In analyzing your own communication as well as that of others, remember these points where breakdowns are likely to occur and attempt to make proper adjustments.

It may be observed that the dynamics of the communication cycle are complex and involve many diverse processes and components. Remember that these factors are usually not considered separately in everyday communication. It is their coordinated effort that produces effective communication. You must be aware of the many facets of communication and strive to integrate the processes into meaningful, workable patterns. By achieving this integration, you may become a truly effective communicator.

QUESTIONS FOR DISCUSSION

1. Why is the communication process often referred to as a "cycle?"

2. Why is interpersonal communication dependent on successful intrapersonal communication?

3. What problems arise when a communicator misinterprets feedback from his audience?

EXERCISES

[Forms for completing the exercises marked with an asterisk will be found in the *Worksheets for Speech—Interpersonal Communication* (San Francisco: Chandler Publishing Company, 1967).]

1. Make a list of communication breakdowns which you have experienced in each of the following areas: (a) the message (b) reception of the message (c) interpretation of feedback. How many of these could have been avoided?*

2. (a) Define the terms presented in the model of intrapersonal communication. (b) Repeat this exercise with the model of interpersonal communication.*

3. Compile a list of breakdowns which you have experienced or observed in areas other than those listed in Exercise 1 above. Suggest ways in which these breakdowns might have been avoided.

4. Using the models presented in this chapter as guides, develop a pictorial model of the interaction process in a discussion group.

5. Find three examples of messages which could be both primary and complementary stimulus messages, depending on the situation.

6. Auxiliary messages may be classified into two categories: (1) Those which positively affect communication and (2) those which negatively affect communication. Cite specific examples of each type of auxiliary message.

7. Prepare a report on the similarities and differences between intrapersonal and interpersonal communication. Consult the suggested readings at the end of the chapter.

8. In a brief paragraph describe an interpersonal communication incident in which you were the originating communicator. Label each part of the incident according to the terms presented in the model of interpersonal communication.

9. Compare the cognitive processes of encoding and decoding stimuli with the use of secret codes in the military and secret service.

10. Prepare a report on the physiological processes of reception and transmission. Consult suggested readings at the end of the chapter.

SUGGESTED READINGS

Ayer, A. J., "What Is Communication?" *Studies in Communication,* London: Martin, Secker and Warburg (1955), pp. 11–28.

Barker, Larry, and Gordon Wiseman, "A Model of Intrapersonal Communication," *The Journal of Communication,* XVI, No. 3. (September, 1966), pp. 172–179.

Berlo, David K., *The Process of Communication.* New York: Holt, Rinehart and Winston, Inc., 1960, "Model," p. 72.

Deutsch, Karl W., "On Communication Models in the Social Sciences." *The Public Opinion Quarterly,* XVI (Fall, 1952), pp. 356–380.

Johnson, F. Craig, and George R. Klare, "General Models of Communication Research: A Survey of the Development of a Decade." *The Journal of Communication,* XI (March, 1961), pp. 13–26, 45.

Katz, Elihu, and Paul Lazarsfeld, *Personal Influence.* New York: The Free Press of Glencoe, 1964. Part One, Chapter VI, "Interpersonal Networks: Communicating within the Group," pp. 82–116.

Nilsen, Thomas R., "Interpersonal Communication: A Conceptual Framework." *Central States Speech Journal,* XV (February, 1964), pp. 31–35.

Osborn, Alex F., *Applied Imagination* (rev. ed.). New York: Charles Scribner's Sons, 1957. Chapter XII, "The Value of Copious Ideation," pp. 146–155; Chapter XIII, "Periods of Incubation Invite Illumination," pp. 156–167; and Chapter XIV, "The Time Factor in Ideation," pp. 171–174.

Ruesch, Jurgen, and Gregory Bateson, *Communication: The Social Matrix of Psychiatry.* New York: W. W. Norton and Company, Inc., 1951. Chapter XI, "Individual, Group and Culture: A Review of the Theory of Human Communication," pp. 273–289.

Schramm, Wilbur, *The Process and Effects of Mass Communication.* Urbana: University of Illinois Press, 1955. Chapter I, "How Communication Works," pp. 3–26.

The Originating Communicator | 3

Socrates stressed the importance of knowing yourself, of knowing your strengths, weaknesses, potentialities, your aims, purposes, and heritage. This self-concept begins with a self-inventory. The purpose of this chapter is to help you understand yourself and the bases from which you communicate. Guides will be suggested to lead you to this understanding, but you alone must be the one who will use these guides and bring about the kind of understanding that is necessary for communication. How much do you know about yourself? You will probably reply that you know yourself very well. It is true that you have lived with yourself for perhaps 20 years, but it takes time and effort to understand the real you. If you are typical, you probably do not have this understanding. For instance, do you know what size stocking you wear? Are your arms the same length? What are your basic prejudices, likes, dislikes? What is your mother's middle name? What does your name mean? What is your basic philosophy? What are your goals in life? Many of the above questions probably could not be answered immediately. By the time the answers were found you would be different. Even as you receive the message written here, you are no longer the same individual; new thoughts and ideas have been added to your storehouse of knowledge and have set in motion all kinds of relationships, each affecting the other.

For purposes of clarification in this discussion, think of your-self as an originating communicator. In reality you are a part of a continuing process that began with man's ability to symbolize and will continue as long as man exists. The influences of the ages precede your communication, and you affect the communication of men who will live after you. That influence may be so infinitesimal that it cannot be discerned, but on the other hand it may change the course of a life, of a nation, of the world. More likely than not it will change the lives of several people close to you—your parents, your classmates, your husband or wife, your children.

As an originating communicator you need to know the mechanism that affects communication. This mechanism influences each step in the communication cycle and often creates breakdowns by its very nature. From the time the stimulus affects you to the actual transmission of the message, you as an originating communicator are in the process, consciously and subconsciously, of weighing each step according to your life orientation. Even as no two fingerprints or no two snowflakes are alike, so no two personalities are alike. All that has happened to you in the past influences your communication, and makes you a unique communicator.

Because of these complexities, the search to know yourself is not an easy task. Sometimes it is painful to look at yourself and to realize who you really are. However, this process must be begun if you are to communicate successfully. At this stage of your life thousands of programs, similar to computer programs, have already been set up in you; when you are communicating, your ideas will follow these programs. The responding communicator likewise follows his programs, so your understanding of his life orientation as well as your own is important. Communication is not a separate entity superimposed on your mechanism for transmission, but is an integral part of you as an individual—it is you. It is flavored, shaped, and fashioned by you and of you. It is impossible to separate the communication from you or you from the communication—for what you communicate is yourself. Communication by its very nature is subjective and you cannot be completely objective about it. The closest you can come to objectivity is to understand the part you play in the communication process, the way you have flavored it, and the part of the communication that is you. To be able to do this is to understand your life orientation, to understand your self.

YOU AS A REALITY

To be able to understand *you,* you must first ask the question, "Which you?" You are different at various times and under different circumstances. You are known to be one you to your friends, another to your teachers, and another to yourself. Even this self known to you may really be selves. The one you know just now and the one which is the result of your accumulated years of living—each has its own personality. For every role there is a different you. These yous that you live and cope with are called *realities.* From among the many realities there are three basic ones important to you and your communication.

These realities are classified as structural, predictive, and subjective. They are not mutually exclusive, yet each has distinctive characteristics that must be recognized. No disagreement is to be had with those who say there is an ultimate reality with which all must deal, but this reality will not be considered now in its relationship to communication. Perhaps as you learn to know yourself you will see the important part it plays in your choices.

STRUCTURAL REALITY

Structural reality is that reality which must be contended with in terms of solid matter. The scientist suggests that what usually is considered solid matter is not really solid at all. However, when you try to walk through a closed door or a wall, you find there is that which appears to be solid. A lamppost may not be solid matter, nor your car, but if you try to pit one against the other something happens. The same principle applies in communication, for if you try to ignore certain basic premises, the end result may be unrewarding. The analogy holds that if on a physical basis you are able to synchronize molecules to bring about the desired result, you may also synchronize opposing views in communication and be successful. In each case the degree of success depends upon the ability to integrate; molecules (ideas) on one hand and life orientations on the other. An understanding of the structural reality of each *object* is the first prerequisite to successful communication.

As a communicator you must take the structural reality of the

situation into consideration before you communicate. You may
say, "I know the facts and I am going to prove my point to the
boss." However, many individuals are required to operate in a
very rigid framework of communication regardless of the way
they feel or perceive a given situation. The boss has been given
certain rules to follow by his board of directors. The representative to the United Nations must act as he is told by his country.
Your girlfriend operates in a frame imposed by her parents that
is as rigid verbally as a wall is physically. Because of this type
of inflexibility it is possible to win many a battle and yet lose the
war; you may prove your point, but lose your job or a friend.

Structural reality exists regardless of whether you recognize
it or not. It is up to you to find where it exists in the communication situation. There are times that you will want to depend
on your facts or information alone, but remember that these may
not be sufficient for communication. You must face structural
reality at all times and be able to work within its framework. It
is similar to predictive reality in the sense that you often will
try to predict what the structural reality will be.

PREDICTIVE REALITY

Predictive reality is that future reality which you determine
before the event occurs. The communicative self tends to avoid
entirely new situations and therefore tries to predict what a
future situation will be like on the basis of past reasoning from
attributes to substances, or determining the unknown on the
basis of the known.

Before you came to college you developed a predicted concept
about college life. Friends who had never been to college gave
you advice, college graduates told you what you could expect,
and you added your own expectations. From these different
points of view you formed a concept of college life, a predictive
reality of college, but when you arrived you probably learned
that college was not entirely as you had pictured it.

Although predictive reality is not always accurate, it serves as
a protective mechanism for the self in new situations, making
adjustment to reality easier. Most often the predicting is done
below the conscious level which makes it more difficult to under-

stand. Predictive reality always deals with probability and the accuracy of your prediction is based upon the similarity between the observed facts and those which are not known. Factors may change and you must be willing to take this change into account. Predictive reality is always hypothetical; therefore, adjustments to the real communication setting are necessary.

Communication on interpersonal and intrapersonal levels is the only means you have of making the realities the same. A young couple spends many months during the first part of their married life adjusting their predictive reality of marriage with the marriage that is actually theirs. Perhaps both of them thought marriage would be a utopia where a great deal of time would be spent together. When they find they do well to have one evening a week together, they can either adjust or become frustrated. Adjustment is made easier through deep understanding and proper communication.

Regardless of the communication situation in which you participate, you will bring your own predictive reality along with you. These predictive realities are given to you by your life orientation which is influenced by your culture and your past involvements. You must first realize this predictive factor, and then make an effort to help yourself and others adjust. However, to feel that everything is fine because predictive realities have been adjusted to structural realities could mean a third area—subjective reality—had been ignored.

SUBJECTIVE REALITY

Subjective reality is the reality within an individual that he has formed for the most part by intrapersonal communication. It is the reality you discover on an interpersonal basis of communication.

Several psychologists have discussed ideas similar to subjective reality and Kurt Lewin in his field theory relates somewhat this same concept in working with groups.[1] His concept is referred to as the *phenomenological position* and states that the phenomena

---

[1] Kurt Lewin, "Frontiers in Group Dynamics," *Human Relations*, Dorwin Cartwright (ed.), (New York: Harper and Brothers, 1951), pp. 5–41 and 143–153.

towards which the individual should direct his attention are those which the individual subjectively perceives, not what the observer perceives. If you are to discover the reality from which each individual operates then you must discover what reality is to him—his subjective reality.

A breakdown in communication can occur when you depend on your own subjective reality. In a recent conversation, an executive of a large corporation related his own frustration about the communication process. He had discussed policy with a group of younger executives and was very pleased that they all seemed to agree at the end of the week. To test himself, each person wrote what he had understood the agreement to be. The executive found that only two of the seven listed the same conclusions, and no one agreed with his version of the policy. Had this disagreement not been discovered, each person would have gone away with his own subjective reality of what the agreement had been.

If you have ever carried on a love affair by correspondence, you know the difficulties that come from your own subjective reality. As long as you feel that all things are fine, the letters sound wonderful, but let a little rift come between and then reread the letters. See how many new ideas you are now able to read into the letters. Even your mood when you receive a letter can make all the difference in the message.

Subjective reality is your interpretation of the world about you. When a student comes for counseling, the counselor must look at the problem from the student's point of view. A major responsibility of the counselor is to aid the individual as he adjusts his subjective reality to a structural reality.

F. P. Kilpatrick and the transactional psychologists contend that your perception comes from you, not from your surroundings.[2] As a perceiver you decide what and where an object is. You make the object what you choose to make it in the light of your individual experience and purpose. You can only perceive that which you have experienced and choose to perceive.

[2] Franklin P. Kilpatrick (ed.), *Explorations in Transactional Psychology* (New York: New York University Press, 1961), p. 40.

What you know is not only what you have been taught but what you have perceived. A successful communicator realizes that each person carries within his mind a picture of the way life is and that for the most part he lives by this picture. Subjective reality tends to make a person feel secure because he is able to manipulate all the variables and make life work out as he pleases. If you want to communicate with this person you must penetrate his world, his ideas of what reality is—and in turn he must penetrate yours. When these worlds slip by each other as two ships pass on the ocean at night, communication has not taken place. Realities must be perceived and there must be some kind of basic understanding in regards to life orientations, or words will serve only as barriers to communication.

LIFE ORIENTATION

You are born into the center of a small world which for the most part is interpreted in terms of pain and pleasure. As you grow you must learn to be *a* center rather than *the* center. It is through this growth that the real you emerges. The real self evolves through the process of perception and is primarily a learned activity of the organism. You are motivated to behave in terms of the world as you perceive it and this world is the product of your past. Sociologists generally agree that every human being is different from every other human being, and that all are influenced by at least three great forces: (1) inherited characteristics, (2) past experiences, and (3) the present situation. The sum total of these influences determines your life orientation.

You have had two parents, four grandparents, eight great-grandparents, and so forth. Within five generations you are the development of 62 persons; add another five generations and you have more than 1000 ancestors who have contributed their protoplasm, their characteristics, their life orientations to your life orientation.

The habits you have now are determined by the ways you have behaved in the past. Your biography determines your action. It determines your way of perceiving life, and of interpreting all the events that come your way. You truly are a "part of all that you have met," but which part is determined by you and your method of perceiving. Interpreting events makes you what you are, and communication is the means by which this process takes place. Any communication is determined on the one hand by the total makeup of the person at the moment, and on the other hand by the total situation in which he finds himself. The communication is a joint product of factors in the individual and factors in the situation. An excellent example of how four people are able to view the same event is quoted below.

"Men are comic!" she said, smiling dreamily. Not knowing whether this indicated praise or blame, I answered noncommittally: "Quite true."

"Really, my husband's a regular Othello. Sometimes I'm sorry I married him."

I looked helplessly at her. "Until you explain—" I began.

"Oh, I forgot that you haven't heard. About three weeks ago I was walking home with my husband through the square. I had a large black hat on, which suits me awfully well, and my cheeks were quite pink from walking. As we passed under a street light, a pale, dark-haired fellow standing nearby glanced at me and suddenly took my husband by his sleeve.

" 'Would you oblige me with a light?' he says. Alexander pulled his arm away, stooped down, and quicker than lightning banged him on the head with a brick. He fell like a log. Awful."

"Why, what on earth made your husband get jealous all of a sudden?"

She shrugged her shoulders. "I told you men are very comic."

Bidding her farewell, I went out, and at the corner came across her husband.

"Hello, old chap," I said. "They tell me you've been breaking people's heads."

He burst out laughing. "So you've been talking to my wife. It was jolly lucky that brick came so pat into my hand. Otherwise, just think: I had about fifteen hundred rubles in my pocket, and my wife was wearing her diamond earrings."

"Do you think he wanted to rob you?"

"A man accosts you in a deserted spot, asks for a light and gets hold of your arm. What more do you want?"

Perplexed, I left him and walked on.

"There's no catching you today," I heard a voice say from behind.

I looked around and saw a friend I hadn't set eyes upon for three weeks.

"Lord!" I explained. "What on earth has happened to you?"

He smiled faintly and asked in turn: "Do you know whether any lunatics have been at large lately? I was attacked by one three weeks ago. I left the hospital only today."

With sudden interest, I asked: "Three weeks ago! Were you sitting in the square?"

"Yes, I was. The most absurd thing. I was sitting in the square dying for a smoke. No matches! After ten minutes or so, a gentleman passes with some old hag. He was smoking. I go up to him, touched him on the sleeve and ask in my most polite manner: 'Can you oblige me with a light?' And what d'you think? The madman stoops down, picks something up, and the next moment I am lying on the ground with a broken head, unconscious. You probably read about it in the newspaper."

I looked at him, and asked earnestly: "Do you really believe you met up with a lunatic?"

"I am sure of it."

An hour afterwards I was eagerly digging in old back numbers of the local paper. At last I found what I was looking for: a short note in the accident column:

UNDER THE INFLUENCE OF DRINK

Yesterday morning, the keepers of the square found on a bench a young man whose papers show him to be of good family. He had evidently fallen to the ground while in a state of extreme intoxication, and had broken his head on a nearby brick. The distress of this prodigal's parents is indescribable.[3]

This story illustrates how individuals do not perceive the same set of events at the same time from the same point of view. Differences in experience acquired early in life tend to compound themselves because each new stimulus is perceived largely in terms of what has gone on before.

All types of communication play a part in creating you, but in the last analysis it is on the level of intrapersonal communication

---

[3] A. Averchenko, "Point of View," *This Week Magazine* (August 16, 1947), p. 2. Reprinted from *This Week Magazine*. Copyright 1947 by the United Newspapers Magazine Corporation.

that you make final evaluations. It is not just the experiences that you have, but the way in which you evaluate them that determines their impact on your life. Similar difficult situations can come to two people, but one may accept them positively and grow while the other yields to self-pity. Any time you make the same mistake twice you have not properly evaluated the first situation. While there are some who live and learn, there are many who just live.

Intrapersonal communication is at the basis of every evaluation you make in the process of becoming a mature individual. You react to communication because of what you are, and each evaluation affects the other until they are not easily distinguishable. The important thing is not only to know how you react under certain communication situations, but to know *why* you react as you do. It is not easy to understand all your deeper motivations—professional help is needed for this—but you can understand many motivations if you are willing to search yourself and your background. Since the meaning of words is not in the words but in you, then you must know what you are and how you affect meaning.

Many of the general semanticists would suggest that an important basic premise with which to begin your study is that every individual is unique—a unique organism as a whole and a unique organism as an environment. Another premise is that no individual is isolated, but that he operates in terms of relatedness. It is in relationship to others and to things that you develop and grow. In your personal development it is this relationship that is important, not the people or circumstances themselves. A third premise, stated elsewhere, is that man is not a static being but a dynamic one in which change is ever present.

If you are to be a good originating communicator or a successful responding communicator each of these premises must be examined in relationship to yourself and to communication. Each individual is unique; any communication directed to that individual or originating from that communicator must take this premise into account. This does not mean that there are no universals to which a communicator may address himself, but these universals must be directed in terms of the individual and not the masses. It is true that security and ill health are universal concerns of older people, but not all older people worry about security or ill health. A successful communicator looks for differences as well as similarities.

You behave in certain ways and most of the time you behave within a pattern. However, since you are not a robot, you do not always behave in the same way. It is not easy to predict the way you are going to behave. If accurate prediction were possible, the social sciences would be more hard-core sciences than they are. For instance, constants in mathematics and elements in chemistry that remain the same and can be controlled and manipulated are not present in human beings. The physical sciences suggest that for every cause there is an effect, but in human relationships the same cause does not mean that the same effect will emerge. All of this illustrates the uniqueness of man. For example, a new idea that will cost money presented to the boss by phone at 3:00 a.m. will not get the same reception as it would at 10:00 a.m. in a scheduled conference, or the same reception if presented to him at 10:00 a.m. after he has been told by the board of directors that costs are too high and he must find ways to cut them.

In addition to the uniqueness of the communicator the relationship of other factors should be considered. A successful communicator will observe as many personal interactions as possible to see what effects they have on his communication. Of vital importance to your understanding are the ways you handle relationships within yourself and within the communication situation. Circumstances and events are important, but your method of seeing relationships is even more important. It is not easy to discover how you handle relationships or how you are unique, but this can be done as you try to determine your own life orientation and the factors that make you *you*.

UNDERSTANDING LIFE ORIENTATIONS

The first step in understanding yourself is to understand the cultural backgrounds of your family, which influenced every part of your early life. If your grandparents are still living, examine your parents' reactions in their homes; listen to the grandparents as they tell about your own parents as children. Determine such things as the power structure in the home, loyalties, customs and habits, methods of discipline, respect expected toward parents, and the success the grandparents feel in having reared their children. Of greater importance is the reaction of your parents to these elements. Some adults who rebelled against their background as children are more lenient with their own children in these areas. A child commanded to do difficult chores may rebel against these restrictions and when he becomes a parent may give his own child very few chores; on the other hand a parent who sees real value in duties may devise chores for his child as a matter of discipline. An understanding of these concepts is essential if proper communication is to take place in the home and within the family.

Another very important area to study in relationship to the grandparents is the area of failures within their family situation. Failures sometimes seem to have a deeper influence on thinking and lives than successes. Grandparents who lost money in real estate or savings and loans during the depression have tried to teach their children not to venture out too far in business deals. The failures during the depressions are still an influence in many people's thinking today. Study these failures and fears that have come down from one generation to the next. Do not simply study the circumstances or the events, but focus your attention on the relationships. To understand why Mother and Dad are the way they are in relationship to their parents might be the first step to understanding yourself and your own life orientation.

Most people of your age have not taken the time to examine the structure of their home, but this is necessary if you are going to understand your communicative behavior. This task is not easy, but as you reflect upon these matters you may be better able to understand yourself. The first view to take of your home is a bird's-eye view. What is the general atmosphere and what are the basic communicative patterns? Is it a home where conflicts are discussed in a sensible way, or one where irritation keeps the home in constant turmoil? A family in which the members are

soft-spoken and calm will have a different effect on an individual than one in which there is constant shouting and turmoil.
A student suggested that the first criterion for a husband was
that he be kind, soft-spoken, and would never yell at her. She
had had so much shouting in the home that she did not want
this in her life. A person who has never been shouted at in
the home will react differently to a boss who tries to emphasize
his communication by shouting than will the person who is used
to being shouted at. Generally, if a home atmosphere is one of
trust and love, a person will react to communication with a
certain amount of trust. Since trust is so basic to many communication situations this background has a direct influence.

The findings of several studies have illustrated the influence
of a broken home on one's outlook. However, one should not
forget that the relationship between mother and father in a
home that is not broken is important as well. A wife who does
not get along with her husband and relates her fears and frustrations to her daughter may prejudice the girl's marriage. If a
mother imposes her concept of men upon her daughter, the girl
will probably examine the men she dates from her mother's
point of view. Perhaps in the early years of marriage when
communication is easier she will forget this influence, but as the
communication between her and her husband begins to break
down she will compare her situation with the ideas her mother
has given her. Communication patterns are deep channels of
thought, and once a stimulus is imposed, it will tend to follow
the channel. An understanding of what is going on is the first
step in changing a pattern.

Again the importance of relationships can be seen when working with other individuals. You will examine their behavior in
relationship to other behaviors you have known. Communication aids you in examining these relationships and in seeing
how they correspond to reality. Knowing your own life orientation gives you a yardstick to use as you check these relationships.

Although subject to the same atmosphere and many common
factors, each individual in a home lives in a unique environment. Certainly, a girl who has six brothers and no sisters does
not live in the same environment that her brothers live in. The

eldest in a family does not have the same environment as the youngest. The number of years between children is worthy of consideration.

A family of three children with 2 years difference in each child's age will perhaps be a closer knit group than one in which there is 6 years difference between each child. The child who comes along 10 or 12 years after the rest of the family has many influences on his life which differ from the early members of the family. Search out the factors that make you unique in your environment.

The kinds of training you received in the home, at school, and perhaps from church have influenced your way of thinking as well as your patterns of communication. The way your nervous system reacts to communication involving the home, school, or church has been conditioned by this orientation. You will not always be able to keep your nervous system from reacting in a certain manner, but you can gain insight and understanding which can prevent many breakdowns in communication. A student told of a discussion in which birth control was suggested as a possible solution for taking care of poverty. The student realized that her strong negative reaction to this idea stemmed from her religious training. She also realized that perhaps others had differing backgrounds, so their thinking would be different. A little understanding on her part prevented a serious breakdown of communication. In time she was able to express her ideas clearly and without emotion.

As you are working to understand your orientation, study the schools you have attended and their influence on you. Pick out the teachers who have contributed most to your personal philosophy. Examine influences of other students and select experiences which you vividly recall and determine their effect on your present beliefs. Always keep in mind that the goal is to obtain a better understanding of yourself and your communication background.

It is important to examine both the pleasant circumstances and tragic events which have happened to you. However, it is even more important to examine your reactions to these circumstances and what you let them do to you. Sometimes a trivial incident can have profound effects on you, if you let it. For example, a girl who hated parties was asked if she knew why. She replied that it all went back to her sixteenth birthday party. In the family there was a very fine ring that was to be passed on to her when she was old enough to wear it. At 16 she insisted that she was old enough even though the ring was much too large for her finger. Her mother finally let her wear the ring. She lost the ring at the party and was never able to find it. From then on parties were a symbol of misfortune and her reactions were unbelievable to those about her. She quarreled with her boyfriend about going to parties and often became ill to avoid going. Her communication pattern in regards to parties was formed by this experience.

Although it is often easy to recognize how patterns were formed, it is not so easy to do something about them. Keep in mind that reactions are learned behavior, and consequently may be changed by relearning different behavior patterns. For the most part, behavior is caused and man acts in response to some stimulation. Both external and internal stimuli make an impact on a person's nervous system as visual, auditory, olfactory, tactile, gustatory, or organic sensations. You continually evaluate the impact of these happenings, although, for the most part, you are unaware that you are doing so. Your intrapersonal communication handles evaluations according to your way of perceiving them.

Your habits, prejudices, experiences, abilities, physiological-emotional state, likes and dislikes, education, hereditary factors, and attitudes influence your evaluations and thus influence your responses. A change in your evaluation pattern or a rethinking at any step in the process will enable you to alter your communication reaction. No, it is not at all easy to do, but for many it is necessary if you want to prevent breakdowns in communication and the tension, anguish, friction, misery, and danger which so frequently follow. Often you cannot change your circumstances, but you can change your reaction to them, and your reactions to your reaction. Your life orientation does not just play a part in the way you behave; your life orientation is you and must be understood.

As you look at yourself and your life orientation do not forget to look at the positive aspects, for they also help your evaluations and aid you in being a successful communicator. A positive outlook on life will often create positive attitudes. Attitudes are even more important than facts at times. How you think about a fact may defeat you before you ever do anything about it. You may permit a fact to overwhelm you mentally before you start to deal with it actually. On the other hand, a confident and optimistic thought pattern can modify or overcome the fact altogether. This positive attitude is often an aid to communication, since positive evaluations are made of circumstances rather than negative evaluations. Every evaluation becomes a part of you and, sooner or later, the results of that evaluation will be evidenced in your communication and will be a part of your communicative self.

ADAPTING TO LIFE ORIENTATION OF THE RESPONDING COMMUNICATOR

All the events that have happened to you and your reactions to them make up your life orientation at the present moment. To be a successful communicator you must first understand yourself, what you are, and how you react. The second step is to understand the responding communicator and his life orientation. It is important that you understand your own life orientation thoroughly. Perhaps it is impossible to understand to the same extent as your own the life orientations of your responding communicators. However, in certain face-to-face contacts, such as husband-wife or teacher-student, it would be wise to understand each other's life orientations as much as possible. For your boss, specific rather than general understanding may be required. A larger audience must be understood in broad terms, although people are influenced as individuals, not as crowds.

Preceding any important communication an attempt to understand the kind of ground on which your communication will fall is essential. The depth of analysis depends on the amount of time you have and the importance of the communication. The life orientation of others is just as important in their lives as your orientation is in yours. Learn to interpret the thoughts, feelings, and moods of others through their words, tones, inflections, facial expressions, and movements.

Never try to communicate to a larger audience unless you have made a special effort to understand their common life orientations. There are these basic facts that must be known: age, sex, educational background, general intelligence, special interests of the group, size of the audience, and reason for their coming together. Even more important than the vital statistics are the ideas and events that catch their interest, take their time, and control their lives. If you are to communicate, you need to touch the needs, concerns, fears, deep emotional feelings, and goals of your audience. Most of the concerns of life change with age and time. There are certain universal needs (see Chapter 8) —freedom from fear, freedom from want, security, desire to be loved, ego preservation, altruistic feelings, and self-preservation—present in most individuals. However, all individuals do not interpret these universal needs in the same manner. This is where an understanding of life orientations is essential.

A teenager wants freedom from the fear of ridicule by his peers; an older individual wants to be free from the fear of financial dependence on others; a person in West Berlin wants freedom from fear of bodily harm. Fear of failure to a successful individual may not be as strong as the fear of failure to one who has known little success. On the other hand, one who is successful may have a fear of failure and loss of prestige, and one who has failed a great many times may by now accept failure. Your interpretation of the ways these universals affect the life orientation of your audience is extremely important. The success of your communication depends on the accuracy of your interpretation. Here your life orientation begins to exert an influence as you make these interpretations. Be careful not to superimpose your own life orientation on the life orientation of your audience.

Before you communicate, a last-minute analysis is always in order. Situations may change from what you have determined and you will need to adjust to these changes. Events may happen just before your communication that will change life orientations and your audience's reception. A speaker was to give a humorous speech during the lunch hour at a factory and he had thoroughly analyzed his audience. After he had failed miserably with the speech, he then explored the situation further. He was informed that a worker had been killed in the plant that morning and the workers were just not in the mood for a humorous speech. Life orientations had been changed by this one incident and he had not adapted to the new situation.

A speaker must constantly be utilizing his feedback and must be flexible enough to make further adaptations in his communication. A fellow who says, "I would never say that to my girlfriend because she would not like it," has learned reactions and adjusted. Families soon learn areas of sensitivity and avoid them if they want to keep communicating. They show an understanding of the importance of the life orientation, often without really knowing what they are doing. A good salesman will adapt his sales pitch as he moves along and will not use the same line of reasoning with everyone. All these examples illustrate the need for flexibility in adapting to your audience's life orientation.

A good communicator will complete the communication process by evaluating the success of his communication and making observations for future use. It takes real effort to be objective, and it is easy to blame failure on others, but you will not learn this way. Regardless of how right you thought you were, if the person did not respond as you wanted, then you failed in achieving your purpose. A careful analysis of the response to your communication will point out patterns that you may be following because of your own life orientation. These may need to be changed.

These concepts are not to be misconstrued as the sophistic philosophy of communicating which suggests that the end justifies the means. There are those who teach that you should find out what the person wants and give it to him even if you must stretch the truth. Chapter 7 on evaluation shows the fallacy of this philosophy. The point to be gained here is that adjustments are made only within the framework of an individual's ethical responsibility. Change is made not just to accomplish your goal but to make sure you have done all you could to get your communication understood.

Understanding life orientations is basic to communication because you communicate from and to this background. The criteria for evaluation comes from the life orientation itself and every communication is evaluated by these criteria. Your method of communicating and your process of preparation is determined by your life orientation. One of the greatest assets in knowing your life orientation comes from knowing yourself and knowing how other people think and react. A desire on your part to understand others makes communication possible. If an individual does not want to understand your message you cannot communicate with him regardless of how many techniques of communication you may know. You need to know him so you can make him want to understand. Adapting to the life orientation of others helps you to be flexible and willing to listen to other points of view. Paradoxically, a deeper understanding of others will also help you to understand yourself.

YOU AS A SOURCE OF KNOWLEDGE

An understanding of your own life orientation will also aid you in assessing yourself as a source of knowledge in communication. It will help you to know your assets and liabilities, your strengths and weaknesses. This knowledge can help you to strengthen the weak points and capitalize on the strong ones. In communication it is often better to say "I do not know" than to act as a storehouse of knowledge when your knowledge is meager. As you communicate you will want to be correct and accurate in the way you handle ideas. As an intelligent communicator you first make an inventory of your knowledge about a subject, then you are willing to do research in depth on your topic. You study all sides of an issue and consult authorities to observe the plan in practice as well as understand the theory. In reality you become an authority on the subject you are trying to communicate. A communicator must be sensitive to all that is around him, ever learning new ideas and facts.

The importance of communicating with your peers will be stressed throughout this text. An understanding of yourself will make clear the thinking of your peers. The subjects that you will be interested in will more than likely be the ones that interest them. At least these areas will serve as starting points for you. You should be able to find common fears, likes, and dislikes through an understanding of your own life orientation. Be careful not to sell yourself short as a source of knowledge for your communication.

ORIENTING YOURSELF TO THE SPEAKING SITUATION

Probably no phase of your college education will affect you more than will your courses in speech. Here your ideas are openly examined, your personality is demonstrated, and your performances are evaluated through written and oral criticism. Your personality will affect your speaking and your speaking will, in turn, affect your personality. In few other subject areas will your teachers or your peers get a more basic understanding of you. Thus you will want to prepare yourself to meet this challenge.

Your first task is to evaluate your attitude toward the speaking situation. Some students have said, "You can make me take speech, but you won't teach me a thing." With this attitude their statement is true for you cannot be taught unless you are willing to be teachable. Speech is an area which you will get more out of than you put in. There is an additive factor which simulates a geometric progression because you are learning both an art and a science.

A recent Gallup Poll suggested that your greatest fear is the fear of criticism from your peers. You know this to be true because in your college career you are probably conforming to the standards set by your peers in order to avoid their criticism. The speaking situation places you under a surveillance which can create fear evidenced in many peculiar ways. Even seasoned speakers experience varying degrees of uneasiness. This uneasiness is often termed *stage fright* and a great deal of research and experimentation has been conducted in this area. References to this research may be found at the end of this chapter. Most people will not need this extra help, although you should know that your instructor is ready to help you when you need it. Some basic changes in your thinking can help you in your adjustments.

First of all remember that this fear is normal and is a common experience. As you look at the other students in the class you will say, "Well, they seem to be perfectly at ease," and most of them will say the same about you. In other words, the manifestations of the fear are never as noticeable or as dramatic as they seem to you. Fear is a way that nature has of stimulating the very best that is in you and if you respond to that challenge you will succeed.

These feelings are not peculiar to the speaking situation. If you remember your first date you will recall many of the same symptoms that you experienced the first time you spoke in public. In fact you may have many of those same feelings as you date now. Fellows relate that they really fear being turned down when asking for a date. Experience helps to take fear away in dating in the same way that practice can help remove fear in speaking.

Since the actual speaking situation contains the elements of a performance, many feel that it must be flawless and forget that they are in a learning situation. Accept the speaking performance as a learning situation and regard it as practice. In the normal learning situation you expect both failures and successes. For example, in learning to bowl there may be times you will miss all the pins. Yet you are willing to accept this, analyze your problem, try to correct it, and improve your score. While speaking before your class if you make several mistakes in the introduction, just start over. A student was demonstrating how to hit a golf ball which required him to have a relaxed stance, yet one of his legs was shaking until he could hardly stand still. He slapped his knee hard with his hand and said, "You behave." The class laughed with him and his knees stopped shaking. He used the situation as a learning experience and succeeded. Accept the fact that you will be learning, build on the successes, and learn from the failures.

Research findings suggest that your greatest tool for overcoming fear is adequate preparation. When you do not know the material as you should then you have both content and delivery to worry about. Since the content is within your control before the speaking situation, understand it thoroughly so that it does not become a problem when you are speaking. It is important to start early and spread your preparation over an extended period. One hour a day for a week spent on the preparation of a speech will be more beneficial than 12 hours spent on it the night before it is to be given. (For a suggested practice schedule, see Appendix C.) Speaking must be a part of you if it is to be successful. Many students try to acquire a quart of knowledge and then return a quart when they speak. Preparation in speaking should resemble the filling of a large reservoir. Your audience should receive the *overflow* of your knowledge. It is possible to read only one article and digest it for the class in a speech. You may even get by with it, but you know its emptiness and most of the time your audience will know as well. Thus lack of adequate preparation is one of the main causes of fear.

Do not speak because you have to say something, but speak because you have something to say. When you have an important message that you want to communicate and you feel strongly about it, you generally will have few problems with delivery. The act of communicating affords you opportunity for expression which you will find in few other situations. Your audience will get to know your innermost thoughts, beliefs, and opinions. If you approach each assignment as "just another assignment," that is the way it will appear. However, if you select subjects that interest you, information that you would like to know, and subjects about which you have deep convictions, you will not be just speaking but you will be communicating. When there is this deep desire to communicate there is little room for fear.

A great many times nervousness is caused by tension in posture which may cause a knee to shake or a hand to quiver. For some reason students feel that the instant they reach the lectern they must start speaking. After you reach the lectern you should pause to collect your thoughts. A deep breath before beginning to communicate often helps to relax you. During the speech a little movement will also help you to be more at ease. However, be careful not to pace like a lion in a cage.

In a classroom situation students often develop fear by delaying their performance as long as possible. When volunteers are called for students engage in activities hoping that they will not be asked to speak. Some students will go through this procedure four or five times hoping that there will not be time for them to give their communication. If you often feel nervous try volunteering to speak first. This positive attitude will help conquer your fears. "Fear knocked at the door. Faith opened it, and lo, no one was there."

Your speech class will become a closely knit group and there will be a great deal that you can do to help yourself and others. If you will give each speaker the kind of attention you would like to receive there will be a permissive atmosphere for speaking. If you whisper to your neighbor or joke with him, the speaker may think he is being ridiculed and this will increase his tension. Respond to each speaker with positive feedback, and this response will encourage him and aid his communication. A brief compliment after class may go a long way toward building self-confidence in a speaker who is having difficulty in expressing himself. Speaking is a cooperative enterprise. Your responses will help create the proper atmosphere for learning, which, in turn, will make it easier for you to speak.

Remember that your speech class is a learning situation. You are acquiring new skills and techniques and should be willing to accept the accompanying responsibilities. If you experience failure in class it is not disastrous because you will have additional opportunities to succeed. Later a failure might cost you your job or a good friend, so be willing to learn from your mistakes. Develop a proper attitude toward communicators and the communication situation. Be willing to spend the time in preparation that is needed. Learn the real joy of acquiring new knowledge and the fun of sharing it with others. Accept your intense feelings as normal reactions to a new situation which involves every bit of you in a special way. Accept every opportunity to speak that comes your way and be willing to be the first to speak in class. Endeavor to be the kind of responding communicator you would desire for your communication and help develop a permissive atmosphere for communicating. If you are willing to invest your time, your energy, your abilities, and yourself in the communication situation, you will receive wonderful returns on your investment not only now but in the years to come.

QUESTIONS FOR DISCUSSION

1. What criteria should a person use in determining which reality is present in a particular communication situation?

2. Discuss communication as subjective rather than objective. What are the factors that make it either subjective or objective?

3. What are some of the ways a class can discover the life orientations of other members of the class?

EXERCISES

[Forms for completing the exercises marked with an asterisk will be found in the *Worksheets for Speech—Interpersonal Communication* (San Francisco: Chandler Publishing Company, 1967).]

1. List three goals which you feel your parents have set for your family. List three goals in similar areas you might want for a family of your own.*

2. Find three important recent national issues and record how you think the members of your class would feel about these. Form a brief questionnaire on the issues, administer it to your class, and compare the results.*

3. List viewpoints you hold about which you think others would differ and then try to see why they do.

4. Choose one student in the dorm who "rubs you the wrong way" and inquire about this person's background. After you have done this note how this person changes in your perception.

5. Read what you can about the setting of Henry W. Grady's speech, "The New South," given December 8, 1837, and describe how he adapted to his audience.

6. Classify the students on your floor who are introverts or extroverts and then state the predominate characteristics of each.

7. List the three greatest pressures that you have felt in the last 6 months and try to analyze how they affected your communication.

8. List five of your personal opinions that have changed in the last three years and try to determine the forces that changed your mind.

9. Have your parents tell you how you have changed since you were younger.

10. Take time to answer the question, "Who am I?" Write a description of yourself including your five most important characteristics. Ask a close friend to list your five most important characteristics and then compare notes.

SUGGESTED READINGS

Clevenger, Theodore, Jr., "A Synthesis of Experimental Research in Stagefright." *The Quarterly Journal of Speech,* Vol. XLV (April, 1959).

Haney, William, *Communication Patterns and Incidents.* Homewood, Ill.: Richard D. Irwin Company, Inc., 1940. Chapter 3, pp. 12–40; Chapter 4, pp. 41–72; Chapter 9, pp. 162–183.

Hilgard, E. R., *Theories of Learning.* New York: Appleton-Century-Crofts, Inc., 1956. Chapter 1, pp. 1–14.

Hill, Winfred F., *Learning: A Survey of Psychological Interpretations.* San Francisco: Chandler Publishing Company, 1963.

Hollingsworth, H. L., *The Psychology of the Audience.* New York: American Book Company, 1935. Chapter 3, "Types of Audiences," pp. 19–33.

Kilpatrick, Franklin (ed.), *Explorations in Transactional Psychology.* New York: New York University Press, 1961.

Robinson, Edward, "What Can the Speech Teacher Do About Students' Stagefright?" *The Speech Teacher,* Vol. VIII (January, 1959).

Schultz, Alfred, "On Multiple Realities." *Philosophical and Phenomeno-logical Research,* V (1945), pp. 533–575.

The Message Organized | *4*

WHY ORGANIZE?

Organization is an integral part of society. You are organized in your eating, sleeping, working, and playing habits. If some event interferes with your organizational plans you tend to become frustrated and angry. If your plans follow your habitual organizational patterns, you find yourself in a more receptive frame of mind, more satisfied with life, and more free from worry and anxiety.

Similarly, organization should be an integral part of communication. Effective organization can reduce frustrations for both the originating and the responding communicators. When a message is not carefully organized, the responding communicators tend to lose interest, and become confused. When a message is effectively organized, the communicator feels more confident and speaks with greater ease. This need for organization in communicating applies to both the prestructured and the semistructured communication situations. The relative importance of organization to both the originating and responding communicators should be considered first.

ORGANIZATION HELPS THE ORIGINATING COMMUNICATOR

Organization is essential to the originating communicator in developing materials into a meaningful cohesive unit. Imagine a motion picture in which the climax of the action is shown before the plot is developed. It is just as absurd to imagine a

63

communication with the conclusion at the beginning and the introduction at the end. A clear and carefully planned pattern of organization can help you detect inconsistencies in assertions and illogical sequences of ideas. Of course you realize that the introduction precedes the body of the speech and that the conclusion follows. But you may fail to realize that organization must be carefully structured within each of the component parts of the communication. This internal organization enhances the clarity and preciseness of the message, making the presentation more meaningful.

A definite plan of organization provides guidelines for your presentation by giving you a comprehensive overview of the message. Organization gives you a security because you know the elements of the communication form a cohesive unit designed to convey effectively the primary stimulus message. The knowledge that your presentation is well organized aids self-confidence. A communicator whose mental processes are free from worry about the structure of the message can devote more energy and expression to its delivery.

ORGANIZATION HELPS THE RESPONDING COMMUNICATOR

Organization aids the originating communicator in unifying the presentation, and is of prime importance to the audience. The organizational pattern of the communicator should serve as a guide to the responding communicator. It should help the responding communicator follow the communicator's thought patterns and perceive the important elements of the message. Without an organizational framework, the responding communicator may lose interest and consequently miss the important concepts.

Organization is an important aid to learning subject matter. Studies concerning the relationship between organization and learning have indicated that an important relationship exists between the two. For example, Wheeler and Perkins reported the following findings as a result of their studies: [1]

---

[1] Raymond Holder Wheeler and Francis Theodore Perkins, *Principles of Mental Development* (New York: Thomas Y. Crowell Company, 1932), pp. 292–296.

1. The more easily recognized the plan of arrangement, the more quickly learning takes place.

2. The longer the content to be learned, the more necessary becomes orderly arrangement in learning.

3. When orderly arrangement is expected but fails to appear, its lack causes confusion.

4. Learning is most effective when the orderly arrangement is explicit as possible and is deliberately explained to the learner at the beginning.

These findings, though not conclusive, indicate that under many circumstances organization can make learning not only more effective, but more pleasurable for the audience. As an originating communicator you must feel a need to communicate. The more easily you can make the responding communicators understand your message, the greater are your chances to obtain a favorable response and fulfill your original need to communicate. In many instances organization provides the key to understanding. In summary, organization aids responding communicators in two ways. It helps them follow the communicator's progression of thought and makes learning more efficient and effective.

ORGANIZING THE PRESTRUCTURED COMMUNICATION

There are basically two kinds of communication situations in which you participate. One is the formal or public speaking situation, and the other is the informal or conversational situation. Although organization is essential in both of these situations there are several differences between their organizational structures. For example, in the public speaking situation the communicator usually has ample time to research, develop, organize, and prestructure the message. However, in the conversational situation you generally have little time to develop your thoughts. In conversation the organization is semistructured at best. For purposes of discussion the public speaking situation will be called prestructured and the conversational situation will be termed semistructured. Since the prestructured communication situation is one of the major concerns in this text, this will be discussed rather completely. There are seven basic steps which you should follow in organizing the prestructured communication.

1. Determine the purpose of the message.
2. Select the organizational pattern of the communication.
3. Select the main ideas.
4. Arrange the ideas.
5. Prepare the outline.
6. Prepare the introduction.
7. Prepare the conclusion.

DETERMINE THE PURPOSE OF THE MESSAGE

There are three different purposes which you should formulate before proceeding to organize the message—(1) the general purpose, (2) the specific purpose, and (3) the personal purpose. First determine the *general purpose* of your message. Is it to inform, entertain, stimulate, or convince? The way you organize the communication will depend on which of these general purposes you decide upon. (See Chapter 8.)

Once the general purpose is known determine your specific purpose for communicating. The *specific purpose* (key idea) should state clearly and concisely the exact message that you want to impart to the audience. It should be stated in a single complete sentence. For example, if your general purpose is to convince, your specific purpose might be: "Courses in comparative government should be taught in high school in order to help combat communism." The specific purpose of a communication to inform might be: "Advertising is a rapidly growing field with many opportunities for young college graduates."

Finally, after the specific and general purposes are determined, discover your *personal purpose* for communicating. The personal purpose is the reaction you hope to obtain from your audience. This purpose can range from desiring a specific audience response toward you to obtaining their social approval. In the communication to convince mentioned above the personal purpose might be: "I want my audience to use their influence to have a practicum in government so that I might be better prepared in my chosen field of endeavor." Another personal purpose of the same communication might be: "I want to let the audience know that I am a civic-minded citizen." You may have more than one personal purpose for communicating, but you should have only one general and one specific purpose. When more than one specific purpose is included in a communication each usually suffers. You may have seen riders in the circus who ride two horses at the same time by straddling the two. The rider runs the risk of falling between the two and could easily end up not riding either one. A rider who rides one horse at a time runs less risk of falling off and is more likely to complete his journey successfully. The same principle holds true with regard to the specific or general purposes of communicating. When you try to accomplish only one purpose at a time you stand a better chance of successfully completing your communication journey.

SELECT THE ORGANIZATIONAL PATTERN OF THE COMMUNICATION

A prestructured communication should resemble a highway. It should begin at a definite point, continue from that point along a specific path, and eventually come to an end. The three divisions in a communication are usually labeled *introduction*, *body*, and *conclusion*. No matter how complex the organizational pattern might be, it will always contain these three basic elements. In most informative and entertaining communications this simple organizational structure will be sufficient. However, a more complex framework is usually necessary when preparing the persuasive communications. One organizational pattern with which you should be familiar was developed by John Dewey.

Dewey suggests a problem-solution approach to organization.[2] His proposed pattern includes the following steps:

1. Attention-getting introduction
2. Statement of the problem
3. Possible solutions for the problem

---

[2] John Dewey, *How We Think* (Boston: D. C. Heath and Company, 1910).

4. The best solution (s) for the problem

5. Appeal for audience action to carry out the solution.

This pattern is not only useful in preparing the communication, but can also be modified for use as an agenda in any problem-solving situation. (See Chapter 9.)

In applying Dewey's method to the organization of your message you must develop fully each step in the sequence. For purposes of brevity the steps may be remembered as (1) attention (2) problem (3) possible solutions (4) best solution and (5) action.

The *attention* and *action* steps will be discussed later in this chapter as types of introductions and conclusions respectively.

The *problem* step is designed to convince the audience that something needs to be done, decided, felt, bought, sold, or the like. This step must illustrate vividly where a need exists as well as the effects of this need on you and society. Furthermore, in this step of the prestructured communication the need should be made to seem vital and realistic to the individual members of the audience. It must be related to their life orientation so that they can feel the need in their own lives. The problem might be poverty, lack of education, graft in government, a need for funds for operating expenses or for a new dartboard in the recreation room. In each instance, present the need and convince the audience that it is not being satisfied effectively or efficiently under the *status quo.*

The *solutions* step in Dewey's sequence involves the presentation of solutions to solve the expressed need or problem. At this point a variety of possible plans of action may be presented. Even solutions which have obvious drawbacks should be presented so that the relative advantages of your proposed plan or favored solution will stand out. A point-by-point comparison of possible solutions is often desirable to demonstrate logically the values of and weak points of each solution.

In most instances you will advocate one solution over the other alternatives. This is called the *best solutions* step when integrated into the organizational pattern of a persuasive message. You should make the audience feel that though a variety of possible solutions exist your proposed solution will satisfy the need quickly and satisfactorily. Upon successful completion of this step the audience should feel confident that your plan will do the best job of solving the problem.

Presentation of the *best solutions* step can be approached either positively or negatively. In the positive approach you help the audience see what will happen if your favored solution is put into action. For example, you might suggest: "Imagine the smiling faces of the starving Viet Namese children when they receive the CARE packages that your dollars will send." The negative approach would treat the same topic in this manner: "Imagine the forlorn faces of the starving Viet Namese children when they find the CARE truck is empty—not enough dollars were sent to fill the truck." This fourth step should be extremely vivid and should contain strong emotional appeals. Paint a verbal picture in the minds of the audience so that they can perceive the values your solution would have in action or the unpleasant effects which could result from not letting your plan be put into action.

Figure 5 helps to show the relationships between the two organizational patterns.

CONVENTIONAL DIVISIONS	DEWEY'S THOUGHT PATTERN
Introduction	Attention
Body	Problem Possible solutions Best solution
Conclusion	Action

FIGURE 5. ORGANIZATIONAL PATTERNS

The organizational pattern you choose will depend largely on the subject matter, the general purpose, and the specific purpose of your message. The pattern of organization chosen must be suitable for your particular speech. No one pattern is best for all communication situations. To slightly adapt an old saying, "Orderliness is next to godliness." This is especially true in preparing the prestructured communication.

SELECT THE MAIN IDEAS

Once the over-all organizational pattern is established, the next step is to select the main ideas for the body of your presentation. Begin by making a list of all possible points that are related to your general topic. Next, select those important points representative of your topic to be your main points. In selecting these points there are several considerations you must make. First, do the main ideas accomplish the specific and general purposes of your presentation? Many of the ideas which appear on your list of possible main points are generally related to your purposes, but only those which will convey your message effectively should be selected.

Secondly, the main points should be relatively few in number. As a general rule, the number of these points should be from two to five, depending upon the length of the communication. When the number of points exceeds five it is often hard for the audience to remember all of the ideas. At times when the number of main points exceeds five, it is possible to reclassify them into more general groups, thus reducing the number of main points. In rare instances you may have only one main point in your communication. This could occur when the time is limited. Usually, if you have done adequate research in preparing your message you will find that most problems have many facets and that a single main point will not adequately develop the topic.

The main points should be considered in relation to the length and type of communication you wish to present. It was suggested earlier that a short communication will have fewer main points than a longer one. Likewise, an informative communication may have more main points than a communication to stimulate or convince. The subject matter is also extremely important in deciding how many main points you should include in the body of your presentation. If you find that you have too many main points in your communication it may be necessary to go back and limit your topic.

Make sure that the main points are really the most important ones in your communication. These must be the thoughts and ideas that you want your audience to remember. It is your task to make sure that the main points will make a lasting impression upon the audience. These points should not be subtle or hidden but should be made abundantly clear to the audience.

You must decide if the main points in your communication are mutually exclusive. If some points overlap you should re-examine them and develop subpoints. An example might help to illustrate the above statement. A student originally selected the following main points for his speech:

A. Federal aid to education
B. Donations by individuals to education
C. Donations and grants by industry to education
D. State aid to education
E. Local aid to education.

Upon checking his main points he discovered he could increase clarity by regrouping them in the following manner:

A. Governmental aid to education
   1. Federal support
   2. State support
   3. Local support
B. Grants and donations to education
   1. Donations by private individuals
   2. Donations and grants by industrial firms.

In the first list, the student had points which were not mutually exclusive. By regrouping the points he made his presentation more meaningful. It is usually better to group related ideas so that the audience may understand related concepts and ideas more clearly.

From a practical viewpoint consider the main points you select in light of your knowledge of the subject. This includes the degree of conviction you have concerning the subject as well as emotional involvements which may be present. If the topic is unfamiliar select those main points which may be researched and supported by evidence rather than by relying on personal examples.

Finally, in selecting the main points consider the life orientation of your audience. Specifically, examine the responding communicators' knowledge of the subject matter, interest in the topic, and attitude toward your specific purpose. If you neglect consideration of these factors you are guilty of disregarding the knowledge you have gained concerning the dynamic process of communication. The responding communicator not only determines *how* you deliver your message, but also determines its content. If this is hard to comprehend, imagine a physics professor trying to explain the nuclear fission process to a class of kindergarten pupils. Not only will his language be affected by his audience (how he says it) but the message itself (what he says) will be vastly different from one that he might deliver to a group of his colleagues. The consideration of and adaptation to the audience cannot be overemphasized. A communicator who considers the life orientation of the audience is much more likely to achieve the specific purpose than one who disregards the audience in the selection of main points, subpoints, and supporting materials.

ARRANGE THE IDEAS

The over-all organizational patterns of the prestructured communication have already been discussed. The arrangement of the ideas in the body of the message is quite similar to the over-all patterns of organization. This internal arrangement may take many forms. It would be impossible to list all the patterns and orders of arrangement which may be used in the body of a speech. Several of the most common forms which are available to you as communicators will be discussed.

Among the patterns which are frequently used to arrange the main points of a speech are: who, what, why, when, how, where; past, present, future; symptoms, prevention, cure; spelling a key word; political, economic, social; and physical, mental, spiritual, emotional. You can devise your own pattern of arrangement similar to these based on the particular needs of your message. Note that these patterns are not mutually exclusive. These and similar patterns may be grouped into more general classes. These general patterns are often termed *orders of arrangement.*

Topical order is the most common order of arrangement. It is simply the division of any subject into its component parts and the presentation of each division as a main point in the communication. An example of topical order would be brass, woodwinds, percussion, and strings when discussing the orchestra. Another example of the use of topical order is the division of matter into the classifications animal, vegetable, and mineral. Many of the orders which follow are also forms of topical order.

Chronological order is the arrangement of main points as they occurred in time. For example, in describing a recent vacation you might give a day-by-day description of events which occurred from the time you left home until the time you returned. A historical speech will usually utilize this order of arrangement.

When you arrange the main points by location you use *geographical order,* termed *spatial order* by some writers. A communication describing a beautiful landscape might begin by mentioning the green pines on the near slope of the mountain, move to the brown-and-white log cabin halfway up the mountainside, and conclude with the icy mountain top covered with snow in the far range of mountains. This is one form of spatial order—the describing of a scene or event as the observer saw it, location by location. Another use of geographical order is the division of the communication according to the places where events occurred. A communication on the Civil War might describe the different locations where famous battles took place. You might describe a foreign country in terms of various regions or cities. This type of order is commonly used in travelogue films.

Another form of arrangement is the *order of definition.* In this order the communication is an answer to a question asked in its title. For example, in a communication to inform entitled "What Is Jazz?" you might order your points by answering the question:

A. Jazz is an American tradition.

B. Jazz is a composite of many musical forms.

C. Jazz is an improvisation on a simple melody.

The order of definition has limited use and is a form of topical order.

In the *order of comparison and contrast,* similarities and differences among two or more concepts are shown. In a communication describing the characteristics of a good teacher, the communicator might compare and contrast the qualities needed by teachers and salesmen:

Comparison and contrast:	A. Salesmen must be familiar with their product. B.Teachers must know their subject.
Comparison:	C. Salesmen and teachers must have similar personality traits.
Contrast:	D. Salesmen and teachers have different goals.

The technique of comparison and contrast may also be used in relating supporting material to the main points of the communication. (See Chapter 6.)

The *order of cause and effect* is a form of arrangement in which the topic is divided into the causes and effects of a particular problem or event. In a communication on the rise of communism in Cuba the communicator might divide his speech into the causes which gave rise to communism in that country and the results of communism on the people of Cuba. Cause and effect is another method of relating supporting material to the main points of the message.

Logical order is the arrangement of the points in ascending order. In this form of arrangement you arrange the points in the order in which they would logically occur. When giving instructions on how to bowl, the communicator demonstrates how to grip the ball before he explains how to release it. In a speech on the passing of a bill in Congress you would not consider the percentage of vote necessary for passage before you explain the process of drafting and presenting the bill. In logical order the sequence of events is the pattern of organization.

The final order that will be discussed is termed *psychological order*. This form of arrangement is based upon the probable reaction of the responding communicators. Some authorities insist that the most important point should be presented first because it will make an initial impact on the audience. Other authorities suggest that the most important point should be given at the end to make a lasting impression. Both sides of the question have merit and this issue is discussed below. The psychological order suggests that your points must be arranged in such a way that they will achieve maximum impact. The following is an example of the psychological order of arrangement:

Topic: *Our Fraternity Needs a New House*
Important point: A. More room for social functions
Minor point: B. More attractive surroundings
Most important point: C. More pledges would be attracted

Psychological order is becoming popular as a form of arrangement. Much conflicting research has been conducted to determine the way in which points of varying degrees of importance affect attitudes.

In deciding whether to use major arguments at the outset of a communication or save them for the climax, consider the initial position of the audience. Such audience factors as motivation, initial interest, and ease of learning will alter the audience's perception of your arguments.

Hovland and his colleagues provided a comprehensive synthesis of research in this general area which is both interesting and valuable to the student of communication.[3] It is not the

---

[3] Our discussion and summary of research in organization follows, with some adaptation, Carl I. Hovland, Irving L. Janis, and Harold H. Kelley, *Communication and Persuasion* (New Haven: Yale University Press, 1953), Chapter V, pp. 134–174.

purpose of this text to present a detailed presentation of research in persuasion, but a brief summary of previous findings might prove helpful. Interested students should study the original sources of research cited in the suggested readings at the end of the chapter.

Research in the area of arranging the points of the speech in the most effective order center around three major problems. These will be discussed separately.

Drawing the Conclusion versus Leaving It Implied

What are the effects of drawing the conclusion for the audience as compared with leaving the conclusion implied? Studies regarding this question have differed in their findings. Cooper and Dinerman found that implicit messages (those which let the audience determine the conclusion) influenced the more intelligent members of a group while the less intelligent members failed to understand the message.[4] Hovland and Mandell, however, did not discover this relationship between intelligence and drawing the conclusion for the audience. They did find that over twice as many subjects changed opinions in favor of the communication when the conclusions were drawn by the communicator than when conclusions were left to the audience. Apparently the relative effectiveness of the two procedures depends on three major factors: the kind of communicator, the kind of audience, and the kind of issue.

1. Kind of communicator. A communicator who arouses suspicion is generally less effective when he draws the conclusion for the audience.

2. Kind of audience. The more intelligent members of the audience will probably need less explicit conclusions than the less intelligent.

3. Kind of issue. If there are strong emotional attachments to the issue the audience may examine the arguments and implications more carefully. In this case it may be more effective to

---

[4] Eunice Cooper and Helen Dinerman, "Analysis of the Film, 'Don't Be a Sucker:' A Study in Communication," *The Public Opinion Quarterly*, XV (1951), pp. 243–264.

let the members of the audience draw their own conclusions. If the implications of the issue are easy to see, however, it probably does not make much difference whether you draw the conclusions or not. A nondirective approach where no conclusions are drawn may be most effective when suggestions are met with strong resistance.

Hovland and Mandell concluded that, in general, it is more effective to state the conclusions explicitly in persuasive communications than to let the audience draw its own conclusions.[5]

Proposing a Conclusion versus Giving Both Sides

What are the relative effects upon opinion change of discussing only those arguments for the proposed conclusion as opposed to discussing both sides of the issue? In studying immediate changes of opinion Hovland, Lumsdaine, and Sheffield noted no difference between one-sided and two-sided communications in the amount of opinion change they produced. However, when they divided their audience into subgroups on the basis of several factors they did find some differences.

1. They found that a communication giving both sides of the issue was more effective for an audience initially opposed to the communicator's point of view.

2. A one-sided communication was more effective for audiences initially in agreement with the communication.

3. Better-educated audiences responded best to a communication presenting both sides of the issue.

4. A two-sided argument was more effective among the better-educated audiences regardless of their initial position concerning the communications' point of view.

5. Among audiences which were already convinced about the issue at hand and which were less educated, the one-sided communication was most effective.[6]

---

[5] C. I. Hovland and W. Mandell, "An Experimental Comparison of Conclusion Drawing by the Communicator and by the Audience," *Journal of Abnormal Social Psychology*, XXXXVII (1952), pp. 581–588.

[6] C. I. Hovland, A. A. Lumsdaine, and F. D. Sheffield, *Experiments on Mass Communication* (Princeton: Princeton University Press, 1949), p. 203.

Lumsdaine and Janis studied the same problem in terms of the long-range effects produced by the communications over an extended period. They also studied the effects of presenting counterpropaganda after the original communication had been presented. The following results were obtained:

1. A two-sided presentation is more effective in the long run when the audience is exposed to counterpropaganda regardless of its initial position.
2. A two-sided argument is most effective when, regardless of subsequent counterpropaganda, the audience initially disagrees with the communicator's position.
3. A two-sided communication is less effective when the audience initially agrees with the communicator and is not later exposed to counterpropaganda. When the possibility of counterpropaganda arises a one-sided argument is generally most effective.[7]

In summary, a one-sided argument will sway audience opinion more effectively regardless of initial position, but if counterpropaganda is given this effect may be lost. If the initial communication is two-sided it will generally be more lasting, especially if counterpropaganda is given.

Different Orders of Presentation

What are the effects of different orders of presentation of arguments in persuasive communication? It is in this last area of research that findings have been most contradictory. Most investigators have compared the relative effectiveness of what they term the "climactic" versus the "anticlimactic" order of presentation. The climactic order begins with the least important arguments and builds to the most important—that is, the climax. The anticlimactic order begins with the most important and proceeds to less important arguments.

Sponberg was among the first to investigate the relative effec-

---

[7] A. A. Lumsdaine and I. L. Janis, "Resistance to Counterpropaganda Produced by a One-Sided Versus a Two-Sided Propaganda Presentation," *The Public Opinion Quarterly*, XVII (1953), p. 311–318.

tiveness of climactic and anticlimactic orders of presentation. He concluded that the anticlimactic order was best.[8] Cromwell, defining strong arguments somewhat differently from Sponberg, found the climactic order to be most effective.[9] It appears that the advantages of the two orders depend upon the particular condition under which the communication is given.

1. The climax order will be favored on an issue with which the audience is familiar and about which they have deep concern.

2. The anticlimax order is favored with unfamiliar topics and with uninterested audiences.

In summary, there is little basis for preferring the climax to the anticlimax order in the presentation of arguments in a communication. Such factors as learning, past associations with the arguments, and acceptance of the communicator can influence which order of presentation is most effective in a given situation.

The above types of arrangement are a few of the most commonly used. Since organization is essential to clear understanding, some form of arrangement should be used when organizing the main points of the message.

Subpoints of a communication may also be organized according to one of the orders discussed above. The order used for arranging the subpoints may differ from the order used in arranging the main points. The degree to which the subpoints need to be organized depends upon the subject matter and time limitations. Having decided upon the important task of arranging the main points and subpoints of the message you are ready to include these in your speech outline.

PREPARE THE OUTLINE

Many students in English and speech classes regard outlining as busywork. Since outlines are frequently required as homework

---

[8] H. A. Sponberg, "A Study of the Relative Effectiveness of Climax and Anti-Climax Order in an Argumentative Speech," *Speech Monographs*, XIII (1946), pp. 25–44.

[9] H. Cromwell, "The Relative Effect of Audience Attitude of the First Versus the Second Argumentative Speech of a Series," *Speech Monographs*, XVII (1950), pp. 105–122.

in these classes students often write the theme or speech and then write an outline from the completed work. This practice is similar to taking a trip without knowing where you were going and then drawing a map of the route after you reached your destination. You usually have a destination and secure a map of the route to follow. Likewise, you should know your destination in communicating and develop an outline to help you reach your goal.

There are several purposes for outlining a message. One purpose is to help note inconsistencies in reasoning and examples. An outline can also help relate major and minor points and let the communicator discover where main points overlap. Another purpose of the outline is to help the communicator gauge the length of his presentation. In many instances this timing is of great importance. Outlining can help the communicator perceive exactly how much material he is planning to develop in the allotted time. Other purposes of making outlines are to evaluate the importance of ideas, to evaluate the arrangement of the main points, and to inspect examples and supporting materials.

A good outline is the recorded culmination of the preparation and development of the message. The outline should not be a straitjacket. It should be a flexible working guide for the communication presentation.

There are three common methods of preparing outlines. The first is the *topical outline*. In this form of outlining all the main points and subpoints are in the form of single words or phrases. In a long communication where it would be cumbersome to write all the main points and subpoints in sentence form, the topical outline might be most appropriate. It is usually better to be more complete in your outlines than too sketchy. An incomplete outline may not be clear upon reading it after a delayed interval of time. It is likely to be of insufficient depth for an effective presentation.

A more complete outline form is the *full content outline*. In this type of outline all main points, subpoints, and supporting materials are stated in the form of complete sentences. The value of this approach lies in the refined language and style. It also insures that your examples and illustrations are complete. It is quite embarrassing to begin a story only to discover halfway through that you have forgotten the punch line. The full content outline can be detrimental if you read from the outline rather than make the material meaningful. If this barrier is overcome, the full content outline can be a useful tool in structuring your communication.

The *logical brief* is frequently used by lawyers and debaters, but it may also be used as an outline for the persuasive communication. In constructing the brief there is no one best method to follow, but a few suggestions might be helpful. The brief should contain only complete statements or phrases. In this respect it is a compromise between the topical and the full content outlines. In the brief a consistent pattern of symbols should be used to represent each statement. Each statement should be preceded by a single symbol in order to show its relation to other statements.

Each main point must be reinforced by supporting material. Sources of supporting evidence should accompany each point. The brief is a device for presenting a point-by-point analysis and synthesis of ideas when preparing your materials for the communication. It is a convenient way to arrange your supporting materials into a clear, logical order. The brief can also help you test logical proofs, assuring you that your thinking moves from point to point in a coherent manner. The main disadvantages of the logical brief are that it is often rigid and time consuming.

Regardless of the type of outline used a uniform set of symbols must be employed. The symbols shown in Fig. 6 are usually used to represent the statements in an outline.

There are several general rules which should be observed in preparing a meaningful outline:

1. The title, general purpose, specific purpose, and personal purpose should precede the outline.

2. The divisions of the outline should be labeled according to the organizational pattern selected.

3. A uniform set of symbols should be used to designate main points, subpoints, and supporting materials. (See Fig. 6.)

```
I.  .   .   .
    A.  .   .   .
        1.  .   .   .
            a.  .   .   .
                (1)  .   .   .
                    (a)  .   .   .
                    (b)  .   .   .
                (2)  .   .   .
            b.  .   .   .
        2.  .   .   .
    B.  .   .   .
        1.  .   .   .
            a.  .   .   .
                (1)  .   .   .
                    (a)  .   .   .
                    (b)  .   .   .
                (2)  .   .   .
            b.  .   .   .
        2.  .   .   .
II.  .   .   .
    A.  .   .   .
    B.  .   .   .
    C.  .   .   .
```

FIGURE 6.   OUTLINE SYMBOLS

4. There should usually not be more than five main ideas in the body of the outline.

5. Each subpoint in the outline should be proof, explanation, or support for the main idea to which it is subordinate.

6. There is no formula for the proper length of an outline.

7. The outline should be neat, with proper left-hand margins.

If you consider the outline as a map to guide you in presenting the most effective communication possible, you will be more likely to reach your destination—that of achieving the desired response from your audience.

PREPARE THE INTRODUCTION

Include in your outline an attention-getting introduction. The basic purposes of the introduction are to *achieve common ground* with the audience, to *arouse attention, attain interest,* and to *preview* what you plan to communicate. The introduction is of utmost importance because it projects a first impression to the audience. On the basis of this first impression they will make preliminary judgments about you as an individual, the subject matter which you are going to present, and whether or not they are interested enough to listen to you. The time you spend preparing an effective introduction will be some of the most valuable time spent in preparing your entire message. The attention step suggested by Dewey was presented earlier in this chapter. This step involves making the audience want to listen. Several methods of gaining attention will be mentioned later, but a word of caution should be expressed at this time. The attention step should be related to your subject matter and be meaningful to your entire speech. Some communicators enjoy gaining the attention of their audience through the use of vaudeville tactics such as lighting a fake firecracker, firing a blank gun, or throwing paper airplanes into the audience. These devices usually gain attention, but they may create resentment among the audience. Another questionable device is to tell the audience a deliberate lie and later tell them that it was only a joke designed to scare them. For example, one communicator began his presentation by stating, "I just heard a bulletin which confirmed that the United States has just been attacked by Red China." The communicator later admitted his lie but said that he wanted to let the audience know how they would feel if this really were true. Did he gain attention? Yes, but at what cost to the audience? A communicator must gain the attention of the audience, but should be fair in doing so. Another disadvantage of the sensationalized attention-getting step is that it draws attention to itself and you lose the continued interest of the audience. There are several accepted ways of introducing a speech. Some of the more common of these techniques are discussed below.

A *startling statement* is an excellent means of arousing audience attention provided the above warning is heeded. The statement should arouse audience attention and should be an integrated part of the speech. An example of a startling statement would be, "Statistics indicate that one out of four people in this room will die of cancer." Again, remember that you have the responsibility to make sure that your statements are true and based upon substantial evidence.

A *quotation* can often provide an effective means of introducing a message. The quotation should be appropriate to the communication and should relate to the specific purpose. A quotation which sounds "nice," but which does not fit the specific purpose is useless. Quotations are generally taken from books, plays, speeches, or radio or television. If the quotation is not well-known to the audience you should document it, and perhaps give some of the qualifications of the author.

Stories can be used as another form of introduction. The stories should, of course, be in good taste and should be related to the life orientation of the audience. The stories may be true or hypothetical, depending on the nature of the communication. When using a story for an introduction carefully plan a transitional phrase to relate the story to your specific purpose. If you plan to use a humorous story it is wise to have more than one in case the first story falls flat.

"What would you do if a stranger walked up and handed you a check for a million dollars?" This is an example of the type of introduction called a *rhetorical question*. A rhetorical question is one which you really do not expect the audience to answer. You ask it to provoke thought and to arouse interest. Although this is an attention-getting type of introduction, there is one consideration which you should keep in mind. Someone in the audience, especially if the group is small, might actually answer the question. Be prepared to handle this situation if it should occur. Usually, however, the audience will realize that the question is rhetorical in nature and that it is not meant to be answered.

Another device for introducing a speech is a *reference to the occasion*. This type of introduction is common in after-dinner speeches, dedication speeches, and recognition speeches. The following is an example of this type of introduction:

> There have been few instances in history which equal the importance of this gathering tonight. We are here to select a man to be president of the United States in a period during which internal and external pressures are struggling to divide this great country of ours.

The occasion does not have to be of national scope to be important. Occasions which afford an opportunity for a prestructured communication are generally important. A reference to the occasion helps make the responding communicator feel important and a vital part of the group or organization.

Regardless of the type of introduction that you select make sure it fulfills the purposes of the introduction and is appropriate to the rest of the communication. An introduction which is effective will achieve rapport with the audience, gain their attention and interest, and begin the communication smoothly.

PREPARE THE CONCLUSION

The final step in preparing your presentation is to develop an effective conclusion. The conclusion serves to unify the component parts of the communication. It should promote goodwill among the audience, provide inspiration for them to carry out the proposed plan of action, and provide a restatement of the main points of the message. The introduction provides a first impression, whereas, the conclusion provides a final or lasting impression. In persuasive communications do not neglect to include an action step. Without this appeal for action the audience will lack direction. You may have heard the story about the irate man who threw one shoe at a howling alley cat, and consequently, his neighbors could not go to sleep because they kept waiting for him to throw the other shoe. Without the action step your audience might keep waiting for you to "throw the other shoe." Once you present a problem and present a plan for it, then show your audience what to do in order to carry out the plan. Without a suggested direction or a challenge to act, the audience may fail to respond to your communication in a positive manner.

The most common form of the many varied types of conclusions is the *summary*. The summary is usually a restatement of the main points of the message in somewhat different terms. The summary should be brief, clear, and vivid. Keep in mind that one of the main purposes of the conclusion is to cement the main ideas of your presentation in the minds of your audience. The summary helps to achieve this function. It may, in addition, be used in conjunction with several other types of conclusions.

One of these types which can be used with the summary is called the *illustrative conclusion*. This can take the form of an anecdote or story. In this type of conclusion an illustration is used to convey your specific purpose. It may be an example of your ideas put into action, or a hypothetical illustration of how the situation could be changed if certain steps were taken. The illustrative conclusion also serves to paint a mental picture in the minds of your audience which will help them to remember the message you are presenting.

Patrick Henry stated, "Give me liberty, or give me death!" This is probably one of the classic examples of a type of conclusion called *statement of personal intention*. In this form of conclusion state what you personally are going to do about the problem. The implication is that you believe strongly enough about your topic to do something about it and you hope that the audience will follow your lead. Statements of personal intention usually contain emotional language and are structured to incite the audience to action.

A type of conclusion similar to the statement of personal intention is the *emotional appeal*. This emotional appeal is a direct request to the audience to set upon the problem at hand. An example of this type of conclusion might be, "Won't you care enough to give to CARE so that a starving child in Viet Nam can know the feeling of a full stomach for the first time in his life?" The appeal should contain vivid language and is used most frequently in persuasive communications. Like the selection of the introduction, the conclusion must be chosen with the specific purpose of the communication in mind. The type you choose is dependent upon a complex of factors unique to your individual presentation.

In summary, remember that the prestructured communication is composed of several distinct parts. These divisions, however, must be combined in such a way that the communication seems unified. The responding communicator hears the communication as a unit and is usually unaware of its individual components. You must realize that your purpose in communication is not simply to present a speech, but rather to make that speech communicate your message to the audience. The communication must be structured with the concept in mind that the whole is greater than the sum of its individual parts.

ORGANIZING THE SEMISTRUCTURED COMMUNICATION

In the prestructured communication situation there is usually ample opportunity for organization. This opportunity is not always present in the semistructured communication situation. As a general rule in informal or conversational situations your thoughts must be organized in a relatively short time. Continual revision of your thoughts and ideas is necessary. Upon casual consideration it might seem impossible to organize the semistructured communication but this is not necessarily true. Many of the rules which apply to the prestructured communication also apply to the semistructured communication situation. Both contain a general and a specific purpose for communicating. A personal purpose is also present in both situations. There must usually be an introduction, a body, and a conclusion in each. The exception to this occurs in interpersonal conversation when the communicator shifts rapidly back and forth from originator to responder. The differences between the two communication situations are also evident. Generally in the semistructured situation, there will be little or no time to choose a pattern for arranging the main points of the communication. It is possible, however, to begin with no distinct pattern in mind and evolve a pattern as the conversation progresses. You should be familiar with the patterns explained in the previous section so that these patterns will come to mind easily when needed. Several specific suggestions might aid in organizing the semistructured communication.

The first suggestion is to utilize the *incubation period*. In other words, take ample time to think before you begin to communicate. Some communicators have a tendency to move their mouths into high gear before their brains get out of low. There is absolutely nothing wrong with pausing a few moments before replying to a question, or before starting to talk. These few seconds may make the difference between a coherent and meaningful communication and a disorganized and trite statement.

During this incubation period you can search for associations and related ideas. Your past life orientation includes many personal examples and illustrations which can be included in the conversation. This device of association is especially effective when initiating a conversation with someone whom you do not know very well. If you are told that a person is from a particular city, think back and gather all the associations that you have regarding that town. If you find a person has certain hobbies or interests you can search for associations you have about these.

If you know in advance you will be meeting a strange person in a conversational situation it might be a good idea to do some research about his home town, interests, occupation, and hobbies. This does not imply that you should spend a great deal of time gathering information, but rather, finding areas and interests you might have in common. A few well-chosen questions can enhance a conversational situation. A request for advice or the focusing of attention on something unusual in the surroundings aid in achieving common ground. If you spend a little time in preparation before semistructured communications you can make the meeting more pleasant for yourself and others.

CHECKS FOR CONVERSATION

When initiating the conversation you can usually organize your thoughts in advance. However, if someone else initiates it you must organize your thoughts as you proceed. Check the following points about your contributions to the conversation:

1. Are my remarks really interesting to those present?
2. Is my humor in good taste?
3. Are my remarks appropriate to the subject?
4. Are my ideas expressed clearly and concisely?
5. Do I listen to the remarks of others?
6. Do I relate and adapt to the life orientation of my audience?

If you are familiar with these questions they can be used as checks while you are engaged in conversation by simply asking them of yourself. These questions can be used as criteria for the remarks you make during semistructured communication.

Some of the classical rhetoricians advocated the use of *topoi* or topics of conversation. They suggested memorizing several bits of information concerning many diverse topics. When it came time to talk, all the communicator had to do was weave these bits of knowledge into the presentation. This technique has some obvious drawbacks, but it also has some good points. A quotation or fact inserted in semistructured communication can add ethical proof and interest. The insertion of these into conversation will greatly aid in achieving your specific purpose and will add spice to communication. Another suggestion is to keep up with current affairs. Reading current newspapers, magazines, and books regularly can pay real dividends when you are thrust into a semistructured communication situation. Current affairs rank high on the list of topics usually discussed, and if you are well-informed you should have no trouble making intelligent contributions to the conversation.

If you do not have organizational patterns established in your daily activities it is very unlikely that you will do an effective job of organizing communication. It might be worthwhile for you to sit down and evaluate the ways you spend your time, the ways you approach your studies, the ways you plan your weekends. If you find organization lacking in these areas it might pay to begin organizing here. Organization is a habit, yet it is not a cure-all. Organization can, however, help you to get more out of life and to use more efficiently the little time you have. If you can establish some organizational habits which suit you individually, it will be a simple second step to apply those same habits to your communication activities.

Another word of caution should be included at this point. Realize that everyone does not have a pattern of organization, especially in their communication. If you try to impose your organizational pattern upon a presentation you hear, you are likely to become confused. It is especially difficult to take notes in the same pattern for every communicator you hear. You should be flexible in both your listening and note-taking. Remember that organization can be of great aid to the responding communicator; but as a responding communicator you must realize that all originating communicators do not have distinct organizational patterns.

QUESTIONS FOR DISCUSSION

1. What ethical considerations must a communicator make when using an attention-getting device? What ethical considerations must be made when using a psychological order of presentation?

2. Why is an outline of the message to be presented necessary? What conditions determine the length and type of outline used?

3. In the semistructured communication setting how does one's organization differ from that in a prestructured setting?

EXERCISES

[Forms for completing the exercises marked with an asterisk will be found in the *Worksheets for Speech—Interpersonal Communication* (San Francisco: Chandler Publishing Company, 1967).]

1. Select a general topic and phrase five specific purposes for five

different speeches on that topic. List three main ideas under each specific purpose.*

2. Listen to a radio speech, sermon, or other prestructured speech and analyze the introduction and conclusion. State what kinds were used and criticize both the selection and the development of those which were chosen.*

3. Prepare an outline for a one-point speech containing at least four subpoints with sufficient proof for each. Repeat this with a different outline form.

4. Clip five advertisements from a current popular magazine and for each one list the factors of attention employed. Explain how they are used.

5. Prepare a talk based on a carefully developed outline. Ask the class to jot down your main points and subpoints as they come through. Check to see if differences occurred between your own outline and those observed by the audience.

6. Select an article in a popular magazine and outline it. Begin by phrasing the purpose and finding the main points.

7. Outline any of the speeches in the magazine *Vital Speeches*. Do a thorough job, and be sure that your outline corresponds in detail to the model outline in the chapter.

8. Prepare a brief list of magazines which might contain source material for a speech on "The Space Race." Of the magazines cited which would have the highest credibility or authoritativeness? Organize the list in the order in which they would be of most value to the speech, down to the least valuable.

9. Investigate the origin of the word "organization." How does this knowledge concerning the original meaning of the word relate to the process of arranging the materials in a speech?

10. Prepare a report comparing the organization of a speech to the preparation of a written theme. What are the similarities and differences?

SUGGESTED READINGS

Baker, Eldon E., "The Immediate Effects of Perceived Speaker Disorganization on Speaker Credibility and Audience Attitude Change in Persuasive Speaking." *Western Speech Journal*, XXIX (Summer, 1965), pp. 148–161.

Black, John W., and Wilbur E. Moore, *Speech: Code, Meaning, and Communication*. New York: McGraw-Hill Company, Inc., 1955. Chapter 18, pp. 182–199.

Hovland, Carl I., Irving L. Janis, and Harold H. Kelley, *Communi-cation and Persuasion*. New Haven and London: Yale University Press, 1963. Chapter 4, "Organization of Persuasive Arguments," pp. 99–134.

Mudd, Charles S., and Malcolm O. Sillars, *Speech: Content and Communication*. San Francisco: Chandler Publishing Company, 1962. Chapter 8, "Outlining," pp. 117–149.

Olson, Donald O., "Confusion in Arrangement." *The Speech Teacher*, XIII (September, 1964), pp. 216–219.

Ryan, Earl H., "That First Awful Minute." *Today's Speech*, I (October, 1953), pp. 16–17. (An entertaining discussion on the introduction of a speech.)

The Message Symbolized | 5

Symbolic formulation involves the selection of appropriate symbols and is vital to any communication situation. Symbols clothe ideas and make them understandable. In everyday communication, both verbal and nonverbal symbols are the means by which you express your ideas, endeavor to understand what others are trying to say, and attempt to understand what you mean. Symbols are the medium which enables you to conduct your business affairs, form friendships, worship, learn new ideas, develop new formuli, explore new areas, and express your likes and dislikes. Symbols also help you to respond correctly, establish the appropriate mood, and make interaction with others possible. In other words, symbols enable you to adapt to and change your environment.

SYMBOLIZATION

The symbolic process is the means by which you, as a human being, are able to let symbols stand for ideas, events, places, and things. Although most of the time words are the primary concern in communication, the symbolic process includes nonverbal as well as verbal symbols. If a fellow squeezes his girlfriend's hand and she squeezes back, communication occurs through a nonverbal symbol, a symbol that has been given meaning by our culture. Communication takes place even if he squeezes her hand and she does not return the squeeze. Most human reactions, both present and future, are controlled by symbols. Life often seems to be a process to obtain and accumulate symbols that provide feelings of accomplishment and success. Good clothes, orna-

93

ments, new homes are symbols of wealth. Rags and shacks seem to symbolize poverty. Since symbols are an integral part of your life orientation, they need to be studied and understood.

Symbols need to be controlled so that they do not control you and determine your daily life. A girl who assumes that a person with freckles is homely and then considers herself homely because she has freckles is letting herself be controlled by the symbol. The mature individual differentiates between *structural reality* and symbols and reacts to symbols as only representations of events in the real world. At the present time a military command in the form of a few symbols could cause the destruction of civilization. Perhaps even more important is the knowledge that a few poorly chosen symbols can disintegrate a human spirit. Many a G.I. felt his world give way not so much as by the shelling and the dangers of combat, but by the words "Dear John." Personal destruction is always more real to the individual. Even though reactions to the symbolic process are often incorrect, the process is still basic to human communication. The first step involved in the control of symbols is to understand and to recognize the symbolic process. Once this has been achieved then you are ready to implement this knowledge into your communication patterns.

Keeping in touch with *structural reality* is basic to control over the symbolic process, and symbolic control is basic to effective communication. The relationship between symbols and reality should be the same as the relationship between a map and the territory it represents. Alfred Korzybski used this analogy and suggested that the relationship should be considered in three ways: (1) the map is not the territory (the symbol is not the thing symbolized) ; (2) the map does not represent all the territory (symbols cannot say all there is to be said about a thing) ; (3) the ideal map would have to include a map of itself (symbols are self-reflective) .[1] Korzybski based many of his theories of general semantics on these ideas. These theories expanded semantics to include the behavioral aspects of language and meaning.

---

[1] Alfred Korzybski, *Science and Sanity*, 4th ed. (Lakeville, Conn.: Institute of General Semantics, 1958), p. 58.

THE TRIANGLE OF MEANING

Ogden and Richards in their book, *The Meaning of Meaning,* have helped to clarify meaning.[2] Of particular interest in the understanding of communication is their triangle of meaning, which illustrates the relationship between language and symbols. The triangle presented in Fig. 7 is an adaptation on theirs.

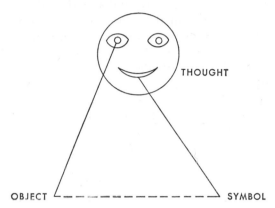

THOUGHT

OBJECT   SYMBOL

FIGURE 7. THE TRIANGLE OF MEANING

Meaning usually starts with a thought. A person thinks of an object with four legs, a wagging tail, and a moist nose. He thinks of this object in relationship to other objects and the mind sorts out the symbol *dog*. The thought, object, and symbol form the parts of the triangle. Each point of the triangle could be discussed at length, but in communication the important concepts to remember are these: There are definite relationships between thought and object, and between thought and symbol; however, the relationship between object and symbol is only inferred and the inference must be recognized. The symbol and the object symbolized are never exactly the same, just as a map and the territory it represents are independent of each other. The thought (perception) can even cause your concept of an object to be different from that of someone else.

The triangle of meaning aids in the understanding of other

[2] Charles K. Ogden and I. A. Richards, *The Meaning of Meaning* (New York: Harcourt, Brace and Company, 1946), p. 11.

concepts about language. It illustrates the risk you often take in communicating when you assume that the other person thinks of the same object you have in mind when you use a symbol to represent that object. When you use the symbol *rose,* a variety of ideas immediately come to the minds of your responding communicators: petals, thorns, colors, scents, four, "mighty-lak-a," compass, war of the, long-stemmed, American Beauty, of Picardy, climb up to her window, Billy, and the ring, dew on the, the yellow of Texas, or any of thousands of others. In word-association tests when the word *rose* is used, the word most commonly associated with it is red. Similarly many people think only of orange juice when the word *juice* is mentioned. They know there are other kinds of roses and juices, but the immediate response is one of red or orange.

Your life orientation, as discussed in Chapter 3, determines your response to a certain symbol. This is best illustrated by the responses of two students in a class. When asked what came to their minds when the symbol *rose* was used, a girl replied, "I think of a beautiful little white cottage with a thatched roof on the hilltop surrounded by a beautiful blue sky with fleecy white clouds. All around the cottage are beautiful beds of flowers which are encircled by a white picket fence. Over the gateway of the picket fence is an archway that is covered by beautiful red roses." In the same class a fellow replied to the word *rose* by saying that he thought of dirt. Life orientations, philosophies, and other patterns are reflected in these two replies. As a communicator you cannot take for granted that your audience will have the same referent (object) in their minds when you use a specific symbol, or that they will even associate the proper referent with your symbol. The learning of language is a complicated process. It is not sufficient to say that the symbol and the thing symbolized are not the same thing. A knowledge of the way you have learned symbols and the structure of language will give you insights into communication.

THE STRUCTURE OF LANGUAGE

LEARNING WORDS AND SYMBOLS

Few stop to consider how they learned a word or the way in

which they are learning new words and symbols now. Yet this process is so basic to understanding communication that you must be constantly aware of it. A word or symbol is usually learned in context rather than in isolation. This context is not always verbal, but may take the form of feelings, hopes, and aspirations. The meaning you attach to a word learned in this way is usually referred to as the connotative meaning. The connotative meaning of a word is the relationship between a word, an object, and a person. The connotative meaning is personalized; you attach personal meaning to the word as a result of past experiences. The denotative meaning of a word is the relationship between a word and an object and is concerned with structural reality. Sometimes this is called the historical or dictionary meaning of a word.

The establishment of connotative meanings for symbols may have lifelong effects. On the way home from school a boy learned a new word from his friends. The boy used this word at home. His parents, however, did not share his enthusiasm and promptly suggested that if the word were used again, he would be punished by having his mouth washed out with soap. As the boy grew older that word carried many connotations with it that dated back to this incident. Although its effect is not always discernible, the setting in which a word is learned often colors the word. Therefore, the learning of words or symbols must be considered an individual matter. This is another example of the importance of understanding your life orientation in order to communicate effectively.

WORD MEANINGS

A word is not a container like a glass. Words do not contain meaning within themselves, but are sounds in the air or marks on paper. One general semantics concept is that the meaning of words is not within the words, but within the individual. Since individuals have learned the same word in slightly different contexts, they have different meanings for the word. There are words which are frightful to some people and yet do not produce fear in others. To the individual who has had tuberculosis, the mention of "T.B." can bring reactions which would not be present in another individual who has not had the disease. The word *dead* might produce certain emotional responses within an individual who has just lost a loved one and yet not produce the same reaction two or three years later. Individuals are usually thought of as being different yet uniqueness in terms of reactions is not often comprehended. A communicator must be sensitive to feedback and constantly check the reactions of others as well as his own reactions, or as a student put it, "you need to keep your antenna up."

HIDDEN ASSUMPTIONS IN LANGUAGE

Communication is made more difficult, if not impossible at times, because of the silent or hidden assumptions that lie buried in language. In communicating, it is not enough to reason well; your reasoning must begin with correct premises. The connotative associations that are learned with a word, or a symbol, are disguised as premises or assumptions upon which you base your communication. The feeling that snakes are fearful, awful, and to be despised becomes attached to the symbol snake until you may react to the word *snake* as to a snake itself. These feelings are often generalized to an assumption that suggests all snakes are frightening and dangerous, while in reality many snakes are harmless.

Many times reactions are transformed into assumptions about racial and color characteristics. Some people's ideas about foreigners, Jews, Negroes, or Christians are based upon prejudices associated with the word, or symbol. One of the difficulties with these assumptions is that they are often below the threshold of consciousness and are not brought to the conscious level without a great effort. These hidden assumptions are ingrained in the nervous system and control the communication process, which in turn affects the nervous system. Language has conditioned your nervous system for the most part, which will control your reactions to the language of others. As you think, so you speak; as you speak, so you think.

LANGUAGE AND YOUR NERVOUS SYSTEM

An analysis of language does not reveal all the characteristics of the nervous system, but it is difficult to discuss, shape, mold, change, or interpret your nervous system without language. Since language is the medium of interpretation, you should be constantly aware of the role it plays in your life. Also, understanding the way in which your nervous system operates will help you to understand your reactions to language. A bit of criticism given at one time will not have the same effect as a bit of criticism at another time. There are some areas within individuals in which a certain stimulus will generally evoke the same response. However, the connotative meaning in language will often alter the response when the time or circumstance changes.

A study of your life orientation should include the effect words, symbols, hidden assumptions, and language concepts have on you. An understanding of your life orientation will often give you a clue to the reason you react in a particular manner. More than half the battle is to recognize the reason for a reaction, even if the reaction cannot be altered. There are areas in which it is possible for a communicator to choose language that is appropriate to the responding communicator's nervous system. Listen to a boy who talks with his sister before he leaves the house and then listen to the same boy as he talks to his girlfriend on a date. He probably has altered his language to fit the nervous system of his date to produce the desired effect.

As you gain an understanding of language and its effect on your nervous system you will realize that words are only symbols and that to discover meaning you must properly interpret the symbol. This understanding will enable you to have symbol reactions to language and not signal reactions. If, in the course of a conversation, someone talks about "dirty labor leaders" and your father is a labor leader, you will not have a breakdown in your communication if you will realize that (1) the other individual is speaking from his nervous system, his background; (2) you are interpreting from your nervous system, your background; and (3) both of you may be correct to some extent. Communicators must recognize their sensitive areas and understand how they affect symbolization for them if they are to communicate successfully. They must also know and understand the sensitive areas of the responding communicator's life orientation if they are to move or change his nervous system.

You learn to interpret your world and yourself through language. This interpretation starts as you begin to learn words, their meanings and associations. Assumptions and concepts are soon built deeply into your nervous system. Communication is like the waters of a river; the flow of language controlled by past patterns forms new patterns for other language to flow over, as the river follows and enlarges its bed. Many rough places could be taken out of the flow of communication if you realized that it was your nervous system which created the rough place and not the language.

THE PROCESS OF ABSTRACTION

The process of abstraction is your response to your environment. You *abstract* (pick out, respond to, are sensitive to, pay attention to, are disturbed by) certain stimuli and do not abstract the rest. A large portion of this process is carried on in the subconscious or at the inattentive level. Your responses to certain stimuli frequently are pushed into the subconscious by habit patterns. One of the first steps in breaking a habit pattern is to bring the stimulus to the conscious level so that you are aware of it. The process of abstracting, then, is not unfamiliar in the sense that you have never tried it. It is unfamiliar in the sense that for the most part you are not conscious of abstracting.

Abstracting is an inclusive term, encompassing the integration of sensory avenues and the associative process of the central nervous system. You do not see, feel, hear, taste, touch, or respond in other ways just in terms of the object itself, but in relationship to your previous experiences. The object is never the thing itself, but an interaction between your nervous system and the object. Your nervous system abstracts certain qualities and leaves out or supplies others. In this sense abstracting is related to the process of perception. What you will abstract (perceive) at any given moment depends on many factors. These factors include (1) your ability to discriminate, (2) the structure of the abstracting organism, (3) your position at any particular time in space, (4) your abstracting details from a total situation, and (5) your life orientation, which predisposes you to abstract in a manner consistent with itself.

ABSTRACTING ACCORDING TO ABILITY
TO DISCRIMINATE

Your ability to discriminate depends upon the way you have learned to discriminate. A professional taster of cream can detect onion flavor more accurately than a layman. A musician can easily identify a "sour note" in a concert, but would not necessarily be able to tell when cream is "sour." The discrimination learned from your past training, then, is a main factor in your process of abstracting.

ABSTRACTING ACCORDING TO THE STRUCTURE
OF THE ORGANISM

The structure of the organism also can determine the extent of learning. The color-blind individual would not be able to discriminate colors, regardless of how much training he might have. A blind man's ability to abstract would differ from that of a person who could see. However, a defect in one sense organ may lead to a keener perception in others. An account is given of a newly married couple attending a party. All were shocked when a blind person suggested that their marriage would not last more than 6 months. He was told he was wrong because he could not see their many signs of affection, but he replied, "I have been able to hear the tone of their voices as they speak to each other." They were divorced within 6 months. Thus, the organism may enhance or limit the process of abstraction.

ABSTRACTING ACCORDING TO THE POSITION
IN SPACE

Your position in space can make a difference in what is perceived or abstracted from verbal and nonverbal contexts. The manager of a supermarket will hardly perceive the employees' eating on the job in the same way as an employee or the owner. What a difference exists between seeing a car wrecked, and seeing your own in the same condition. Your mood often determines your position in abstracting. Blissful newlyweds do not abstract problems from events as readily as they may later. If, in one week a student gets three exams back on which he receives two A's and a *D*, the single low grade is much easier to take than if he received *D*'s on the two previous exams. In the latter case, he might abstract, "I am a failure;" in the former case he might abstract, "Oh, well, I'll do better next time." What you abstract from a situation is influenced by your position at that time and determines your reaction to that situation.

ABSTRACTING DETAILS FROM A TOTAL SITUATION

Usually, you abstract details from a total situation. The process of identification works from specific to general more often than from general to specific. As has been discussed earlier, identification is significant to all levels and plays an inherent role in abstracting. It is probable that you use the inductive process in reasoning more than the deductive process (see Chapter 6), at least when identification is involved.

ABSTRACTING ACCORDING TO YOUR
LIFE ORIENTATION

Basic to all of the ways you abstract is your life orientation. For the most part your life orientation is a self-perpetuating mechanism. It predisposes you to abstract in a particular manner, which in turn reinforces your life orientation. You enjoy being correct in your perceptions, and hence, you alter *subjective reality* to make them true. An individual who says "I do not think I am going to like her," in many cases will abstract details that will reinforce his first impression. If a girl has been told that a certain boy is "fresh" before her first date with him, she will probably abstract from his actions characteristics that reinforce this impression. For this reason, a person whose life orientation has taught him to dislike Negroes, Jews, or other groups finds it difficult to abstract anything good about these people. At this point, he becomes a slave of the abstracting process and stops learning; no longer does he have new experiences, but just repeats old ones. He does not learn but just rearranges his prejudices.

ABSTRACTION AND COMMUNICATION

Discussion of the five abstracting areas helps you to know the reasons why you respond to your environment in certain ways.

As a mature communicator your task is to relate the world of nonwords to the world of words as closely as you can. An understanding of abstraction helps you to see the framework of your intrapersonal communication and the possibilities for distortion of any event or happening. It is not possible to develop a perfect, one-to-one relationship, but you can know that it is only *a* relationship based on the limited experience of your nervous system. Once this is understood, then the next step is to know something about the levels of abstraction and their use in the process of communication.

The process of abstracting has been illustrated in several ways starting with Alfred Korzybski's structural differential.[3] S. I. Hayakawa explains the process by utilizing an "abstraction ladder." [4] Regardless of the way it is illustrated, knowledge about abstracting is needed by each individual who hopes to communicate. The communicator who is aware of the process of abstraction not only says something; he communicates.

LEVELS OF ABSTRACTING

NONVERBAL LEVEL

The various illustrations mentioned earlier help in understanding the different levels of the abstraction process. This knowledge aids the communicator in identifying and noting change. The first level of abstraction is called the nonverbal level and is the level known to science since it ultimately consists of atoms, electrons, protons, and neutrons. At this level, structure is ever-changing and an object can be identified through scientific instrumentation.

The object level of abstraction is also nonverbal. In fact, language can block communication on this level. Sometimes an understanding look by a husband, after his wife has broken a piece of china, transmits deeper meaning than words. Most of life's deepest experiences are at the object level where language is meaningless. A communicator who sharpens this level of abstraction will better understand people and be more able to

---

[3] Korzybski, *op. cit.*, pp. 386–451.
[4] S. I. Hayakawa, *Language in Thought and Action* (New York: Harcourt, Brace & World, Inc., 1964, pp. 165–170.

reach them. Harry Weinberg suggests that this is the world of the artist and poet—the portal to mystic experiences and transcendental visions which great works of art, literature, and music can evoke.[5] This is the level of abstraction on which you live your most intimate and personal life. It is the most important level of experience, for it is the level of feeling and sensation and emotion. Animals cease abstracting at the nonverbal level and only man has the ability to move to the next level of abstraction—the verbal level.

THE VERBAL LEVEL

Man is a predicator as well as one who has dominion and these two attributes enables him to use symbolic language. The verbal level, with its plotting, planning, theorizing, and predicting, operates in the final analysis for the sake of the nonverbal level and not vice versa.

The verbal level of abstracting can be divided into many levels of description: naming of objects and the higher orders of inference, generalizations, and class terms.

The Naming Level

The first of the verbal levels might be called the naming level. At this level, one attaches a name to an object for identification. A communicator may find it necessary in using a symbol to leave out many characteristics and invariably suggest others which he may not have intended. For example, an individual who suggests, "All you need is an attorney to help you," to a person who has distorted ideas of what an attorney might do may find that his message is not accepted. It is important in communication to know that words, symbols, and names do not always evoke the same referent. Whenever characteristics are left out and agreement is not reached on the few understood, there will be a breakdown. This is why a functional definition is often the most appropriate one. If the name of a product describes what it will do, communication is enhanced.

---

[5] Harry Weinberg, *Levels of Knowing and Existence* (New York: Harper and Brothers, 1959), pp. 58–59.

The Inferential Level

The inferential level, which consists of class terms and classes, leaves out more details and characteristics. It is well to keep in mind that class terms are man-made and can have all the infallibility that seems to be inherent in man. These are high-order abstractions created by man for his convenience by noting similarities and disregarding differences. Communication so depersonalized becomes meaningless and stereotyped. The communicator must deal with a universal truth, but in a personalized manner. A television or radio personality may be speaking to millions, but unless each listener feels he is being spoken to, the communication will not be successful. Again the premise needs to be stressed that the way in which you classify an object determines your reaction to it. The discussion of an extensional orientation, which follows in the last part of the chapter, will show many ways of seeing differences as well as similarities.

The Higher Levels

The highest level of abstracting deals with inferences and generalizations. At this level statements can be made about statements. Here, it is easy to become far removed from reality and truth. At this level both the responding communicator and the originating communicator have tremendous responsibilities to make sure that statements can be referred to lower levels of abstraction. Many examples of the use of high-order abstractions are found in the speeches at a political convention for the nomination of a presidential candidate. Platitudes and clichés seem to be the order of the day to stir up emotions for the cause. A great deal of meaningless hot air can be produced at this level of abstraction.

A good communicator can function at all levels of abstraction. To be able to do this the communicator must be able to identify the different levels and know why he indentifies each level as he does. In short, you must know your own life orientation as well as the life orientation of your audience in order to select meaningful levels. For example, a wife fixes an anniversary dinner with a blend of the elements of all the different levels of abstraction in order to achieve her goal. If she used only flowers, candles, and soft music, she would not communicate as much as when she adds his favorite steak done to perfection, golden brown French fries, and a crisp garden salad. Then she has taken into consideration all the levels and has blended them into a whole as the orchestra conductor does with musicians and musical instruments to create the desired effect.

ADJUSTING TO AN EVER-CHANGING WORLD

Life exists in an ever-changing world and to communicate successfully, you must be aware of this basic concept of change. To complicate the picture even more, you are not a static being, but a dynamic ever-changing process. This change is not at the same rate or in the same areas, so it is imperative that you discipline yourself in such a way as to take change into account. In this area feedback is especially significant. Feedback is necessary for adjustment on an interpersonal level (with others) or on an intrapersonal level (within yourself). When change is indicated it is not enough just to change, for change must be accompanied by proper adjustment. For instance, when mixing paint you do not just add coloring, but you add coloring according to the amount of paint you have and the shade you desire. Likewise adjustments are always made in relation to something else and accurate feedback is necessary to determine the degree of that relationship.

EXTENSIONALLY ORIENTED COMMUNICATOR

The communicator who fails to recognize and properly interpret feedback may blunder and create a breakdown in communication that is difficult to repair. Students were discussing a current problem when one of the students said something about "dirty Jews." A Jewish student in the group was hurt by this remark, but the speaker did not notice this and continued in the same vein. The speaker soon lost his audience. His listeners became hostile toward him, and their sympathy was extended to the Jewish student. Had the speaker been aware of the reactions to his remark (feedback) immediately, the breakdown might have been avoided or at least have been made less disastrous.

Sometimes individuals are spoken of as "being out of touch with the world" or "being out of touch with reality." Most of the time when this occurs individuals have not taken *change* into account and they are living in a world that has eluded them. Unless parents take change into account they will not be able to communicate with their children. Breakdowns in communication between a parent and a child often occur because the father still thinks of his daughter as his "sweet little girl of seventeen," when daughter is now married and has a family of her own.

It is not always easy to see change and even more difficult to adjust to it when you do perceive it. Very often you are aware of change, but do not know how to do anything about it. In communication it becomes the originating communicator's responsibility to make the changes necessary to complete the communication. A successful communication is one in which adjustments are made back and forth until each communicator understands the other.

EXTENSIONAL DEVICES

The general semanticists have established certain rules to help an individual in this effect to adjust to his changing world. These are often called "rules for a flexible extensional orientation." Korzybski divides them into "working devices" and "safety devices." [6] Whatever these devices are called, they refer to methods of being aware of change, for relating assumptions and statements to their facts or, in Korzybski's language, making the map fit the territory. These devices are as follows: (1) indexing, (2) dating, (3) etc., (4) quotes, and (5) hyphen.

INDEXING

Indexing relates similar things to their unique circumstances. Hasty generalizations may cause communications to go astray. With indexing in mind the communicator would not refer to all

---

[6] Korzybski, *op. cit.*, pp. 1–18.

labor unions as the same, but would know that labor union $_1$, is not labor union $_2$, or is not labor union $_3$. Likewise, the teacher who would communicate with his class understands that class$_1$ is not class$_2$, or is not class$_3$, even if they have the same call number and go under the same course description.

DATING

Dating helps one to adjust to events as they are now and not as they used to be. A new supervisor is appointed for a section of workmen and the men do not respond in the same way because they recognize that there is a change. A minister who thinks that he has the same congregation every Sunday morning will not be able to communicate with his people unless he has taken into account the difference in the makeup of the audience, the events that have changed his congregation, and other factors. A Germany of 1943 is not the Germany of 1949, or of 1974, and in order for our statesmen to communicate with the Germans this change must be recognized.

ETC.

Etc. helps the communicator to know and understand that no matter how much is said about a subject something must be left out because all cannot be said about anything. The business executive knows that orders cannot cover every detail and realizes that breakdowns may occur in the realms which he did not cover. A communicator is cognizant of the fact that not all can be known about an audience's life orientation so this leaves room for adjustments as the communicator receives feedback from the audience. The mental *etc.* helps the communicator keep an open end to his thinking and keeps him from being inflexible and rigid.

QUOTATION MARKS

Few statements that are really true-to-fact can be made. Most statements contain an element of false-to-fact relationship. Mental quotation marks aid the responding communicator in knowing that most statements cannot be taken at face value. This device can help remind communicators to develop statements which are as clear and concise as possible. It also helps responding communicators make healthy criticisms of what they hear. When both originating and responding communicators are alerted to this problem then the end result can be a successful communication.

HYPHEN

There is often a tendency to create verbal splits in communication, speaking as if an idea or concept must be either black or white. The hyphen makes it possible for you to overcome fallacies in your thinking caused by verbal splits. The doctor in communicating to his patient speaks of mind-body, not mind or body. The teacher thinks of his students not as good or bad, but knows that there is both good and bad present in each.

There are many significant ways in which the extensional devices are useful in your communication. However, one area often neglected is intrapersonal communication. Proper personal communication will help produce better communication on an interpersonal level. This one area is within the complete control of the communicator. Most adjustments to life, to changing events, are made at this level of awareness and in turn adequate adjustments are made to the ever-changing world. Communication on this level brings an awareness at all levels. A Hitler who communicated to himself injustices communicated these injustices to a country, and the results will be communicated from generation to generation and from culture to culture.

Extensional devices are not an end in themselves, but can be a means to an end. As they become a part of the very fiber of your being they can be utilized in all communication situations. Their goal is not to make you wishy-washy, but to make you flexible enough to take the storms of symbols and still remain an integrated individual working toward your goal. In short, they go a long way toward keeping the important, important and the unimportant, unimportant.

MAKING LANGUAGE WORK FOR YOU

Language is a set of tools for building your mental image in the mind of a responding communicator. The closer you are able to make his image conform to yours, the more effective will be your communication. Language is not only your chief means of communicating ideas and feelings, but it is also a tool for reasoning, for transforming experience into ideas and ideas into experience. As a communicator, become acquainted with these tools and learn to use them well.

The first important task of language is to enable you to build the proper atmosphere for the communication. Many a message is lost not so much because of the message, but because its reception is distorted by the communicative atmosphere. The simple words "I love you" have a deeper meaning spoken at the edge of a lake with a full moon reflecting in the water than said at a basketball game. When it is not possible to have the correct physical atmosphere, language can help create the proper verbal atmosphere. For example, several ideas conveyed in meaningful language about how you feel about the person can make even an "I love you" at a basketball game meaningful. A raw, specific idea is apt to fall on deaf ears in a speech or in a conversation if language is not used to create the proper atmosphere. After this atmosphere is achieved proper language must be utilized.

The following guidelines will help in your selection of proper word symbols: (1) Language must be adapted to your audience and the occasion; (2) there must be an economy and accuracy of language; (3) the language must be as vivid and meaningful as possible; (4) language should be properly used with respect to grammar and pronunciation.

Knowing your audience's life orientation is equally important in the use of language. The language of your communication can be adapted to the occasion and your audience only after you know their life orientations. Jesus Christ used language familiar to the disciples and communicated. Unfamiliar terms or the improper use of language can cause your responding communicator to turn you off quicker than any one thing. This has been substantiated by research conducted on listening. Highly emotional words, words of poor taste, and double meaning words, only cause the audience to react to your words, not your message. Each ethnic group, organization, and person has many conditioned words and it is your job to ferret them out and avoid them. In a contest many orations sound beautiful, but have little meaning because the language has not been adapted to the audience or the occasion. Language chosen to fit the college crowd, the church group, or the union men will get your message through to that particular group. Symbols are effective in direct proportion to the strength of the experience your responding communicators can associate with them.

Accuracy in the use of language can mean life or death in a communication on the battlefield, but can also determine the life or death of your message in any communication. A common habit is to use too many words to say the thing to be said. When asked how much notice a man would have to be given to speak, he replied, "If you want me to talk an hour, three days. A half hour, a week, and if it is fifteen minutes I must have two weeks' notice." It takes time to develop concise language, but it is worth the time and effort. Meaning is often lost in a sea of empty words that drown the responding communicator in platitudes and generalities. Be specific in your daily conversations so that all your communication will be to the point.

Earlier in this chapter it was revealed that for the most part, language has feelings attached to it. In fact, language seems to be the best means to arouse a person's feelings. In learning to use language that touches all the senses, develop one point until the responding communicator can see, hear, feel, taste, and touch the object being described. Instead of just saying it was a steak, call it a sizzling, juicy, golden brown, tender steak. The more vivid the image you have in your mind, the more vividly you can transfer this image to your listener. Instead of saying you received a cool reception, check from among the following list the word most appropriate—cold, cool, chilly, frosty, frigid, freezing, icy, glacial, or arctic. Again the term must be appropriate to the audience, for "a chilly reception" in Alaska might not have the same meaning that "a chilly reception" would have in Miami. Knowing the life orientation of the audience enables you to select words that can create the proper image in their minds. Images and words must be based on your audiences' past associations. Try to aid your audience in seeing the object, hearing the sound connected with it, tasting its flavor, smelling the odors involved, and feeling its texture and shape. It is a challenge.

Your language should always be in good taste. There may be

times when you will resort to a colloquialism, a slang term, but these times will be the exception and not the rule. Substandard expressions not only violate good language usage but suggest that you are unaccustomed to the practices of an educated person.

You are often judged as a person on the basis of how you speak. If you use "git," "jist," and "put the feesh in the deesh and poosh it in the booshes" you are immediately judged as a person at least poverty stricken in the use of language. On the other hand, your use of language in good taste portrays you as an individual who is able to relate himself the best way possible to his auditors.

Language as a tool must first be understood and then if you are to become an artisan, a great deal of practice is needed. Every time you open your mouth to speak you have a chance to work with these tools. In another sense, words are likened to stones across a stream; you can use them as stepping stones to get to your destination or you can use them as stumbling blocks that will make you fall flat on your face. The difference is the way you use them.

QUESTIONS FOR DISCUSSION

1. What is the process you would use in retraining yourself in your reaction to a symbol?

2. What are some of the ways that you can determine if your responding communicators have the same referent for a word that you have?

3. What are the elements in language that make it meaningful? Those elements that distort meaning?

EXERCISES

[Forms for completing the exercises marked with an asterisk will be found in the *Worksheets for Speech—Interpersonal Communication* (San Francisco: Chandler Publishing Company, 1967).]

1. List a number of words to which you have a "signal" response and ask yourself why.*

2. Select four words and see how many times you are able to change their meaning by changing the context.*

3. Analyze a situation where two people are no longer speaking to each other and determine what part language played in the breakdown.

4. Make a list of colloquialisms that you have learned since you have been on the campus whose meaning is restricted to college students. For example, "ding," "shot down," "tough," or others.

5. Cite examples where people let words come to mean the actual thing they represent.

6. Write examples from your observations of the extensional devices.

7. List words that give you a feeling of sadness and ones that give you a feeling of joy and then try to discover why.

8. Write two incidents in communication where two people by-passed each other because each held a different meaning of a word.

9. The next time your mood changes quickly make an analysis to see the part words played in it.

10. List five names that you would not name your child and discover the connection with the names that make you feel that way.

SUGGESTED READINGS

Chase, Stuart, *The Power of Words*. New York: Harcourt, Brace and Company, Inc., 1954.

Hayakawa, S. I. (ed.), *Language, Meaning, and Maturity*. New York: Harper and Brothers, 1954.

Hayakawa, S. I., *Language in Thought and Action*. New York: Harcourt, Brace & World, Inc., 1964.

Johnson, Wendell, *Your Most Enchanted Listener*. New York: Harper and Brothers, 1956.

Korzybski, Alfred, *Science and Sanity*. Lakeville, Conn.: Institute of General Semantics, 1958.

Lee, Irving, *Customs and Crises in Communication*. New York: Harper and Brothers, 1954.

Ogden, Charles K., and I. A. Richards, *The Meaning of Meaning*. New York: Harcourt, Brace and Company, Inc., 1946.

Sondell, Bess, *The Humanity of Words*. Cleveland: World Publishing Company, 1958.

Weinberg, Harry L., *Levels of Knowing and Existence*. New York: Harper and Brothers, 1959.

The Message Developed | 6

Ideas are important in communication, but they are not sufficient by themselves. If they are to be communicated, they must be developed. You develop an idea to (1) clarify a point, (2) win acceptance of a point, and (3) make the point interesting and understood. Many good ideas never come to fruition because proper care is not taken in their development. Although there is not a particular way to develop an idea, one that is not developed will produce nothing. The purpose of developing an idea is to expand your thinking, to free the idea.

ADAPTING TO AUDIENCE LIFE ORIENTATION

When you begin to develop an idea, your focus must always be on the responding communicator. Each idea should be developed in terms of an understanding of his life orientation. Jesus Christ, who communicated a message that has changed the world, applied this principle in His teaching. It is not difficult to imagine Jesus as He looked at a yoke of oxen, felt their yoke to see if it were smooth, and then turned to His disciples and said, "My yoke is easy, my burden is light." On another occasion as Jesus rested by a vineyard, He was asked what His kingdom was like. He picked up a vine and pointing to it said, "I am the vine and ye are the branches." When He suggested, "A sower went out to sow . . . ," He communicated with His audience because they had seen the sower go out to sow, and were familiar with this experience. Again you see the importance of knowing the life orientation of your audience. If a contemporary speaker were to say, "A certain sower went out to sow . . . ," not much of an image would be called forth, since not many individuals today would be familiar with the example.

Ideas must be developed in the light of the needs, desires, ambitions, and concerns of your audience. These days it seems that most persons are concerned with "What is there in it for me?" If this is your responding communicator's concern then you must show him how he will benefit personally from your idea. But you must also bear in mind that it is possible to change the needs and wants of your audience and that you are not totally at the mercy of their attitudes. You may have watched a demonstration in a store for something you did not need and have been so skillfully persuaded by the salesman that you were convinced you did need his product and purchased it. He had succeeded in modifying your desires.

Knowing the life orientation of your audience and knowing their basic concerns are only two of the elements to keep in mind as you try to develop a message. Each situation is new and different and you must search out all the complexities involved in the situation. A new idea for packaging a product would have to be developed differently if the product were selling at its highest peak than if sales were at their lowest. A wife who wants a new dress will have to develop her ideas differently depending on whether the budget is balanced or unbalanced, and whether her husband is happy with his work or finds it a real burden. In communication a knowledge of the immediate situation is imperative. Just as a farmer who wants a good crop knows his land well and prepares the soil for the seed, a communicator who wants his ideas to be accepted and to grow knows where the idea will fall and does what can be done to prepare for its reception. He makes sure that the idea gets the right nourishment so that it will develop as he wants it to.

DEVELOPMENTAL DEVICES

Although each idea must be developed appropriately, the same idea can be developed in several different ways. In your communication try to develop one idea in several ways to see which one results in better understanding. The means of developing ideas are most simply called *developmental devices*. Six

generally accepted verbal devices are (1) example, (2) illustration (3) testimony, (4) explanation, (5) statistics, and (6) restatement. Nonverbal developmental devices are discussed in
Chapter 10.

EXAMPLE

The example is one of the basic developmental devices. Very
often someone says, "Give me an example;" if you can, your idea
is made clearer. A good communicator is constantly searching
for useful examples. Examples are usually classified as (1) general examples, (2) specific examples, and (3) hypothetical examples.

The *general example* is used to focus attention on a particular
subject before you discuss its specific parts. You may say, "Automobiles have become a vital method of transportation for many
Americans." This example brings automobiles and the idea of
transportation into your mind's eye. The *specific example*,
"Among United States' 185 million people, 90 million drivers
operate 76 million automobiles on 3½ million miles of roads
and streets, traveling 738 billion miles a year," brings specific
figures to the communication. The specific example must always
involve specific events, places, or things. It is a way of making the
abstract concrete by acquainting the audience with more tangible ideas. Communicators who always deal in terms of "someone
said" or "things this" and "things that" do not forcefully get
their ideas across.

The *hypothetical example* is one that deals with future events
or makes circumstances that do not exist have some meaning.
For example, "When airplanes become as popular as cars, the
Sunday ride will be replaced by a weekend trip to London." The
hypothetical example is an excellent device to use when you are
trying to help your audience visualize the results that will come
if they follow, or do not follow, your ideas or plan. You must
always present something tangible before you go on to the in-
tangible, or you must discuss the present before you proceed to
the future.

All three types of examples should be varied and must always
come from or relate to the life orientation of the audience. The

more they relate to the audience, the better you will be understood. Each time Russell H. Conwell presented his famous speech "Acres of Diamonds," [1] which has been called the "$4,000,000 lecture," he used the same theme but took his examples specifically from the community in which he spoke. Conwell spent days in the community to find his examples before he gave the speech and thus was able to speak in specific terms to his audience. The speech was probably given more times than any other speech and provided the funds for establishing Temple University. The example is a communication tool which you should learn to use well.

ILLUSTRATION

The word *illustration* means to "shed light" and this definition implies the purpose of the illustration. Two basic forms of the illustration are the analogy and the story. In the *analogy* you compare the unfamiliar with the familiar and draw conclusions about the unknown on the basis of the known. "Things equal to the same thing are equal to each other" seems to be the basic premise upon which the analogy works. Ordinarily, analogies are either *literal* or *figurative*. The literal analogy compares objects or events in the same classification. The figurative analogy is an extended analogy and links objects in widely different fields, such as the federal government and a three-legged stool. The distinction is sometimes made on the basis of whether the comparisons are real or fictitious. When a comparison is real and is also somewhat extended, usage has given it a special name, the literal analogy. When it is fictitious and developed at length, it is named the figurative analogy.

Comparisons and contrasts are concerned with showing likenesses and differences among objects, ideas, and situations. The former puts stress upon similarities; the latter emphasizes dissimilarities. The analogy is concerned with comparisons and may be either long or short. If the comparison is extended it is usually called an analogy; if it is compressed it is either called a

---

[1] Russell H. Conwell, *Acres of Diamonds* (New York: Harper and Brothers, 1915).

simile or a *metaphor*. If the terms *like* or *as* are used, it is a simile. The metaphor states the comparison without these terms. "Hitler was like a rat" or "A pretty girl is like a melody" are examples of the simile. Winston Churchill, a master at the use of figurative illustration, used such comparisons as these: "The German eruption swept like a scythe around . . . our armies" (simile); "We shall use these powers without the slightest hesitation until we are satisfied that this malignancy in our midst has been stamped out" (metaphor).

The analogy is very useful in explaining something new or strange. People not only find it difficult to understand new concepts and new ideas, but are usually suspicious of them. Your job as a communicator is to discover ideas familiar to the responding communicator, get him to accept these ideas, and then introduce the new concept. A college student asks his roommate to arrange a blind date for him because he is afraid of being told no. When the roommate obliges, the student asks, "What's she like?" "Well, she is like Susie. You know Susie; she's like her," the roommate replies. "Wonderful," the student responds. However, at 12:30 a.m. he is waiting for his roommate to return. "What did you mean, she was like Susie?" You see, what he thought of Susie and what the roommate thought of Susie were two different things. A real communication breakdown has occurred because of a lack of understanding of life orientation.

Even though analogies are very important in communicating ideas, the *story* has been and perhaps will always be one of the best ways to illustrate a point and kindle interest. There is a real art in telling a good story. A person who wants to communicate will not only learn the principles of this art, but will also practice them. A good collection of stories that can be recalled on the spur of the moment will not only make you a good conversationalist, but will add interest to your message. The stories should always fit you, be in good taste, and be *apropos* for the specific occasion.

Three of the most familiar types of stories are the anecdote, the fable, and the parable. The *anecdote* is a story either humorous or serious, usually with real-life characters. Usually you think of the joke or humorous story when the anecdote is mentioned, but there is a wealth of meaning in serious anecdotes as well. Anecdotes should be chosen so that they are appropriate to the occasion, the audience, and the point to be made. As long as they are in good taste, audiences usually find those stories taken from their own profession or background most interesting and meaningful. A school teacher who hears stories about students does not find it hard to identify himself with the story and to find meaning. The professor who uses illustrations from the lives of his students will communicate his ideas. Anecdotes can help change the mood of your audience and get them to go along with you in spirit as well as idea.

The *fable* is often neglected as a means to illustrate a point. It is a story which is usually set in the animal world; the characters are animals and act and speak like humans. The fable is an excellent way to epitomize the specific purpose of your message. Aesop's fables are perhaps the best known, but are seldom used in the development of a communication. George Orwell's *Animal Farm* is a skillful extended use of the fable.[2] Both the fable and the parable are tools that need to be in the hands of a good communicator.

The *parable* is a device used frequently by Jesus and can be defined as a story from which a religious or moral lesson may be drawn. It does not relate a specific instance, but deals with a universal truth as if it were a specific instance. It is a good teaching device since it provides a background or takeoff point for discussion. Sometimes it will need to be elaborated upon as the parable of the good seed and the tares; other times, as in the parable of the Good Samaritan, one short sentence drives home the point. Its lesson should be obvious to the responding communicator; therefore, it must be related to his life orientation. Sometimes the parables mentioned in the Bible may be put in modern-day parlance to illustrate a point.

The anecdote, the fable, and the parable are the most popular kinds of stories that are used, but you can learn to be creative in developing your own stories. A person who is brave enough

---

[2] George Orwell, *Animal Farm* (New York: Harcourt, Brace & Company, Inc., 1946).

to tell a humorous story on himself establishes credibility with his audience. However, beware of taking too many stories from your own experience, especially when they all end up glorifying yourself. No story can be effective, however, unless it is told well. Both timing and language are important as you paint the scenes of the story. The story must be precise and to the point. A fumbled punch line can ruin even the best story. You need not act out the story for it to be good, but you will need to reinforce it with facial expression, bodily movement, and gestures. A successful practitioner of communication learns to tell a good story well.

TESTIMONY

Another popular device for gaining support is the testimony. Commercials use this device, or perhaps overuse it. It used to be a popular method in churches to spread the gospel, but is not used as much in modern times. If the testimony is to be effective a feeling of kinship must be established. The commercial method of gaining support is through self-projection. The one who testifies for a product usually exhibits certain traits desired by the audience and the manufacturer hopes that by association a desire for his product would be transferred. The young man would like to be the great baseball player as is the person in the commercial; he cannot be that player but he can shave with the same brand of razor blade. In the light of analysis this sounds far-fetched but in practice it seems to work.

Because testimony is only as good as the person who gives it, his reputation and reliability must always be considered before you decide to quote him. Very often *why* a person says something is even more important than *what* he says. Know your source's personal interests, his prejudices, his training and experience, and if he has based his ideas on firsthand knowledge. Very often this background will have to be identified if the responding communicators are going to be persuaded by the statement of the testimony.

Text without context is pretext, and every caution should be taken so that the exact words and the intent of the person being quoted are reported accurately. It is easy to forget to read the word *not* and change a statement, but you will lose in the final analysis because your own credibility is as important as the person's you are quoting. Good research will lead you to the testimony that will be to the point and will support and develop your ideas in the way needed.

EXPLANATION

Explanation is the total process of making something clear, and you can best do it by definition and classification. A definition should be a working definition in the sense that it tells you what to do to manipulate or obtain the object defined. A working definition of a cake is a recipe. Make your definitions in terms of your audiences' life orientation. Classifying an object often helps the responding communicator to pinpoint that which you are talking about. As suggested in Chapter 5, you must always be careful about how you classify an object because the way you classify it will determine your reaction to it.

STATISTICS

Statistics are compilations of numerical facts from which inferences are made about a large population based on a sample from that population. Statistics can be used wisely or poorly. Most people use statistics as a drunk uses a lamppost, for support rather than illumination. As a rule you look up statistics to support the beliefs that you already hold. It is possible to find statistics that will support most any idea. However, if the statistics are meaningful they must meet certain accepted criteria: (1) you must make sure that you are comparing like things, (2) the sample must be large enough to predict on the basis of the entire unit, and (3) the statistics must have been gathered over a long enough period of time.

A student once compared on a percentage basis the increase in the output of steel by the United States and Russia for 2 years after the war. Her conclusion was that Russia was more productive in steel than the United States. The truth of the matter was that the United States increase in steel production was greater than the entire tonnage of steel produced by Russia. Like things were not compared.

A speaker may report that the students on campus want certain restrictions removed. When he is asked how many students he has contacted he usually says, "I took a survey on my floor," which is certainly not a large enough sample for a university of 15,000.

It would be possible to take the income of teachers for the first 5 years after graduation and compare it with the income of doctors for the first 5 years after graduation and conclude that teachers are better paid than men in other professions. However, the second period of 5 years after graduation would be a more accurate time period to show the relative income of the professions.

Statistics can be dry and meaningless material unless you as a communicator reinforce them with visual aids or make them meaningful and clear in terms of your audience. A percentage can often be given in terms of the size of your audience to make the idea more meaningful and interesting to them. Instead of saying that Joe Louis earned more than $3 million as a boxer and over $100 thousand at his last fight you might say that a member of the audience would have to work 20 years at a job paying $5000 a year to earn as much as Louis did in 30 minutes.

Give the statistics in round numbers, as briefly as possible, and as graphically as you can. It is always wise to check your statistics against other sources because statistics are often manipulated to serve particular causes. It may be true that figures do not lie, but liars do figure. A comparison of statistics over a particular period can be very persuasive when used in the correct manner. Statistics are a beneficial tool for developing and supporting your ideas.

RESTATEMENT

Oral discourse is of a nature that it may not be grasped the first time, and the individual may need to have the idea restated so that he is able to understand the message you are trying to communicate. "Tell them first what you are going to tell them, tell them, and then tell them what you have just told them" is a good rule to follow. In restatement you do not just repeat the idea, but you clothe it in new language, use other kinds of developmental devices, or add new supporting materials. The importance of restatement can be seen in any television commercial trying to sell you a product. Repetition is another tool similar to restatement, except that you repeat the same idea in approximately the same words. If the purpose of your communication is informative, repetition will enhance learning.

This brief discussion has given you several ways to develop your ideas. More material is easily available on any of the developmental devices described here. Variety is always the keynote and you will want to add as much interest to each method as possible. Never feel that you are confined to one particular developmental device. While you are practicing during your training period, experiment as much as you possibly can to see the form with which you are more at ease and to see how you can develop the same idea in several ways. Remember that you are not developing the idea for yourself but for the responding communicator.

TYPES OF REASONING

Reasoning is a mental process which begins with something known or believed to be true and reaches other supposed truths which cannot be, or have not been, directly determined by perception. The reasoning you would do in the message you develop for a communication consists of the developing of a convincing arrangement of arguments that bring conviction. Proof is derived from evidence and reasoning. A truth or an inference should be carefully related to an issue through reasoning. The need for caution in the reasoning process is illustrated by the following story.

An excited entomology student had rushed into his professor's office. "Quick, sir," he panted, "come and see what I have discovered." Obligingly, the professor followed his student into the laboratory. The student took a jar of fleas, unscrewed the lid, picked out a flea, put it on the back of his hand and said, "Jump!" The little flea jumped; the student dutifully recorded the data in his notebook. Then took another flea, put it on the back of his hand and said, "Jump." And the flea jumped. "Did you see that, Professor?" queried the student, and again made a notation in his notebook.

Now, he took out a third flea, and using a pair of tweezers he carefully pulled off all its legs. Then he put the flea on the back of his hand and said, "Jump." Nothing happened. He took another flea and repeated the process. Then he exclaimed, "Professor, now do you see what I have discovered? If you remove all a flea's legs, you make it deaf!"

The student used the inductive method, his procedure was empirically sound, and he made a correlation with observation and conclusion. He had done well in testing by replication design to insure that the correlation was not a random one. Although this procedure was faultless, you can see that his conclusion was not causally related.

Reasoning is often classified as either inductive or deductive. *Inductive* reasoning is the process of reasoning from the specific to the general. *Deductive* reasoning is reasoning from a generalization to a specific case. Pictorially, examples would look something like the diagrams in Fig. 8.

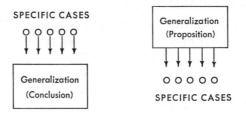

FIGURE 8. INDUCTION (LEFT) AND DEDUCTION (RIGHT)

In reasoning by induction several ideas, examples, and premises lead to a particular conclusion. In reasoning by deduction the conclusion is stated first and then the specific ideas, examples, and premises come later. Although these processes are distinct in theory, they are seldom separated in practice. In actual practice you will move back and forth from induction to deduction several times. This is because conclusions formed through induction often form new premises for deduction. The types of reasoning and their definitions seem to illustrate this interaction.

The most popular types of reasoning are (1) reasoning from example, (2) reasoning from analogy, (3) reasoning from cause, and (4) reasoning from sign. You will remember that reasoning is making an inference, and inferences can be made poorly as well as correctly. The rules you learned for inferences are related to and should be applied to all the types of reasoning. The basic purpose of reasoning is to try to win the responding communicators agreement to your purpose.

REASONING FROM EXAMPLE

Reasoning from example is a form of induction since you group several examples and infer a conclusion from these examples. A communicator who cites examples of girls being molested while a crowd stood around and watched in Chicago, Boston, and New York City is using reasoning by example. His conclusion, that "the American people do not feel that they are their brother's keeper," has been arrived at inductively and is seen as a cause of the examples cited. The examples must be carefully drawn, be sufficient in number, be representative, and the originating communicator should infer only those conclusions which the examples tend to support. The process of indexing discussed in Chapter 5 must be applied if improper generalizations are to be avoided in the reasoning process.

REASONING BY ANALOGY

Reasoning by analogy consists of using the analogy as a means of proof. As defined earlier, the analogy makes comparisons of known features and draws inferences about unknown features. Again the known features must be the support for the conclusion that is drawn. In the example cited earlier a person might further reason that the conditions in the United States are similar to conditions during the Roman Empire. He could also reason since they are similar in one way, they must be similar in other ways. The tests of a good analogy hold true here as well. Are there significant points of similarity? Do the points of likeness outweigh the points of difference? Is the analogy a true representative of its class?

REASONING FROM CAUSE

The process from reasoning by cause consists of inferring that a certain cause is a force that produces an effect. You might extend the analogy of the United States and the Roman Empire by suggesting that since the conditions in the Roman Empire caused it to fall, then similar conditions in the United States will ultimately cause the United States to fall. Causal reasoning may be either cause-to-effect, effect-to-cause, or effect-to-effect. Its purpose is to demonstrate the significant, practical, and effective causes in the subject being developed. As you develop your ideas, you try to show that a given set of circumstances will produce a probable set of consequences.

Questions to be asked about the reasoning by cause are: Did the cause exist when and where it is said to have existed? Was the alleged cause adequate to have produced the effect? Is this the sole or distinguishing causal factor? Could the alleged cause be associated with the effect by chance?

REASONING FROM SIGN

The process of reasoning from sign consists of inferring relationships or correlations between two variables. You argue that two variables are so related that the presence or absence of one may be taken as an indication of the presence or absence of the other.

In the fall when the leaves (attribute) are falling and you take this as a sign that winter (substance) is coming soon, you are reasoning by sign. In reasoning from sign you reason either from attribute to substance or substance to attribute. A plant of somewhat vinelike habit, with trifoliolate leaves, greenish flowers, white berries, and an irritant oil poisonous to the touch is near the wild strawberries you are going to pick. You do not pick the strawberries because you conclude that you would rather not have the strawberries than run the risk of coming in contact with the common poison ivy. Here you reason from attribute (the trifoliolate leaves) to the substance (poison ivy).

SOME CAUTIONS IN REASONING

To guard against false conclusions in reasoning adhere to the following rules.

1. The substance must be identified accurately. During a town meeting, an official proposes that chain stores are harming the community because they are a monopoly. A townsman disagrees

with him, pointing out that technically chain stores do not constitute a monopoly because they do not prohibit free competition. In his reasoning, the first man has failed to identify the substance, in this case the monopoly, accurately.

2. The attribute must be identified accurately. In the excitement of receiving a dozen roses from her boyfriend, a girl must be careful not to assume the boy has serious intentions of marriage. The roses are only an attribute, not to be mistaken for the substance love.

3. The attribute must be inherent in the substance. "Well, what did you expect? He is a preacher's son." This statement assumes that every preacher's son will possess the attribute of misbehavior. This statement is not true.

4. The attribute must be a certain sign of the substance. A hitchhiker's service uniform is not always a sign that he is a serviceman and is safe to pick up.

Perhaps these rules seem contrary to the rules for an extensional orientation (see Chapter 5) but upon close examination you will see that they complement one another.

MILL'S RULES OF REASONING

In dealing with particular instances perhaps you have noticed certain relationships between them. These relationships were stated by John Stuart Mill, English mathematician and philosopher, in the following five rules:

1. The rule of agreement
2. The rule of difference
3. The rule of agreement and difference
4. The rule of residues
5. The rule of concomitant variations [3]

THE RULE OF AGREEMENT

"If two or more instances of the phenomenon under investigation have only one circumstance in common, the circumstance

---

[3] *John Stuart Mill's Philosophy of Scientific Method,* Ernest Nagel, ed. (New York: Hafner Publishing Company, 1950), pp. 211–233. Original work: *A System of Logic* (London: 1843), 3.8.

in which alone all the instances agree, is the cause (or effect) of the given phenomenon." On a college campus where students eat in different cafeterias, an investigation is undertaken to find the cause of an illness among a group of students. In the area of agreement, if all students eating at Shively Hall became ill then the food at Shively Hall could be suspected as being the cause. It is well to keep in mind the caution that reasoning may be logical but incorrect. All circumstances must be examined and you must begin with a correct premise. If the illness suggested above was not of the nature that could be caused by food, then the eating at Shively Hall cafeteria would not have much to do with it. It is better to state the relationship as a causal connection and suggest that it exists if the occurrence of one incident is invariably followed by the occurrence of another in all the varied situations and circumstances in which they can be observed.

THE RULE OF DIFFERENCE

"If an instance in which the phenomenon under investigation occurs, and an instance in which it does not occur, have every circumstance in common save one, that one occurring only in the former, the circumstance in which alone the two instances differ, is the effect, or the cause, or an indispensable part of the cause, of the phenomenon." If all the students at Shively Hall who did not become ill did not eat a salad, then it is possible to list the salad as a probable cause for the illness.

The method of agreement does not always by itself establish a uniform one-to-one relationship between two incidents. A greater degree of certainty can be established by determining the differences. Again the relationship is to be held as only a causal one and other factors need to be checked. When the two methods are combined you are using the agreement-difference method.

THE RULE OF AGREEMENT AND DIFFERENCE

"If two or more instances in which the phenomenon occurs have only one circumstance in common, while two or more instances in which it does not occur have nothing in common save the absence of that circumstance; the circumstance in which alone the two sets of instances (always or invariably) differ, is the effect, or the cause, or an indispensable part of the cause, of the phenomenon." This area is best described by a study that uses a control group in which the activity is handled in a normal way while other groups are given an experimental plan and then the results are checked to see if the experimental materials make the difference.

This method is employed in education and is the plan followed by many experimental theses and dissertations. Since all variables cannot be controlled you need to be careful how you read or report results. A new method that you test may be said to have a dependable and uniform causal relationship if, in all situations in which it occurs, certain results follow and in situations in which it does not occur those results do not follow.

THE RULE OF RESIDUES

"Subtract from any phenomenon such part as is known by previous inductions to be the effect of certain causes, and the residue of the phenomenon is the effect of the remaining causes." A doctor uses this method as he checks the many symptoms until he finally gets to the one that relates most closely to the disease. Likewise, the automobile mechanic uses a process of reasoning by elimination as he checks the fuel system, the ignition system, and other mechanical systems until he deduces the cause of the trouble. This method is one of reducing variables and then looking at what is left over. Its accuracy depends on the ability to assess the many variables that may be involved. If the mechanic does not know how to check out the ignition system then he is not able to exclude it from the possible causes.

THE RULE OF CONCOMITANT VARIATIONS

"Whatever phenomenon varies in any manner whenever another phenomenon varies in some particular manner, it is either a cause or an effect of that phenomenon, or is connected with it through some fact of causation." A merchant finds that his

business increases in direct proportion to his amount of advertising. He then would probably conclude that the advertising is
the cause of the business increase. The more use a high school
student makes of his car the lower his grades; the less he uses it,
the higher his grades. Again the relationship may not be a causal
one and other factors should be considered. To say that the increase in the manufacture of tires has increased in direct proportion to the increase in the production of automobiles, and
therefore one is the cause of the other, might be correct. However, to say that the increase in production of automobiles is in
direct proportion to the increase of the use of tobacco in the
United States, one being the cause of the other, would be incorrect. In life situations you must always be careful of your
conclusions. Where all variables can be controlled as in a laboratory situation then your conclusions have a greater chance of
being accurate. A use of more than one of Mill's canons will aid
you as you search for the cause—the truth.

Several elements have been listed and described that can be
used as you develop your message. Keep in mind that these
elements or devices should never be ends within themselves but
are only means to an end, the end being communication. Your
responding communicator may be convinced against his will but
he will never be pleased. A man convinced against his will is
unconvinced still.

Unless you can sharpen the focus of what you want to communicate, the image will be blurred. You bring this image into
focus by knowing your own life orientation and the areas that
influence you. Just as there are areas in your orientation that
might get your image out of focus, the same is true in the life of
the responding communicator. Knowing his orientation you
select the developmental device that you feel will call up the
image in his mind that will be as close to yours as possible. The
closer the likeness, the clearer the communication. Once you
have been able to transfer the image with some degree of
accuracy, then you have communicated.

It is possible to control to some extent the areas of conflict that
distort the image. Chapter 5 on symbolization points up the fact
that just because you use the symbol "dog" does not mean that

the responding communicator will get the same picture of a dog that you had in mind. A careful selection of specific symbols from his orientation will give you a better chance to reduce the area of conflict.

A story or illustration may give an entirely different picture to the responding communicator than you had in mind when you used it. Sometimes the listener will become absorbed with the subject of the story and not move beyond it. A story that starts "This stupid college teacher" could lose an audience of college teachers regardless of what you did with the rest of the story. A conflicting image will replace the image you are trying to arouse and you will not communicate. The theory of cognitive dissonance suggests that a person works hard to reduce dissonance (see Chapter 8).

As you try to focus a picture in the mind of your listener, use every aspect you can to make this picture a vivid one. The value of an illustration is in the degree of reality it creates. To make the most effective use of the illustration endeavor to employ all the senses. The responding communicator must not only visualize your image but where possible he should also hear, feel, touch, taste, and smell your image. Again life orientation is of prime importance. The smell of new-mown hay would not call forth much of an image to the city dweller, while the grimy metalic smell of the subway might.

The use of visual aids and other nonverbal symbols combined with the verbal symbols will aid in the development of your message. Statistics given verbally are much more meaningful when accompanied by a chart or bar graph that pictorializes them. These nonverbal means of support are discussed in Chapter 10.

Do not forget that these suggestions are merely aids in reaching your goal—the fully developed message. You must constantly be aware of your feedback to see how you are progressing as you communicate the message. If one device does not seem to do the job, feel free to change to another that will. The responding communicator is not likely to listen to something that does not interest him. Catch his mind and his emotions and you will get action.

OBSERVATION, INFERENCE, JUDGMENT

The basic symbolic act, discussed in Chapter 5, is a report of what is seen, felt, or heard. Reports should be capable of verification, and exclude as far as possible inferences and judgments. There are two types of statements you can make about what you observe with the five senses: (1) statements of observation and (2) statements of inference. It is not easy to distinguish between the two because there is nothing in the structure of the language or even the inflection of the speaker's sentence that will give you a cue for proper identificaton. It is easy to utter inferential statements with the false assurance that you are dealing with facts. However, a good practitioner of communication will not only learn the distinctions but will also work to keep them clear in his own communication.

The first step is to learn the characteristics of statements of observation and know where the line is drawn between them and statements of inference. Distinctions can be seen in four basic areas—the origin of the statement, the timing of the statement, the content of the statement, and the verification of the statement.

A statement of observation can be made only by the observer. The very nature of the statement suggests that the person making the statement has actually observed what he is reporting. A statement of inference can be made by anyone regardless of whether or not he has observed the action. Whether the person is once removed from the observation or 100 times removed, his statement is still an inference and must be treated as a statement of inference. This would suggest that most of the statements you make are inferences, and therefore you should be careful just how you make them.

The time a statement is made gives a very good clue as to what kind of a statement it is. A statement of observation can be made only after the observation while an inference can be made at any time, even before the observation is made. The statements used in describing predictive reality are by definition inferential statements and involve a calculated risk.

The content of the observation must stay with what you have

observed if it is going to be a statement of observation. The content of the statement of inference does not have a limitation, and you can infer to the limits of your imagination. The tendency to add a bit of flavor to a statement is ever present in communication, and when you do this you must realize that it is an inference you are making, not a statement of observation.

Statements of observation can be verified and therefore approach certainty, while an inference cannot be verified and involves many degrees of probability. Realizing this difference is essential, for often the lives or personalities of people are at stake in your communication.

As a teacher, executive, shop steward, or in fact in any position where you must make evaluations of others, it is imperative that you distinguish the difference between a statement of observation and an inference. Incorrect reporting leads to improper evaluations and wrong decisions. The ability to give a clear concise report can be achieved if you are willing to work for it. It is one ability that will help you advance in your chosen field.

There is nothing in the structure of the language *per se* that helps you to discriminate between these two kinds of statements. Check statements as to their origin, timing, content, and verification. Once you have done this and want to use a statement of inference, which you will need to do at times, then calculate the risk that is involved before you make the inference. Often the risk will be small and you can afford to take it; other times the risk will be too great and you must be careful of its consequence. The important point is always to be able to identify properly a statement. So very many statements in communication are inferences, so many that communication is often referred to as a calculated risk.

QUESTIONS FOR DISCUSSION

1. What are the elements that make an event or incident stand out in a person's life?

2. What are some of the major fallacies in reasoning and how can one avoid them?

3. What are the steps involved in developing an idea? Discuss specifically how one would go about it.

4. Discuss methods you may use to focus an idea correctly for the responding communicator.

EXERCISES

[Forms for completing the exercises marked with an asterisk will be found in the *Worksheets for Speech—Interpersonal Communication* (San Francisco: Chandler Publishing Company, 1967).]

1. Take one simple idea and develop it through statistics, an analogy, an example, through comparison and contrasts, and through a parable.*

2. Examine several contemporary speeches and bring to class five examples of the speakers' use of developmental devices.*

3. Select five advertisements and determine which statements are statements of inference and which are statements of observation.

4. Start with the figure of the amount of money the United States has spent on Foreign Aid since World War II and put it in terms of college students and their cost of an education.

5. Give one three-minute speech in class in which the idea is developed through one story or illustration. Ask the class to write down what they felt your point was and then you tell them what you were trying to do.

6. Develop one basic concept by the method of induction; then develop it by deduction.

7. Find examples of John Stuart Mill's five rules concerning relationships.

8. Before you ask for your next date, see how many different ways you may develop your request.

9. Find five generalizations made by your roommates in their conversations.

10. Analyze four advertisements using testimony and check to see if the person being used is an expert in the area of the testimony.

SUGGESTED READINGS

Dresser, William R., "Effect of Satisfactory and Unsatisfactory Evidence in a Speech of Advocacy." *Speech Monographs,* XXX (August, 1963), pp. 302–306.

Hildebrandt, Herbert W., and William M. Sattler, "The Use of Common Materials in the Basic College Speech Course." *The Speech Teacher,* XII (January, 1963), pp. 18–25.

John Stuart Mill's Philosophy of Scientific Method, Ernest Nagel, ed., New York: Hafner Publishing Company, 1950. Chapter VIII, "Of the Four Methods of Experimental Inquiry," pp. 211–238. Original work: *A System of Logic* (London: 1843), 3.8.

Mills, Glen E., *Reason In Controversy.* Boston: Allyn and Bacon, Inc., 1964. Chapter III, "The Basis of Controversy," pp. 37–53; Chapter VII, "Reasoning Process," pp. 125–149.

Oliver, Robert T., *The Psychology of Persuasive Speech.* New York: Longmans, Green, and Company, 1942. Chapter 9, "Evidence and Authority," pp. 201–223.

Wallace, Karl, "The Substance of Rhetoric: Good Reasons," *The Quarterly Journal of Speech,* XLIX (October, 1963), pp. 239–249.

Wheelwright, Philip, *Valid Thinking.* New York: The Odyssey Press, 1962. Chapter VIII, "The Truth of Premises;" Chapter IX, "Inducting," pp. 215–240.

Communication Evaluated | 7

At a midwest college, some students decided to conduct an experiment in crowd reactions. The college newspaper reported that Dr. Collerige, distinguished British author and economist, might lecture at the University. In reality there was no such person. To add to the hoax, a student who purportedly had read books by Dr. Collerige wrote a letter to the newspaper maintaining that his views were too controversial to be presented on the campus. This immediately prompted letters to the editor stating that Dr. Collerige should be allowed to speak. Some protestors stated that they had read his books and that there was nothing controversial about them! A student from England was disguised as the nonexistent economist and was ushered to the auditorium for the lecture. His speech consisted of nonsensical sentences and phrases which were vague, obscure, and virtually meaningless. When he had finished, the crowd applauded him loudly; several students even asked him to stay longer and continue discussing his marvelous economic theories and ideas.

This unusual incident is disappointing and frightening to say the least. On what basis did these students evaluate this speaker? They certainly must not have been critical listeners or they would have detected the hoax, or at least would not have been quite so impressed. It seems that their criteria for evaluation were either nonexistent or were badly neglected. Fortunately most communication situations do not involve this degree of absurdity, but it is still necessary that you recognize criteria by which a communication should be evaluated. Without such criteria you could find yourself a victim of propaganda, or misleading communication.

Detecting fraud is not the only reason for studying evaluation. Proper evaluation is important because you make judgments about every communication you hear. Whenever you overhear a comment in the cafeteria line, participate in conversation, listen to a professor in class, hear a distinguished lecturer, or listen to the radio, you evaluate the communication. You make the evaluations according to your own specialized nervous system and your life orientation. The degree to which your evaluations are accurate depends upon your knowledge of the speaker, of his topic, and of the criteria by which communication should be judged.

To become an objective evaluator you need to understand the factors that influence your evaluations. You must understand that the reason you react to certain words and situations may be due to your life orientation. To achieve your goal of evaluating as objectively as possible, you need to compensate for your biases in the application of communication criteria. Having learned to recognize the biases in yourself, try to perceive similar tendencies in others. It is your job to perceive the subjective reality of the speaker, whether or not it corresponds to your own or to structural reality.

The real value in studying evaluation, however, is in learning by critical observation those communication techniques in others which are effective and those which are ineffective. By noting techniques which enhance communication in others, you may acquire methods to improve your own personal communication. Conversely you may observe techniques in communication which prove weak and inconsistent. These may serve as warnings of what not to do. It is through this evaluative process that many of the basic concepts of communication become clearly understood.

PROBLEMS OF EVALUATION

Communication evaluation is not a new concept. Records of rhetorical evaluation date back to the Tenth Century B.C. Before studying some of the theories of evaluation it might be helpful to understand some of the problems involved in evaluation. Fortunately not all the problems that follow are present in every evaluation situation. However, recognize the influence that each of these problems may have on your evaluation.

EVALUATION AND BIAS

A person who believes in capital punishment is going to be more likely to favor a pro-capital-punishment speech than someone who is opposed to it. This bias, of course, should not affect his evaluation of the communication, but it very likely will. It is the task of the evaluator to recognize his own biases and compensate for these in the evaluation of a communication.

One of the most widely recognized forms of bias which can affect the rating of evaluators is termed the *halo effect*. Thorndike, the originator of the term, found that "ratings were apparently affected by a marked tendency to think of the person in general as rather good or rather inferior and to color the judgments of his qualities by this general feeling." [1] The halo effect occurs most often in the following areas:

1. In a trait that is not easily observable
2. In a trait that is not frequently singled out or discussed
3. In a trait not clearly defined
4. In a trait involving reactions with other people
5. In a trait of high moral importance [2]

Thus it is imperative that evaluators be familiar with the criteria for evaluation in order to avoid the presence of the halo effect in evaluative judgments. There may be situations, however, in which the halo effect is not detrimental. When the object is to make a general evaluation of the speech as a whole, the halo effect need not be entirely discounted (see point 4 below).

PERSONALITIES AND EVALUATION

Sometimes a person might seem to "rub you the wrong way." You may not like his looks, his dialect, his dress, or his language.

---

[1] E. L. Thorndike, "A Constant Error in Psychological Ratings," *Journal of Applied Psychology*, IV (1920), pp. 25–29.

[2] P. M. Symonds, "Notes on Rating," *Journal of Applied Psychology*, IX (September, 1925), pp. 188–195.

Again, attempt to recognize your initial prejudices to make the most objective evaluation possible. It certainly is not fair to the speaker to judge him on his appearance or dialect any more than it is fair to judge an automobile race on which car is the prettiest or sounds the best.

One investigator studied the relationship among knowing a person, liking a person, and judging him as a speaker. He discovered that:

1. The better-liked students are judged to be better speakers.

2. The better-known students are apparently liked better.

3. The better-known speakers are judged to be somewhat better speakers.

4. There is apparently a slightly closer relationship between liking a person and judging him as a speaker when he is known only in class than when he is well-known.[3]

This evidence strongly suggests that personalities do play an important role in the effect your communication will have on others. However, as an objective evaluator you should strive to elminate the personal influence of the communicator and make your evaluations in an objective and impartial manner. Though objectivity is difficult to accomplish, it provides more meaningful feedback to the communicator and helps him to make more realistic self-appraisals of his performance.

DISAGREEMENT CONCERNING THE QUALITIES OF A GOOD SPEAKER

Theories of evaluation differ, some closely resemble each other and others exhibit few similarities. Realize that most listeners have no specific theory of evaluation. They know only their personal likes and dislikes about a communicator and often judge a communicator without specific criteria for evaluation.

In New York the problem of the selection of appropriate criteria for communication resulted in a legal dispute. The role

---

[3] E. H. Henrikson, "The Relation among Knowing a Person, Liking a Person, and Judging Him as a Speaker," *Speech Monographs*, VII (1949), pp. 22–25.

of correct pronunciation of words in determining what consti-
tuted effective speech for teacher certification was questioned.
Though no definite consensus was formed, the question was an
extremely important one. What relationships may be found
among pronunciation, articulation, voice, gestures, content, and
delivery? An answer to these questions would solve many of the
problems of speech evaluation. But one speech educator has
stated, "The yardstick for measuring speaking skill has not
been found. The perfect yardstick will probably never be
found." [4] This statement by no means implies that speech cannot
be measured objectively in the classroom. It simply indicates
that perfection in evaluation has not been and probably never
will be attained. When human evaluative processes are utilized
there is always a possibility of human error.

EVALUATION AND THE TOTAL IMPRESSION

The criteria for evaluation may relate specific factors involved
in communication, but it is their combined impact that will affect your judgment of the effectiveness of the communication.
Criteria are only effective in helping you base your total impression upon accepted standards. The criteria alone cannot adequately describe all of the elements necessary for effective
communication evaluation.

Several factors determine the total impression the evaluator
will form about the communication. Some of these have little to
do with the speech itself but are a function of the psychological
and physiological state of the evaluator. These factors include
the evaluator's sensory capacities, alertness, concentration, listening ability, knowledge of what to look for, lack of bias and
prejudice, freedom from fatigue, ability to interpret, and ability to record observations quickly.[5] All of these factors affect the
communication evaluator and help to form his total impression
of the communication.

---

[4] Wayne Thompson, "Is There a Yardstick for Measuring Public Speaking?"
The Quarterly Journal of Speech, XXIX (1943), pp. 87–91.
[5] Franklin Knower, "What Is a Speech Test?" *The Quarterly Journal of
Speech,* XXX (1944), pp. 485–493.

OTHER EVALUATION PROBLEMS

In addition to the four problems discussed above there are other factors which may adversely affect communication evaluations. These include change in the criteria by which evaluations are made, the motivation and instructional "set" of the evaluator, any deviation from the expected performance of the communicator, an increase in the number of criteria to be evaluated, and an increase in the number of general judgment categories. These problems must be considered when contemplating the evaluation of interpersonal communication.

One effect of studying evaluation should be to make you more aware of its value and, consequently, more willing to receive speech criticism yourself.

GOALS OF COMMUNICATION

Delta Sigma Rho-Tau Kappa Alpha, an honorary forensic and speech fraternity, emphasizes three goals of communication. These goals serve as criteria in the selection of a speaker of the year:

1. Communication must be *intelligent.*
2. Communication must be *effective.*
3. Communication must be *responsible.*

It is upon these three basic goals of communication that the approach to criticism and evaluation will be based. They represent specific characteristics that a communicator should possess. A desirable communication will exhibit all three of these criteria. The basis for these goals was formulated many years ago by rhetoricians and orators in Greece and Rome. Their teachings provide groundwork for contemporary views on speech criticism and evaluation.

EARLY RHETORICAL THEORIES

The earliest of the rhetoricians were the Sophists. Corax and his student, Tisias, formulated a system of rhetoric as early as 465 B.C. in Greece. The system was an outgrowth of the way in which legal disputes were settled. Trials were public and similar to modern town meetings, with each party in the dispute presenting his own case. The crowd acted in the capacity of a jury, awarding the decision to the most persuasive speaker.

A weakness of the Sophistic theory was that the end result justified the means through which it was accomplished. To the Sophists, winning the case, or procuring the desired results, was all-important. The methods used to accomplish the goal often really did not matter. Their disregard of the intelligent and responsible qualities of communication led to unethical practices in speaking. Fortunately this theory is not widely accepted today, for as you can see it stresses only one of the three goals of communication—effectiveness.

Plato (427–347 B.C.) realized the basic flaw in the Sophists' theory of communication and attacked it strongly. He advocated that the formal training in communication the Sophists stressed was unnecessary. Plato believed that if a man knew the truth and had a sufficient body of knowledge, he would become persuasive. Plato's theory was almost the exact converse of the theory of the Sophists. Though he emphasized intelligent and responsible communication, he did not stress effectiveness. You probably have encountered people who were experts in their field, but who could not effectively communicate their knowledge or ideas to others.

Two Roman rhetoricians, Cicero (106–43 B.C.) and Quintilian (First Century A.D.), developed theories of rhetoric that were based on the responsible qualities of a communicator. To them an effective communicator was "a good man, speaking well," implying that if a man possesses high ethical standards and expresses himself clearly then he will be persuasive. This theory was valuable because it emphasized the responsible and effective qualities of communication, but it lacked proper emphasis on intelligence. Again, you can realize that even though a man is responsible and effective, he may lack the necessary knowledge about his subject to present it intelligently.

Aristotle (384–322 B.C.), several years before Cicero and Quintilian, initiated a theory of communication which has had a more profound influence on rhetoric than that of any other theory. He stressed not only the intelligence, character qualities, and skills of an individual, but he added a stress on orderly arrangement of the materials. This arrangement was necessary in order to fulfill the effective quality of communication. His theory, substantiated by modern research, was that the more orderly a presentation, the more effectively and efficiently it may be learned by the audience.

Aristotle's theory, then, is the basis of the thinking of rhetorical critics who demand that a communicator be intelligent, effective, and responsible. Derived from these three essential qualities, the criteria for evaluating communication discussed are compiled solely to provide you with an objective basis for criticism. As an evaluator you must make the final judgment as to which criteria are most important in a given situation.

CONTEMPORARY EVALUATION

The communication model presented in Chapter 2 not only describes the communication process, but also serves as a basis for the establishment of contemporary criteria for evaluation. The three original criteria—intelligence, effectiveness, and responsibility—are the basic framework for the criteria developed below. These criteria have also been tested in actual communication evaluation situations.

ANALYSIS AND ADAPTATION TO AUDIENCE

You will recall that your first task as a communicator is to understand your own life orientation. But once you have acquired this understanding, you then concentrate on adapting to the life orientation of others. To evaluate the degree to which a communicator has adapted, determine if his approach is in line with the knowledge, experience, and socioeconomic background of the audience. A communicator can adapt to the life orientation of his audience by adjusting his topic to a specific level or by properly using interesting examples. Ask the following questions when evaluating this phase of communication:

1. How well did the communicator know his own life orientation?

2. How well did the communicator analyze the audience's life orientation?

3. Did the communicator adapt to these orientations in his presentation?

FLOW OF THE COMMUNICATION

In most instances a communication which is broken, choppy, or interrupted by such vocalized pauses as "uh" and "and-uh", will be less successful than one which flows smoothly. A communicator can help facilitate the flow of communication by preparing concise transitional phrases and sentences to connect his ideas. Controlled delivery and elimination of unnecessary pauses and regressions also help the communicator achieve a smooth flow of communication. In evaluating the communicator's flow of words and ideas ask these questions:

1. How well did the communicator use transitional phrases and sentences to connect ideas?

2. Did the communication move continuously toward the direction of the specific purpose?

3. Was the movement of words and ideas smooth or jerky?

COHESIVENESS OF THE MESSAGE

Chapter 4 discussed methods of arranging thoughts, materials, and parts of the communication. The degree to which the communicator organizes his communication will have an effect on its cohesiveness. The main object of the communicator should be to have his communication organized so well that it appears as a unified whole rather than a combination of individual parts. Ask the following questions when evaluating the cohesiveness of a communication:

1. To what extent did the communicator unify his communication through arrangement of materials, thought units, and language?

2. Were the ideas and parts of the communication an integrated whole or a composite of separate ideas?

USE OF DEVELOPMENTAL DEVICES

You have already studied the various developmental devices which add authority and interest to the communication. The audience, the communicator, and the topic all determine what sort of developmental devices are necessary. A communicator who bases his communication solely on personal experience or hearsay is lacking in those developmental devices which provide support in the form of evidence for his arguments. Similarly, a communicator who has an abundance of evidence might be lacking in those developmental devices which hold the interest of the audience. Ask these questions when evaluating the communicator's use of developmental devices:

1. Did the communicator exhibit a knowledge of the developmental devices?
2. Were the examples, analogies, statistics, and illustrations meaningful in terms of the audience's life orientation?
3. Did the developmental devices appeal to all of the five senses?
4. Was a variety of developmental devices used?

SELECTION OF APPROPRIATE WORD SYMBOLS

Since language is a system of coded symbols, it is necessary that the communicator use symbols which can be properly decoded by the receiver. A good communicator would never transmit the same set of language symbols to two different audiences even though he were presenting the same topic to both. For example, a lecture on conservation would have to be treated differently for an audience of farmers than for a group of conservationists. The key to effective symbolization is adapting to the level and background of the audience. Let these questions serve as guides in evaluating the appropriateness of a communicator's symbolization:

1. Did the communicator make the symbols work for him? Were the symbols accurate and vivid?

2. Was the style of the communication befitting the occasion, audience, and topic?

3. Did the communicator use correct grammar and pronunciation?

4. Were sentence structures in proper form?

5. Were the symbols sufficiently concrete or abstract (depending on the topic) for maximum understanding by the audience?

USE OF COMPLEMENTARY STIMULUS MESSAGES

Many times a visual aid or a graphic illustration can explain a process more efficiently than words by themselves. When visual aids and physical reinforcements such as gestures, facial expressions, and movements are used to supplement the words of the communication, the communicator is much more likely to achieve his specific purpose. Do not forget that effective use of the many different channels available will reinforce the primary stimulus message and enhance the communication. When evaluating the communicator's complementary stimulus message ask the following questions:

1. To what extent did the communicator reinforce his communication with facial expressions, gestures, or bodily reinforcements?

2. Were visual aids used to support the primary stimulus message?

3. Were visual aids used correctly and effectively?

AUXILIARY AND INTERFERENCE MESSAGES

Have you ever been in a communication setting where the voices of persons outside of the room could be distinctly heard through an open door? Did the communicator make an effort to overcome this interference by closing the door or asking someone nearby to do it? Probably not. Some people seem to think that delivering a communication is like a theatrical performance in the sense that "the show must go on" regardless of the obstacles. This is not the case. Communication can take place best in a setting where interference and interference messages are carefully controlled and minimized. It is the job of the communicator to make sure that external distractions or his physical appearance do not interfere with his primary stimulus message and complementary stimulus message. Use these questions as a guide in evaluating these areas of communication:

1. Did the communicator eliminate items which might detract from his communication?
2. Did the communicator handle effectively any interferences that arose during his communication?
3. Was the communicator in control of the communication situation at all times?

GENERAL EFFECTIVENESS OF THE COMMUNICATION

In the final analysis the purpose of the communication is to receive a response from the audience. The primary stimulus message is the primary means through which this response may be gained. A communicator's primary stimulus message should be made abundantly clear to the responding communicators. Interference should be recognized and minimized in the communication system. In addition, the primary stimulus message must be strong enough to pass through the filtering processes of discrimination and regrouping in order to make an impact upon the responding communicator. This important aspect of communication can be evaluated by asking yourself the following questions:

1. To what extent was the primary stimulus message clear?
2. Was the central theme predominant throughout the communication?
3. Did the communicator make an effort to help you know his primary stimulus message?
4. Did the communicator use the most effective medium of transmission available for his primary stimulus message?

FULFILLMENT OF THE REQUIREMENTS OF THE ASSIGNMENT

You are familiar with the classroom situation where it is important that students adhere to such requirements as time length, topic selection, and type of communication. The instructor has a planned program of improvement for the student, and his rules are aimed at helping students learn the maximum amount possible. There are communication situations outside the classroom, however, which also have specific rules which must be followed. For example, if you are asked to speak for 10 minutes on a radio or television program, you must have your talk timed exactly. An extra 10 seconds either way could throw off an entire day's program schedule and prove costly to the station. Or, imagine that you were asked to speak on flower growing to a garden club. A speech on tree surgery would certainly not be an acceptable substitute. In the prestructured speaking situation it is imperative that the communicator adhere to the rules governing his communication. When evaluating the degree to which the communicator fulfilled the requirements of the assignment ask:

1. How well did the communicator observe the time limit and rules set forth by those in charge of the communication setting?

2. Was the communication the type specified in the assignment?

3. Did the communication add to your body of knowledge?

4. Did the communicator indicate that he had probed his subject in sufficient depth?

5. Did the communication appear to have had a sufficient incubation period?

6. Was the communication of sufficient maturity for the audience?

A SAMPLE EVALUATION FORM

In Fig. 9, you will find a sample communication evaluation form which lists many of the criteria discussed in this chapter. This form is one of many used in classrooms and other situations in which communications are evaluated. In completing these evaluation forms the stress should be on objectivity and completeness. If you analyze the parts of the communication according to specific criteria, your evaluation will be more accurate than one based on subjective intuition. In a study by the authors it was discovered that student evaluators tended to rate their peers similarly to the instructor when they followed the suggested criteria on the communication evaluation form, whereas they rated their fellow students differently when they had no criteria of evaluation before them.[6] These findings suggest that it is a good idea to follow the criteria listed rather than to make over-all subjective judgments.

Notice that even though the evaluator marked numerical ratings corresponding to the scale at the top of the evaluation form, he also wrote specific comments. This practice of explaining or emphasizing the ratings on the evaluation form is a good one to initiate in evaluation. The evaluator's comments help the communicator to understand why he received a particular rating and give him valuable feedback to help him improve the next time.

When using a communication evaluation form, it is usually a good idea to write down specific comments during the presentation of the communication. Then, when the presentation is concluded, briefly review your comments and complete the numerical ratings. By waiting until the communication is completed to mark your ratings, you can make a more comprehensive judgment of the presentation. If you try to decide on ratings during the communication, your mind will not be on the message which is being transmitted and you may miss an important part of the presentation.

TOOLS OF SPEECH EVALUATION

Two tools of evaluative methods are most commonly used in the evaluation of communication. These are rating scales and ranking scales.

RATING SCALES

Rating scales may take many different forms but numerical and linear rating scales are most common in the evaluation of communication. Linear scales include two bi-polar terms on the end of a continuum. Along the continuum are intermediary

---

[6] Gordon Wiseman and Larry Barker, "A Study of Peer Group Evaluation," *The Southern Speech Journal*, XXXI, No. 2 (1965), pp. 132–138.

Communication Evaluation

Name John Doe Section 2222 Activity Informative Speech Date April 5 Group 1

Instructions: Place an x in the box which represents your response:

	5. Superior	4. Good	3. Average	2. Poor	1. Inferior
Flow of the communication..........			x		
Selection of appropriate word symbols.........				x	
Use of complementary stimulus messages......	x				
—Over-all transmission of the message...........			x		
Cohesiveness of the message.........		x			
Use of developmental devices.........				x	
—Over-all content of the message.........			x		
Analysis and adaptation to audience..........		x			
Fulfillment of specific assignment........		x			
General effectiveness of communication........			x		

Time_____ Evaluator_____ Total_____

Please write additional comments on the back.

150

Comments

Area(s) where most improvement is needed:

Your presentation was interesting but lacked depth. More concrete facts and illustrations were needed to support your main points. Don't rely too heavily on personal experiences.

Be careful about letting unnecessary pauses interrupt the flow of your communication. These occurred in three different instances near the beginning of your speech. You needed to control the outside noises in the room. Closing the door might have helped.

Area(s) where achievement is greatest:

Your example about the student in financial trouble was well adapted to your audience.

Your freedom from the lecture added to the informal style of delivery. You had excellent eye contact with your audience.

FIGURE 9. COMMUNICATION EVALUATION FORM

points which represent various degrees from the center position (neutral) toward either of the poles. An example of a linear rating scale is given in Fig. 10.

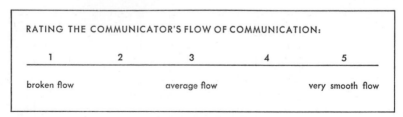

RATING THE COMMUNICATOR'S FLOW OF COMMUNICATION:

1	2	3	4	5
broken flow		average flow		very smooth flow

FIGURE 10.   LINEAR RATING SCALE

An evaluator would circle one of the numbers along the scale which most closely expressed his evaluation of the communicator's flow of expression.

Numerical rating scales are very similar to linear scales except they take a slightly different form. An example of a numerical rating scale is given in Fig. 11. The evaluator simply checks a number from 1 to 5 to indicate his evaluation of the communicator's flow of expression.

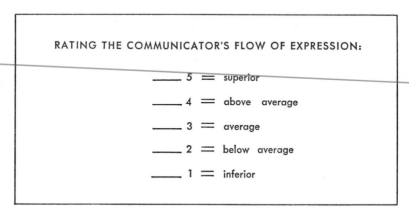

RATING THE COMMUNICATOR'S FLOW OF EXPRESSION:

_____ 5 = superior

_____ 4 = above   average

_____ 3 = average

_____ 2 = below   average

_____ 1 = inferior

FIGURE 11.   NUMERICAL RATING SCALE

The rating scale has been used more than any other instrument in the evaluation of speeches. It has enabled both trained and untrained observers to evaluate speech performance with some degree of accuracy. But rating scales are not without limitations. Perhaps the most common weakness known to raters is *central tendency*. Raters often tend to evaluate speakers in a tight cluster around the midpoint of the rating scale. The extremes at each end of the scale are rarely used. Though most speakers, according to normal curve theory, will be average there should be several students in each class who are significantly above and below average in speaking ability.

Another common error which occurs in the use of rating scales is termed *logical error*. Logical error is often a result of the halo effect mentioned previously in this chapter. Similar ratings are given on traits that seem logically related in the minds of the rater. In order to avoid this type of error, strive to make independent evaluations for each criteria so that you can identify the specific behavior which relates to the criteria being evaluated.

RANKING SCALES

Another method which is often used in speech evaluation, especially in speech contests, is the ranking scale. This type of scale can only be used if a series of communications are presented. Basically, the ranking method involves assigning one communicator as best, one as second best, and so on until the entire series of communicators has been ordered from best to worst. For example, suppose that you heard a series of eight speakers in a row: Linda, Paul, Laura, Bob, Rosalind, Jeff, Susanne, and Ken.

In order to rank these speakers you would need to rearrange the list in the order of their communication ability. Your rankings might look something like this:

Rank	Speaker
1	Susanne
2	Paul
3	Laura
4	Rosalind
5	Linda

6	Ken
7	Jeff
8	Bob

The major drawback of the ranking method is that it tells very little about the true ability of the communicator. If the group in the series are all excellent speakers even the person ranked eighth might be superior in his communication. Rankings are often necessary in competitive speech events when a winner must be declared, but in classroom communication evaluation ratings are probably more useful.

ATOMISTIC VERSUS ORGANISMIC EVALUATION

The criteria suggested earlier in this chapter represent the *atomistic* approach to evaluation, which entails dividing the communication into its component parts and evaluating each part separately. The combination of the evaluations of the specific parts of a communication should ideally represent the value of the speech as a unit. The merit of this approach is that it tends to be a comprehensive and objective system of evaluation. By analyzing the individual factors of communication, you can more clearly understand the intricate processes involved. The opposite approach to criticism of communication may be termed *organismic*. In this type of evaluation the communication is evaluated over-all, as a unit, rather than through its composite parts. This approach also has value because there are often instances when the sum of the parts differs from the whole communication.

Ideally, the communication evaluator should utilize a combination of the organismic and atomistic approaches. By doing so he becomes more objective and more comprehensive in his evaluations. Notice that space for both types of evaluation is provided on the sample communication form. In most instances you will find that the same general evaluation of a speech will be reflected in both the over-all and the composite evaluations. Because of the exceptions which may occur, however, you should attempt to utilize both methods.

ETHICAL RESPONSIBILITY IN COMMUNICATION

The power of symbolization has made man higher than the animals and has given him opportunities not afforded other forms of life. Where there are opportunities there are also responsibilities. Since man has the power of symbolization, he has the responsibility to use it wisely. Inherent in the nature of symbolization is the power of choice. Choice affects every part of man's life, from what kind of shoes he will wear to the kind of world he wants to live in. The power to choose can bring good or evil. Aristotle said that virtue depends on the individual. The same is the case with vice, for where it is in your power to act, it is also in your power to abstain from action. In other words, where you can say "yes" you can also say "no." The power of choice is important since you must accept both privileges and responsibilities if you are to be a successful communicator.

Immediately you will say, "I know some successful communicators who are not ethical." This fact cannot be denied but the truth or falsity of this statement depends on your definition of success. It has been suggested earlier in this chapter that if a communicator is to be successful he must be intelligent, effective, and responsible. Involved in the last criterion is the concept of ethical responsibility. A speaker may be effective and even intelligent, but until he demonstrates ethical responsibility he cannot be considered a successful communicator.

Responsible speaking can be determined by definition, but it cannot be implemented through lip service. As long as you confine your thinking to generalizations the difference between right and wrong may appear clear-cut, but when specific situations are discussed the distinction becomes less lucid. Consequently, it is usually better to work from some basic premises rather than follow a list of specific inflexible rules. Some ideas must be adopted while others should be adapted. The establishment of an ethical framework for communication must reflect your personality and your goals if it is to be meaningful. Most individuals operate simultaneously from two ideas regarding ethics—a system of absolute ethics and one of relative ethics.

Some people attempt to follow only one of the two systems, yet in actual practice, neither is complete within itself. Absolute ethics are eternal, immutable, applying at all times with equal force to all people in all circumstances. Absolute ethics deal with the basic nature of man and are guidelines but leave room for interpretation which, in essence, develops into a system of relative ethics.

Relative ethics are determined by the cultures of the people concerned and therefore are dependent on customs and cultures. Because of this, they vary widely at different times among different people with different circumstances. If a system of relative ethics is adhered to by itself, as you move from culture to culture your system of ethics will change and you will not find much stability. A set of general ethical principles is needed. The first rule to follow is "to thine own self be true." You have within your makeup some absolute ethical standards and, generally, you will need to follow these or risk frustration and despair. However, you will need to adopt a relative ethical standard for yourself. There are areas of your behavior that you cannot let society dictate and other areas where it does not make much difference.

On the interpersonal level communication is most effective where a condition of mutual trust exists. If your responding communicator does not trust you, a marvelous command of language will be of little value. As semanticists suggest, the meaning of words is not in the words themselves but in individuals, so mutual trust must be established before communication can be successful. If the responding communicator trusts you, the wrong words may be used and he will still understand. Trust is developed only as you adhere to high ethical standards over a period of time. This trust develops as you demonstrate a real effort never to betray the confidence of the responding communicator. You do not falsify or misrepresent evidence, and you work hard to recognize differences between fact and inference.

Since communication is a social act it will affect both originating and responding communicators. The power of influence is always present when you speak, and you must accept the responsibility of changing emotions, beliefs, and lives. There are times when this change is minute while other times it may be radical. Other speakers in the past may have contributed evidence supporting a change, or your communication alone may have done so. You never know when your additional evidence or influence will tip the scales to change a listener's attitudes.

There are those who feel that since you have the right to communicate then you have a responsibility to defend the right of others to communicate. You should be interested in all sides of an issue, be willing to hear the other person out.

On an intrapersonal basis, since you and your communication cannot really be separated, you must accept the responsibility of handling yourself. After all, you are the one person who can make sure you have the correct ethical standard for communication. What you are to be you are now becoming, so you must be willing to train now. Understand the limitations of your perceptions. Know the reasons for and the extent of your biases and prejudices, and the influence they have on your communication both as an originating communicator and as a responding communicator. Keep your mind open to learn new facts, and practice new methods. Become an informed individual so that you are an expert on the subjects you wish to communicate. Do not be satisfied with half truths but be interested in all the evidence. Be an honest borrower, giving credit where credit is due.

In the final analysis realize that your training and level of living will be reflected in your communication. Therefore your responsibility is to make your training the best.

The privileges afforded a communicator are wonderful and reflect the sacredness of man. The responsibilities are equally challenging. Train yourself to accept this challenge so that the gift that has been given to man will always work for his betterment in all phases of his life.

In summary, it is both an opportunity and a responsibility to evaluate the communication of others. When you are asked to evaluate communication you should not only look at the over-all speech, but you should utilize specific criteria in your evaluation. Use every opportunity to evaluate speeches in order to improve your listening and observation faculties, as well as learn from the techniques of others. Remember that a good communicator should possess three major qualities. He should be intelligent, effective, and responsible. All speakers who possess these three qualities are not necessarily the best communicators but the best communicators possess these qualities.

QUESTIONS FOR DISCUSSION

1. What relationship exists between the "sophist" theory and present practices in commercial advertising?

2. What bases do laymen usually use to evaluate communication? Are these adequate in light of contemporary communication theory?

3. How can critical evaluation be improved outside the classroom?

EXERCISES

[Forms for completing the exercises marked with an asterisk will be found in the *Worksheets for Speech—Interpersonal Communication* (San Francisco: Chandler Publishing Company, 1967).]

1. Make a list of problems (including those discussed in this chapter) which can negatively affect evaluation of speeches. Suggest a possible solution for each problem.*

2. Prepare a report on the importance of communication evaluation outside the classroom in the "real" world.*

3. Conduct a survey of basic speech texts and copy the evaluation forms presented in each. Present a report on the similarities and differences you find.

4. As a result of your survey in Exercise 3, develop an evaluation form which represents the criteria you believe are most important in effective communication.

5. Using the evaluation forms provided in the workbook, evaluate three of the following five types of speeches and write a brief critique of each:

    (a) a television speaker

    (b) a minister

    (c) an after-dinner speaker

    (d) a convocation lecturer

    (e) a college professor lecturing *

6. After you have given a speech in class fill out an evaluation form on your own speech. Compare your rating with those of the class and the instructor. If differences arose try to determine why (analysis of communication).

7. Make a list of the criteria for speech evaluation which are most difficult to assess. Try to determine what factors make them difficult to evaluate and explain why.

8. Observe a salesman as he succeeds in making a sale and as he fails to sell his product. What factors contribute to his success? To his failure?

9. Prepare a description of the "ideal" speaker based upon the discussion presented in this chapter. What characteristics should he possess? Which ones should he avoid?

10. Evaluate a series of speeches in class utilizing both organismic and atomistic evaluative approaches. Did differences occur between the two types of ratings? If so, which do you think is most accurate?

SUGGESTED READINGS

Bryan, Alice I., and Walter H. Wilke, "Audience Tendencies in Rating Public Speakers." *Journal of Applied Psychology*, XVI (1942), pp. 371–381.

Bryan, Alice I., and Walter H. Wilke, "A Technique for Rating Public Speeches." *Journal of Consulting Psychology*, V (1941), pp. 80–90.

Douglas, Jack, "The Measurement of Speech in the Classroom." *The Speech Teacher*, VII (November, 1958), pp. 309–319.

Fotheringham, W. C., "A Technique for Measuring Speech Effectiveness in Public Speaking Classes." *Speech Monographs*, XXIII (1956), pp. 31–37.

Kelley, William D., "Objectivity in the Grading and Evaluation of Speeches." *The Speech Teacher*, XIV (January, 1965), pp. 54–59.

Robinson, Karl F., and E. J. Kerikas, *Teaching Speech—Methods and Materials*. New York: David McKay, Inc., 1963, Chapter XII, "Determining Grades," pp. 249–261; Chapter XI, "Diagnostic Evaluation, Testing, and Criticism," pp. 218–249.

Thompson, Wayne, "Is There a Yardstick for Measuring Speaking Skill?" *The Quarterly Journal of Speech*, XXIX (February, 1943), pp. 87–91.

The Kinds of   Communication | 8

Four basic reasons for communicating are (1) to make interpersonal contact, (2) to inform, (3) to persuade, and (4) to entertain. Three kinds of speeches will be developed from these reasons—speeches to inform, to persuade, to entertain. Each reason has its counterpart in conversation, or semistructured interpersonal communication. Although you may use these reasons in combination, to be most successful as an originating communicator you need to settle on a single, clear-cut purpose. Essentially, the size of the audience does not make a difference in your purpose, for these reasons apply in a prestructured speaking situation or in a semistructured situation. However, audience size does make a difference in the materials you use, and the manner in which you present these materials.

If you wanted to inform the boss about the operation of a new model, you would not prepare a formal speech, but you would discuss the operation in a conversational manner with appropriate supporting materials. If the boss requested you to present the information to 60 of his salesmen at a convention, you would not convey the materials in the same manner. If he asked you to write an article for the company newsletter, the materials would again take a different form. Your purpose, to inform, would be the same, but the manner in which you fulfill it would be entirely different.

"Chit chat," such as the breakfast table conversation between husband and wife, is sometimes the purpose for communicating, and is referred to as *meta communication*. Its purpose is to pass the time of day, to create some sort of interpersonal contact.

Sometimes if you just purred, barked, or growled and did not use words, you could achieve the same effect. Meta communication ranges all the way from the very important to the ridiculous. A coke date with that very special one is full of "chit chat," yet it is important that all goes well and that there is mutual understanding. On the other end of the continuum the story is told of the man who started out in a receiving line by saying in a friendly manner, "I just shot my wife." All along the line, he received such replies as "Isn't that wonderful" and "I am so glad to hear that." There was no need to convey a specific message, only a need for a feeling of relatedness. Some of the most serious breakdowns in communication occur when these two purposes are confused by one of the communicators. Almost every wife has had the experience of telling her husband at the breakfast table to pick up something on the way home. When he, thinking she was just wanting a listener, did not get the message, there was no bread for toast the next morning. It is imperative that all involved in the communication process understand and agree as to the purpose of that communication.

COMMUNICATION TO INFORM

The informative communication is one of the most widely used forms of communication. In this type of communication you will be giving precise and meaningful information so that you may (1) increase knowledge, (2) direct action, or (3) provide a foundation for judgment or belief. These goals are in harmony with the educative process, thus the basis of informative communications is broad. Although the goals are not mutually exclusive—they differ in direction and intent—they are largely noncontroversial and factual. An informative communication should never be given just to exhibit how much you know, but to increase the knowledge of your audience. Informative reports based on careful investigation make a useful contribution to the body of knowledge in any field. In many fields the desire to increase knowledge is the prime function of those involved—teachers, newscasters, guides, or researchers, for example.

Often the informative communication is used for instructional purposes: how to perform an operation, how to get to a particular place, or how to conduct a particular ceremony or ritual. In these instances, you are in the truest sense directing action. An army sergeant who tells the new recruits how to assemble and disassemble a rifle is directing their action. When someone tells you how to get to Super Hall on the campus, he is directing your action. This directing has not come about through persuasion but through explanation.

The informative communication is basic to your formation of judgments and beliefs. For the most part, you believe the way you do because of the information you have. As you become aware of new facts, you gain new understandings and insights which will alter your beliefs. You may think that one of your classmates is lazy and unconcerned if you see him sleeping in class. If someone tells you he is working an 8-hour night shift to put himself through school, then this information would alter your beliefs about him. Your knowledge of Christians, the Amish people, or the Irish, will determine your opinion of them. To experience Christianity, to live with the Amish, or to visit the Irish would alter your original beliefs. Most of your beliefs stem from the knowledge you have and the way you have organized or interpreted that knowledge. Thinking is a matter of determining relationships and information is basic to that process. Often people believe the way they do because of the information or lack of information they have, and to understand people or beliefs you will need to understand their sources of information.

Three of the most popular methods of implementing the informative communication are reports, instructions, and lectures. Reports facilitate the ongoing of business, industry, government, and education. Fact-finding boards, investigating committees, and boards of inquiry all serve as means of obtaining information. The findings in reports determine the amount of advertising done, the food eaten, the television programs watched, and the progress of society itself. Reports serve an important function in the time-binding process as they enable the passing on of information and give others the benefits of experience. Clear concise reports are essential to survival.

Instructions are essential in learning new operations and

new skills, and are at the very core of the educational system. You will find instructions on every new appliance and piece of clothing, and they are the essence of the "do-it-yourself" society. Thousands of dollars are spent on manuals explaining operations in order to train new personnel and to avert breakdowns in machinery. Men are ever looking for new ways to explain the operation of old processes. Instructions given with the life orientation of the responding communicator in mind will be much more meaningful.

Although the lecture is a tool of our educational system, it has become recognized as a means of communicating information outside the school environment as well. Primarily it is a method of imparting factual information to large groups though its form may be altered to fit the occasion. Whether you are teaching, presenting reports, conducting a demonstration, or giving a book review, conveying precise information is your goal. To achieve this goal follow the journalistic pattern of telling what, where, when, how, and why. Developmental devices are discussed in Chapter 6 but certain ones are better adapted to the informative communication and should be reviewed.

DEVELOPMENTAL DEVICES FOR THE
INFORMATIVE COMMUNICATION

Definition of terms is necessary in an informative communication. You and your audience must have the same point of reference from which to approach new knowledge. In order to establish this point of reference, sometimes it will be necessary to define terms in the introduction. The importance of knowing the life orientation of the audience is again stressed, so that you define unfamiliar terms rather than familiar ones. There are seven basic ways to define. These include: (1) *negation,* or telling what something is not; (2) *authority,* or a statement by a person knowledgeable on the subject being defined; (3) *explication,* or giving the dictionary definition; (4) *function,* or telling what something does; (5) *derivation,* or showing the etymology of the word or concept; (6) *example,* or giving an illustration of the ideas being described; and (7) *context,* or determining the relationship of the word to the sentence.

Statistics are sources of numerical information which when interpreted accurately help to clarify the message. Statistical research should precede determination of the direction of your communication. Do not use statistics just for support, but use them as inquiry into the facts. Many of the ideas on observation and inference (see Chapter 4) apply here as you interpret the facts you find. Statistics are never very meaningful by themselves, so relationships must be shown through analogies, comparisons, and contrasts. Visual aids are excellent means for showing these relationships.

Comparison and *contrast* are excellent informative devices. The first shows how two things are alike and the second shows how they differ. Examples that point up the extremes help you to understand the scope of an idea. The more vivid the details the clearer the distinction between two ideas. Comparisons and contrasts drawn from the life orientation of the responding communicator are most meaningful.

Use of *restatement and repetition* is essential in informative communication. Often you will inform the audience in the introduction what you intend to do, carry out that intention in the body, and in the conclusion summarize what you have done. Although in particular kinds of instruction it might be better to repeat an idea exactly, it is usually much more effective to vary the restatement. Giving the same idea in a different manner will do much to broaden the meaning and insure understanding.

Use of *visual aids* is important in every form of communication, but has a particular significance in informative communication. Since visual aids help show relationships and visualize new material, they provide additional clarity and understanding. The old Chinese adage that "one see is worth a thousand tells" is true when you are trying to impart information. Even the simplest of visual aids can be useful. More detailed visual aid instructions will be found in Chapter 10.

The introduction and conclusion of the informative communication have special functions that increase your audience's receptivity of basic information.

The Introduction. The *introduction* paves the way for under-standing the material in the body of the communication. The scope of the proposition and any difficult terms should be defined and the importance of the subject stated, so that your audience will be both willing and able to understand the information. Also, the introduction should indicate the direction of the com-munication and provide a preview of the main points to be discussed in the body of the communication. As you limit the scope of your topic, relate the information to the needs of the responding communicator.

The Conclusion. The conclusion will very often summarize the main points. It ties together into a unified whole the infor-mation you have presented. Most likely you will want to suggest further applications of the ideas to reinforce their uses, and you will tell where additional information may be secured. You should always look for the best ways to accomplish the special expository functions that the introduction and conclusion must fulfill.

Every effective means must be employed to provide clarity and order in all points discussed and to keep the interest of your audience at a high peak. Proper organization can do a great deal to aid understanding. Inquiry is the foundation of the informa-tive process as you seek to analyze and interpret data. A study of learning theories will aid you as you try to present informa-tion so that it will be assimilated. A great deal of your day is spent in imparting information and you want to be as concise and meaningful as possible. Learn to master this area and you will have gained insights into the educative process which is so important to you at this time.

COMMUNICATION TO PERSUADE

Persuasion is a process of securing acceptance of an idea or directing a course of action by associating it with the responding communicator's beliefs, needs, and desires. Almost every day will find you involved in persuasive communications. Some will be so insignificant that you will hardly recognize them, while others can change your way of thinking, believing, or feeling for a lifetime. It is imperative that you understand persuasion so that you may begin to recognize and control it. The persuader seeks to resolve controversy through the process of advocacy. His goal is to control beliefs, attitudes, or behavior in a predetermined manner. For those who want to study persuasion in more detail, several reference books are listed at the end of this chapter. Also review the material on studies in persuasion in Chapter 4, to relate fundamentals that will help in handling persuasive communications in which you will be involved.

Two basic categories of persuasive communication are the communication to stimulate and the communication to convince. Since these two types are not discrete or opposite it is often difficult to distinguish between them. The difference is more one of degree than of kind because the over-all purpose of both is to persuade. But differences are apparent in audience attitude, the kind of proof used, and the specific purposes of each communication.

The importance of knowing the audience is again emphasized since the type of persuasive communication you develop will depend upon the attitude of the audience towards your specific purpose. In the stimulative communication, most of the responding communicators will give mental assent to your specific purpose, but will not be acting upon it. In the communication to convince, the majority of the responding communicators will disagree with your specific purpose. Most people know that they should study more, have more of an interest in their city government, guard their health, and the like, but most people do not do much about this knowledge and must be aroused to reinforce their beliefs to a point of action. In these cases the stimulative communication will be used. On the other hand, people do not always agree on the right-to-work laws, the value of foreign aid, or which candidate is the best one. A speech to convince is necessary for these types of topics. To fulfill your specific purpose you must change the audience's way of thinking, feeling, or believing.

KIND OF COMMUNICATION	PURPOSE OF COMMUNICATION	ATTITUDE OF RESPONDING COMMUNICATORS	KINDS OF PROOF	USE OF EXAMPLES
Communication to stimulate	To move emotionally, to change an emotion, to reinforce an emotion	Agrees with stimulus message	Emotional, ethical	Use few, but in great detail
Communication to convince	To change an attitude, belief or way of doing	Disagrees with primary stimulus message	Logical, ethical	Use many with little detail

FIGURE 12. PERSUASIVE COMMUNICATION

KINDS OF PROOF

In communication three kinds of proof are usually discussed: ethical, emotional, and logical. Proof by *ethos* or *ethical proof* is that which lies with the speaker either because of his past reputation, or because of elements within the communication which add to his credibility. This kind of proof is used in all types of speeches. The salesman you trust, the minister you are willing to listen to, and the teacher you are willing to counsel with use ethical proof, which is a major factor in persuading you to believe what they have to say. If ethical proof is not present before you speak—for instance, if the audience does not know you—you can establish it by the matter and manner of your speaking. Even an individual's appearance has a great influence on his ethical proof. The clean-looking man who has grey hair and stands straight and tall already has a great deal going for him in the way of ethical proof. Aspects of ethical proof are often conveyed through auxiliary messages (see Chapter 2). This factor must be recognized in all communication, especially the communication to persuade. Quintilian, Aristotle, and Cicero agreed that ethical proof is important in persuasion but they did not agree on how to obtain ethical proof. Recent research suggests that it can be obtained by the character of the individual as well as by what he says as he speaks.

Emotional and logical proof are more limited in scope. In the communication to stimulate, emotional proof is used *primarily* while in the communication to convince, logical proof is used. The term *primarily* is stressed because there will be emotional proof in the communication to convince, and logical proof in the stimulative communication, but the emphasis will be on one or the other.

Pathos or *emotional proof* is that which involves the individual's emotions. Its aim is to substitute one emotion for another, to change or reinforce feelings. Although it is designed to arouse certain feelings, it is not sentimental. It is that "thinking of the heart." You know that you do not have a thinking mechanism in the heart but this term is used to distinguish between logical thinking and emotional thinking. Very often a student couple in counseling will relate how they met at a party but knew they could not date seriously because of "steadies" at home. They say, "We understood our situations to begin with, and we talked about our other obligations on every date. However, something has happened to us now and we think seriously of each other. What do we do?" They were thinking with their heads, but their hearts were not listening. In many areas your emotions do not correspond with your logical beliefs. The knowledge of what needs to be done and the will to do it are two different things. Emotional proof is often used to bring the two together—to stimulate the person to action. This proof is powerful but subtle and suggestion is its most important tool in bringing about results.

Proof by *logos* or *logical proof* is that proof arrived at through reasoned discourse. It is that proof used to group known truths and accepted premises in relationships which will cause the responding communicator to accept new truths or conclusions. It generates new ideas and conclusions from existing facts. Evidence is the raw material of logical proof, and it consists of either observable facts or opinions about facts. Reasoned discourse is the means of conveying the facts and arriving at conclusions as you appeal to the thinking ability of the responding communicator.

The communicator who employs logical proof will utilize statistics, statements of authority, reasoning by example, and analogy to support his ideas. Sources of the material should be cited and actual quotations used when possible. Such phrases as "I think" or "I feel" have little place in this kind of communication. Materials must be employed to hold the attention of the auditor and to get him to reason with you. You get him to agree with you, have his mind operating with yours, and then move on into new areas, letting him continue to reason with you as you proceed.

Supplementary references for additional reading about the kinds of proof and the reasoning process are listed at the end of this chapter. A communicator must be acquainted with many of the techniques of persuasion. However, perhaps equally important if you want to persuade people is an understanding of basic needs, drives, or wants mentioned in the discussion of life orientation.

BASIC NEEDS

No two people are alike, yet there are certain concepts common to all. These universals may be listed in several ways. They are sometimes called drives; the important ones are listed as biological, ego, social and habitual drives. They are also listed as needs basic to mankind, a more practical approach from the point of view of communication. The needs usually listed are (1) need for freedom, (2) need to help others, (3) need for new experiences, (4) need for power and influence, (5) need for recognition, (6) need for response and affection, (7) need for security, and (8) need for workmanship. All human beings experience these needs but not to the same degree or at the same time. Human nature at its source is a ceaseless effort to satisfy inner stresses set up by man's basic needs. The directions these efforts take are determined by the opportunities and thwartings present in the individual's physical and social environment. When there is a reasonably well-balanced realization of his needs, man will do what he recognizes as being right and proper. Communication, both intrapersonal and interpersonal, is the medium through which man expresses a great many of his needs to himself and to his world. Understand these needs and their effect upon man and his communication. A. H. Maslow is the author of an excellent discussion on the hierarchy of needs (see Suggested Readings at the end of this chapter).

Need for Freedom

The basic need for freedom from undue restraints, duties, or domination is a powerful and deep-seated one. Many people today give their lives to maintain this freedom. If your plan takes away some of the freedom enjoyed by your responding communicators, you will need to show how it gives them greater freedom in another area. The struggle for personal liberty on a large-scale basis has received a great deal of publicity. However, one should not forget the personal struggle that goes on for liberty within each individual. Very often in a communication situation the message is completely distorted by this desire for personal freedom. The boss who starts his communication

"Smith, I want you here on your day off. . . ." will not get much of his message across. It is always necessary to think in terms of what the responding communicator feels are his rights and freedoms and then move from there.

Need to Help Others

Helpfulness towards others, sometimes referred to as the altruistic attitude, is more prevalent than many people would want to believe in our pragmatic society. It is at the basis of the Judeo-Christian tradition and is expressed in the ideas "he that loses his life shall find it," "except a grain of wheat fall into the ground and die. . . ." Further evidence of this need is found in the existence of many foundations in the United States and the amount of money given to charitable organizations each year. A man must nurture his self-respect and desire for success if he is to resist emotional disorders. On the other hand, man must also give of his means and energy to the nurture of less fortunate individuals if he is to achieve a proper balance. It seems to be a fundamental principle of mental health that the happiest people and the most mature individuals are those who give their energy to some constructive cause that serves the need of humanity. The smallest package in the world is the man all wrapped up in himself. Therefore it seems that from basic needs and growth the altruistic drive must be implemented. In communication this drive is more often reached through emotion rather than reason, through challenge rather than condemnation.

Need for New Experience

This need is an excellent means to get the attention of your responding communicators and hold it. To avoid "getting in a rut," people try new ideas. This need is stronger, generally, in young people, but many older people remain young by seeking new experiences. Growth and maturity come about through the medium of new experiences. A certain amount of fear of the unknown always accompanies a new experience; when communicating, you will want to reduce this fear and emphasize the new knowledge. Responding communicators enjoy being let in on something new or being taken behind the scenes. Although this need may be emphasized as a strong interest factor, remember your ethical responsibility not to mislead the listener.

Need for Power and Influence

Although there are some who like to live unto themselves, man is gregarious, and he not only enjoys being with others but wants to wield some kind of power and influence over those about him. With some this becomes an obsession and at its furthest extreme produces a Hitler, but obsession is the exception rather than the rule. The ability to "pull strings," to "fix it with city hall," satisfies a basic need in many people. In other areas the need expresses itself in a desire to be in charge of something, to exert leadership, or to have the right to make decisions. Perhaps the strongest manifestation is shown in the individual's desire to make his own choices, to be in control of himself and his own life. Intrapersonal communication can be an important factor as a person decides whether he has the power to make the decision or if the decision has been made for him. In communication you will generally be more successful if you make it clear to the responding communicator that he has the power to choose and that he is not being pushed around. Most people have a deep desire for social dominance or the ability to influence the behavior of others in a face-to-face situation.

Need for Recognition

Closely related to the need for power and influence is the need for recognition. The art of complimenting others, of making them feel good about what they have done, is nearly a lost one. Surveys show that only a very small percentage of workers enjoy their work. Lack of recognition is one of the main reasons more people do not. Some do not put forth an effort because they feel no one cares how they do their work. The successful communicator will learn to employ the art of sincere recognition in a speaking situation. It is a universally recognized tendency of man to seek distinction and individuality. This need is often referred to as the self-esteem or ego need. This driving motive is probably not inherited but it is soon learned or acquired. It is a strong motive; as a communicator, recognize the strength and importance of this need for personal recognition. A great deal of the behavior of a normal person is powerfully influenced by the stress this need develops. The personality becomes maladjusted when one is too severely thwarted in his efforts to secure reasonable ego satisfaction. This need probably causes more breakdowns in communication than any other. In a communication situation where the ego is at stake there must always be some way the individual can "save face," or interpersonal relations will be severely broken. Man cannot live without recognition and proper response from others. This self-motive drives individuals to make themselves appear in a good light. It impels them to make an impression, to be sought after, to gain publicity, to cover up inconsistencies, and to win the praise of others.

Since the desire for recognition is such a universal drive to action, it is the logical motive to employ in dealing successfully with people. You communicate in such a way that people feel more satisfied with their attainments. Often this can be done by being a good responding communicator and giving the originating communicator proper feedback. Sincerity must be at the basis of this motivation or your end goal will not be achieved.

Need for Response and Affection

The need for comradeship, affection, and sex relations is a universal one. Love can move more people than can power. Although it is not always apparent, there is within most individuals the need to love and to be loved. Sincere love will move many an auditor where nothing else would. In our society, so much emphasis on sex has distorted this need, making it difficult to distinguish its true meaning in communication. Recognition, esteem, a feeling of worth are all a part of this need, but the strong factor is the interaction of personalities. It is through interaction by means of communication that this need can be satisfied. You may admire someone, recognize his worth, love him, but until you communicate this the responding communicator will not really know how you feel. "He cared enough about me to ask how I was doing," illustrates the idea that it is good "to care," but there must be the "asking" as well. This attitude can be communicated on a close interpersonal basis or to a large audience. Teachers often make the mistake of feeling they cannot really get to know the students in a large class, so communication fails. The teacher of a class of eight can also fail unless he is able to communicate his interest and his recognition of the need for comradeship. Through communication, you help the responding communicator know that you are interested in him as a person and that this interest is motivated by a sense of love.

Need for Security

Studies today show that security is a basic need. With older people it often becomes the motivating force of nearly everything they do. It becomes the fear that plagues the workman. It involves both individual freedom and recognition. It is one of the most difficult needs to handle in communication because it is seldom forthright and honest. Most individuals who feel insecure will behave in a manner that brings about less security rather than more. A child who feels he has lost security with his parents will often misbehave to get their attention, or an insecure workman will blast out against his company. In communication you will need to recognize behavior that asks for security or questions that are not really points of inquiry. A wife who asks, as she walks out the door to a party, "Is my dress all right?" is often seeking reassurance, not a candid opinion. Since this need is so deceptive it first must be recognized if you are to help fulfill it. With a large percentage of people the need for security manifests itself in a desire for the status quo. Groups resist uncertainty. They prefer the security of the status quo, and they are inclined to reject any change or the insecurity of a divergent opinion, both of which are seen as threats to the group. Individuals who feel you want to change their way of life or their beliefs will often perceive you as a threat to their security. Feelings of insecurity are attached to new ways of doing things while feelings of security come from doing the same thing in the same way. Again the deceptive nature of this need is stressed.

Need for Creativity

The desire to build or make something has received great consideration in the "do-it-yourself" craze in our country. Cake-mix makers fix it so the woman must at least add some water or an egg to the mix so that she can feel that she is contributing creatively. Greater emphasis is given to creativity today and a great deal of research is being done to discover not only the aspects of this need but ways to satisfy it. The first concept to work from in communication is that more often than not creativity is inhibited by social pressures of all kinds and often the way to satisfy this need is to remove the pressure to conform. This need is associated with several of the others because often a person desires to be creative so that he will be recognized by the things he is able to do well. More often than not the satisfaction of this need comes in seeing the finished product. It would seem that challenge and encouragement are the best approaches to take in communication geared to this need.

Unsatisfied Needs

In this discussion some of the needs you will find present in yourself and in your audience have been defined. Efforts to satisfy these needs account for much of man's behavior. The stress that these unsatisfied needs set up in personality explains much of what is called good and bad behavior. Where there are unfulfilled needs in the human organism there will automatically be internal stresses and strains. Therefore as a communicator you are not only interested in the basic human needs in order to move people in a particular direction but also in learning the many possible stresses that can cause breakdowns in communication. Your communication may have nothing to do with security but if your responding communicator is under stress of insecurity, your message may be lost in his frustration. According to the homeostatic theory, a psychological drive—with its many effects on activity, goal selection, and conscious want—stems from an internal disequilibrium. Thus psychological drives are often associated with psychological need. Communication is basic to the training that guides you in making a wise choice rather than following what seems to be a blind urge.

You as a communicator have a responsibility when you seek out these basic needs in order to direct your audience. This responsibility is a serious one because you are manipulating persons when you work with their needs. Use the needs to help communicate your ideas, but be honest in your intent and purpose and accept the responsibility that is yours. Be sure to follow the criteria set forth in Chapter 7 to evaluate your communication.

THE PERSUASIVE COMMUNICATION TO STIMULATE

The stimulative communication is basically persuasive in nature and employs primarily emotional proof to achieve its end. As a rule, controversy is not involved and therefore evidence and argument are not needed. Existing beliefs, loyalties, devotions, and attitudes are being reinforced or the responding communicator is being motivated to action. The stimulative communication is used at dedications, memorial services, commencement exercises, promotional staff meetings, PTA meetings, and meetings of different groups. You will use this kind of communication with your parents, with your pinmate, and with your fellow employees. At times you will want to give your responding communicators a good feeling as you cement loyalties or develop appreciation for a person or institution, as in the speech of praise. At other times you will want to move them to a particular action to give to the Red Cross, to donate blood, to exercise their right to vote, or to donate money.

Since the responding communicator already agrees with your purpose in principle, the content of the communication should be selected to motivate the audience. The style should fit the occasion. Because the vividness of your appeal affects your chances of stimulating your audience, language that will involve the five senses should be employed. These senses are at the basis of emotions and the listener can be moved through them. If you employ these senses skillfully the responding communicator will be able to participate imaginatively in the experiences you present and thereby allow his emotions to be aroused. Ideas may be made vivid by using contrasts, parallelism, and many of the developmental devices.

Introduction. The introduction of the stimulative communication should arouse attention but also emphasize common ground with your responding communicators before you ever try to move them. It must be flexible so that you may transform the audience from their initial frame of mind to the mood you would have them experience. A startling statement or an illustration can help you get attention and create the proper mood. Wise use of the rhetorical question can bring the audience to a common starting point. Do not be afraid to involve the responding communicator emotionally from the very beginning. Even your tone and manner of speaking can be used to great advantage. Often a reference to the occasion is appropriate. Aspirations, desires, affections, and sentiments of the responding communicators should be studied and knowledge of their basic needs is essential.

Body. Perhaps the best organizational form to use for the body of the communication to stimulate is the psychological order. To support the stimulative communication many developmental devices will work, but pertinent illustrations and examples help to involve the audience. Examples should be sufficiently detailed and not too numerous. It is best to give an example or illustration in enough detail that the audience feels the plight of the person or lives the act of the illustration. A stimulative communication on juvenile delinquency can present examples almost as thorough as case histories so that the responding communicator lives, moves, and feels with the person's predicament.

Conclusion. The conclusion of the stimulative communication focuses the purpose of your message. Unless your purpose is clear in your own mind your audience will not be able to visualize what you are expecting of them. An illustration, a personal conclusion, or a stirring challenge are all effective means of concluding your communication. The "dawn of a new day" kind of conclusion, where you end in a positive manner by suggesting the wonderful things that will happen if your plan is implemented, is often stimulating in itself. The communication to stimulate should build emotionally to a strong conclusion. The responding communicator should be ready to act, feel, or believe the way you have directed him. You may seek to inspire devotion, faith, reverence, and respect, or you may want him to march, to pray, to give blood, or to register to vote. Each occasion will certainly dictate modifications in your general approach and direction of the communication. Be sensitive to the emotional reaction and be careful not to negate your purpose by going too far in your final suggestions.

The stimulative communication offers a challenge to the communicator. You must maintain a constant balance of emotions. As the communication proceeds be sensitive to the feedback from the responding communicator. It is easy to fall into sentimentality, to arouse the wrong emotion, to fail to control the emotion that has been aroused and thus lose your responding communicator completely. Once this has happened the intrapersonal communication taking place within the responding communicator will shut you out, and you will be unable to communicate. However, when responding communicators are moved to noble thoughts, actions, and deeds, you can feel a sense of pride in having fulfilled your job as a communicator.

Your ethical responsibility in the stimulative communication is great because of the potential of communication. To call out "Fire" in a theatre may move your audience to action, but if there is no fire, the death of those crushed in the mad rush to the exits is your responsibility. People's emotions should not be toyed with or used to selfish advantage. Your goal should be to produce a lasting effect, not just an immediate response that fades as soon as the emotional atmosphere is gone.

THE PERSUASIVE COMMUNICATION TO CONVINCE

The communication to convince using logical proof is sometimes called the speech to activate or actuate. It deals primarily with the mind or the will and should always have the intellectual dimension. Its basic purpose is advocacy and it is at the core of the decision-making process. Any decision with an either/or alternative will involve the persuasive communication. You will use it when you are dissatisfied with existing conditions or attitudes or conduct of your responding communicator. It is used by attorneys, debaters, legislators, salesmen, politicians, and others. The ultimate goal of the persuasive communication is to get the responding communicator to believe or act on what you advocate. Studies referred to in Chapter 4 should be reviewed, as should be the material on basic needs. It would also be wise for the student of persuasion to study the area of cognitive dissonance developed by Leon Festinger (see suggested readings). Shepherd suggests that "in Festinger's theory of cognitive dissonance he seeks to develop a theory to explain why a person holds a given opinion or expresses a given behavior or changes his opinion or modifies his behavior. He argues that there exists in the human being a drive to maintain a general sense of consonance of one's opinions, ideas, attitudes, and the like, a sense of their being consistent with each other, of going together in a meaningful way. When some aspects of a person's mental life seem awry, seem to be dissonant with other aspects, there is a drive; the person is motivated to reduce the dissonance. The reduction of dissonance may be accomplished in many different ways: a person may ignore some things, he may reinterpret observations he has made, or he may modify other attitudes or opinions in order to reduce dissonance. Man may be a dissonance-reducing organism, but this does not necessarily mean that man is a dissonance-avoiding organism. Some experimental evidence suggests that man does not avoid dissonance and may, in fact, seek it out." Intrapersonal communication is used to bring the real world into line with a person's motives when the real world and one's motives are at odds. But when this is impossible for external or internal reasons, the discrepancy or dissonance can be reduced. As a persuasive communicator these ideas suggest not only reasons for frustrations but also an approach to move your responding communicator.

The communication to convince is best handled when its purpose is framed in the form of a proposition, for example, "Resolved: That Red China Should Be Admitted to the United

---

[1] Clovis R. Shepherd, *Small Groups* (San Francisco: Chandler Publishing Company, 1964), pp. 47–48.

Nations"; "Resolved: That All Foreign Aid Should Be Discontinued"; or "Resolved: That You Should Own a Sweep-ease Sweeper." You do not have to state your primary stimulus message in the form of an assertative proposition but it will help you and your responding communicator understand what you are advocating. Since reasoning is basic to advocacy, any device that will enable you and the auditor to reason together is valuable. Your approach to the communication will be determined by whether you argue the affirmative or the negative side of the proposition.

In the body of the communication, if you argue the affirmative side you must convince your auditor (1) that there is a need, (2) that the change you propose is desirable, (3) that your plan is workable, and (4) that yours is the best plan. This method of persuasion is referred to as a *prima facie* case.

This kind of case is adequate to prove its side until it is refuted. It is logically sufficient to establish a high degree of probability in favor of your proposition. You work to have evidence and reasoning to support all the main points listed above. General usage suggests evidence that appears to support its point is also *prima facie*.

If you want to argue the negative side of the proposition you may argue (1) that there is not a need, (2) that the plan is not desirable or practical as it now stands, (3) that the statement of the proposal is not valid, (4) that there is a need, but it is better to repair the existing plan, or (5) that you agree with the need but would like to present a counterplan. This procedure, which the debater will recognize as the outline for an affirmative or negative case, seems the best way to approach the persuasive communication to convince.

As the communicator you must first have the issues perfectly clear in your mind and then find evidence to support them. The evidence must be clear, concise, and relevant, and your arguments should be based on sound reasoning. Cite source material and make frequent use of statements of authority, examples, statistics, and analogies. In every type of communication avoid generalities; be specific. Unlike the stimulative communication, the examples should be short and direct. More examples with less detail are needed to change the individual's way of thinking.

Introduction. The introduction of the communication to convince serves a special function since your audience will not agree with your purpose and you will need to persuade them to listen. Your own credibility is very important when the audience does not agree with your ideas at the outset. Try to find a common point of departure, build common ground, common understanding before you attempt to present your message. Even the responding communicator's process of perception may be a barrier to change and you must deal with his subjective reality. The introduction may serve as a means of synchronizing life orientations, of making the responding communicator see your proposal as a means to his existing goals. The introduction must be flexible enough to adjust to audience reaction so that your responding communicator will have tuned you in on his wavelength before you proceed.

Body. John Dewey's thought pattern (see Chapter 4) is among the best organizational patterns to use for the persuasive communication to convince since it follows the logical pattern of reasoning. Organization is even more important in persuasion than in other types of communication. The logical order is one of the best to follow in the body of the message. In this order, Point *B* will depend on Point *A*, and Point *C* on Point *B*, as was suggested in Chapter 4. The psychological order could be used as well, and you may reason inductively or deductively depending on which you think is the best approach for your particular responding communicator. It is imperative that you know as much about your responding communicator as possible because you must convince him on the basis of his desires or needs.

Conclusion. The conclusion of a communication to convince demands that you be sensitive to the responding communicators. It is easy to oversell and thwart your purpose. Since action is usually your final goal, it is wise to present some available means of action and urge the responding communicator to accept the challenge. Also, the presentation of the action step must be carefully timed. The action is your primary concern in the conclusion of the communication to convince because you know that the action taken or not taken will have a definite effect. Make acceptance of your proposed plan of action as easy as possible. Emphasis placed on the benefits is the more positive way of getting action. If you build the proper relationship between yourself and the responding communicator then an effective way to conclude is with a statement of your personal intention. This does not have to be actual participation but can be achieved through the means of suggestion.

The question is often raised, "Should I present both sides or just my own?" Although you will need to know the life orientation of your responding communicator, studies seem to point to the fact that if the responding communicator is intelligent he will usually want to know both sides of the issue, but if he is not so well-educated it is better to just give your side. Generally, the extremely hostile audience will listen to both sides better than one not so hostile.[2] If you do give the opposite point of view be careful not to reinforce it too much, but rather use it as a basis from which to reason to your side.

Several reference books are listed at the end of this chapter for additional studies in persuasion, for persuasion is part of your way of life. The content of your communication is the one area that is within your most immediate control. The audience's opinion of you, their own background of experience and established beliefs, their habits of thinking, and their immediate reaction are all factors that influence the outcome of the communication, but are not so easily regulated. You must learn "to discover *all* the available means of persuasion," as Aristotle has said, and use them. The focus of the persuasive communication to convince is the mind—a powerful, stimulating, and awesome mechanism. The facts it works with are objective data about which there should be little question, but conclusions it reaches are subjective judgments, open to endless differences of opinion. Your mind is not omniscient, so you must receive ideas from your responding communicators as well as direct ideas towards them. Through this interaction of minds the persuasive communicator hopes to achieve lasting results.

---

[2] Carl L. Hovland, Irvin L. Janis, and Harold H. Kelley, *Communication and Persuasion* (New Haven, Conn.: Yale University Press, 1963), pp. 112–129.

COMMUNICATION TO ENTERTAIN

A desire to entertain should be present in almost every communication and often good ideas are lost because the communicator did not add the element of entertainment. However, there are occasions when an audience wants only to be entertained. This is not to say that entertainment is the only goal but this is the general feeling the responding communicators will want to have as you finish. If you are able to give them excellent information or to challenge them or to give them a sense of well-being in the process, then you have succeeded. The communicator who is able to achieve this combination will be sought after for informal conversational situations as well as for special occasions when people get together and want a speaker.

A popular misconception is that the communication to entertain must be hilariously funny and that the joke is the only material you use in building the communication to entertain. Humor can be an important element but a collection of unrelated jokes is hardly the definition for a communication to entertain. Another misconception is that the originating communicator must appear stupid, cute, or a real joker. It is possible for you to do an excellent job with this communication and still maintain your credibility. You do not have to be a television or night club comedian to use the communication to entertain.

The communicator who wants to entertain must possess the qualities of any good communicator, but some qualities must be developed to a greater degree. The communicator must be able to transmit vitality and life to his audience. Animation, gestures, and movement must be free and meaningful. A quick mind, sensitivity to the responding communicators, the ability to adapt to reactions and a certain amount of take-over ability is imperative. If you write down your ideas or are tied closely to your notes you may not be successful. This kind of communication takes a great deal of practical experience in working with audiences and understanding the communication situation, yet is very rewarding when well done.

Introduction. The opening ideas of the communication are important not only to get you started, but to create the atmosphere you must have to be successful. There should not be any question in the minds of your responding communicators concerning your purpose. A permissive atmosphere is needed for the communication to entertain and this must be accomplished in the introduction. A warm feeling of satisfaction must be achieved in the minds of the responding communicators—a feeling of satisfaction towards the originating communicator, the occasion, and themselves. A recognition of the occasion in terms of the listeners will often aid in obtaining these feelings. Avoid poking fun at the person who introduced you unless you are on close friendly terms. Most of all avoid making the introduction or the ideas seemed canned. Always appeal to the highest motives and you will never need be ashamed of the results. Make the introduction flexible enough to have your audience with you before you move into the body of the communication.

Body. It is difficult to make positive suggestions about the body of the communication to entertain because it must be framed in the life orientations of your responding communicators more than any other communication. The most important idea is that you should be brief. Preciseness of language is employed so that words are not wasted; you move quickly from one idea to another, and you always want to leave your responding communicators wanting more. This task is difficult because by its nature the communication to entertain elicits more response from your audience than any other communication and it is difficult for a communicator who is getting a good response to be brief. Communications of this nature usually are only a part of the program and often the responding communicators are wanting to leave by the time you speak. Brevity is another means whereby you can endear yourself to your audience, rather than letting them endure you to a bitter end.

The purpose of your ideas seldom is to impart knowledge but to elicit an immediate interaction with your responding communicators. You will favor the novel and vivid over the familiar and the exact, the active and lively over the dull and dead materials. Careful explanation is omitted in favor of lively description, novelty, and humor. Actual dialogue, unexpected phrasing, human-interest stories, imagination, and overstatement are just a few ingredients of the successful communication to entertain. The art of telling a good story is imperative and the ability to blend all the ideas into a unified whole will aid in achieving your purpose, which should always blend with the purposes of the group and the occasion. Interesting, unusual, or amusing daily experiences of yourself or your audience add variety. Those examples which serve to show the absurdity of your ways or such sentiments that make the listener aware of the possible charm or pleasure of your relations with your fellows will provide excellent content. Humor is an art which you will need to study if you want to use it. Emotions will be high in the communication to entertain so you will want the audience to empathize with you. A generous stock of ideas should be developed for your entertaining communication. In most situations you may be more effective if you only use 50 per cent of your materials. The ability to select while speaking that which is truly appropriate will make you the kind of entertaining communicator who will be invited again.

Conclusion. The conclusion of the communication to entertain should let you finish on a high point with your responding communicators asking for more. It must be brief—often the best conclusion is an excellent story or illustration that leaves your responding communicators in a roar of laughter, or in a highly emotional state. With so many tensions present in individuals, the communication to entertain can afford an excellent respite from the pressures of life and should always be viewed with this purpose in mind. Become a part of your responding communicator's lives and for a few brief moments, laugh, cry, love, aspire, or just enjoy life with them and both of you will leave with a good feeling of time well spent.

QUESTIONS FOR DISCUSSION

1. What are some of the basic needs of college students today? How does communication fit in with these needs?

2. In what ways does persuasion affect your day-to-day decisions?

3. What are the criteria to be used in judging communication so that

you know the person has a message for you and is not just wanting to pass the time of day?

EXERCISES

[Forms for completing the exercises marked with an asterisk will be found in the *Worksheets for Speech—Interpersonal Communication* (San Francisco: Chandler Publishing Company, 1967).]

1. Study a speech as reported in the *Wall Street Journal* and the headlines of four other newspapers about the same speech.*

2. Take five major national issues and frame them into the form of debatable propositions.*

3. Secure three examples of advertisements using the "hard sell" and three using the "soft sell" approach.

4. Read a speech in *Vital Speeches* and find examples of the three kinds of proof.

5. Give a "This I Believe" speech as a stimulative speech, then as an informative speech. Explain how your life orientation has helped you develop these beliefs.

6. Report three additional examples of meta communication.

7. List four different approaches you can take to convince your parents to give you something you want.

8. Analyze critically a poor purchase you made recently to see what factors persuaded you to buy it.

9. What are four factors in your life that would add credibility to your speaking?

10. What were the teaching methods of your most effective teacher? Contrast and compare them with methods you would use in informative speaking.

SUGGESTED READINGS

Cronkhite, Gary Lynn, "Logic, Emotion, and the Paradigm of Persuasion." *The Quarterly Journal of Speech,* L (February, 1964), pp. 13–18.

Festinger, Leon, *A Theory of Cognitive Dissonance.* Evanston, Ill.: Row, Peterson and Company, 1957.

Fulton, R. Barry, "Motivation: Foundation of Persuasion." *The Quarterly Journal of Speech,* XLIX (October, 1963), pp. 295–307.

Jones, Morris Val, "A Speech of Definition." *The Speech Teacher,* V (January, 1956), pp. 37–39.

Maslow, A. H., *Motivation and Personality.* New York: Harper and Row, 1954. Chapter 8, "Higher and Lower Needs," pp. 146–154.

QUESTIONS, EXERCISES, READINGS

Mudd, Charles S., and Malcolm O. Sillars, *Speech: Content and Communication*. San Francisco: Chandler Publishing Company, 1962. Chapter 17, "Speaking to Inform;" Chapter 18, "Speaking to Persuade," pp. 325–363.

Tompkins, Philip K., "Organizing the Speech to Inform." *Today's Speech*, VII (September, 1959), pp. 21–22.

Group Communication: Discussion | 9

Group discussion has become an essential socialization and problem-solving force in modern-day free societies. Committees, panels, and conferences are playing an increasingly important role in government, business, education, and industry. Group discussion is a current research area in sociology, social psychology, and communication. Although many times the discussion group or committee is a group of the unfit, chosen by the unwilling, to do the unwanted, it need not be this way. Discussion operates on the basic premise that a group of people thinking together are able to accomplish more than a number of individuals thinking separately. It is the art of thinking independently, yet cooperatively, in solving a problem.

Group discussion is an effective teaching technique for presenting subject matter to a class. Through discussion, members of a class participate in a kind of communication which can be applied outside the classroom. A person giving a speech controls the speaking situation and limits himself to the materials he plans to present. A discussion is not controlled by one individual and may develop along many different lines. Therefore a student's preparation for discussion must often be more thorough than for a speech. If discussion is to be successfully practiced, its philosophy and place in the decision-making processes should be understood.

METHODS OF DECISION MAKING

A list of the three most important methods of decision making would include (1) the method of authority, (2) the method of advocacy, and (3) the method of inquiry. As might be expected each of these methods has certain advantages and disadvantages.

METHOD OF AUTHORITY

If your primary purpose is to make a decision and implement it, then the method of authority is the quickest way to get the job done. However, it is almost impossible to develop continuing leadership and attain long-range goals with this method. The method of authority not only lacks adequate means of perpetuating leadership but contributes to its own ultimate breakdown as it excludes minorities that may become majorities.

METHOD OF ADVOCACY

The method of advocacy is the most widely used decision-making process in free societies. It operates on the basis that thinking, articulate people are able to make the best decisions. Practitioners of this method never consider decisions derived as ultimate truth but rather as that which was wise and expedient at the time the decision was made. The method of advocacy is often difficult to employ because participants must be willing to suspend judgments until all ideas are heard. All parties must be willing to abide by the majority decision, while realizing that the minority opinion may become the majority opinion.

METHOD OF INQUIRY

The method of inquiry is usually an activity practiced in small groups, requiring the participants to maintain sober unbiased thoughts. It would be too time-consuming to adhere to the method literally, although some Quaker groups use it almost entirely in their meetings. Any group using the reflective-thinking method considers controversy as a problem that is not to be debated, but solved through investigation and deliberation. The method of inquiry has often been termed the scientific method and is best exemplified by problem-solving group discussions.

RATIONALE OF DISCUSSION

A complete understanding of group discussion is not possible without a grasp of the four basic relationships which clarify the rationale of discussion. These relationships include (1) inquiry and advocacy, (2) reflective thinking and intentional reasoning, (3) criticism and propaganda, and (4) cooperation and competition.

INQUIRY AND ADVOCACY

Inquiry is a key word as you proceed from problem to solution on any level. You must search until you have all of the pertinent and necessary facts available. Advocacy begins where inquiry ends. Through inquiry you arrive at some tentative conclusions, usually stated in the form of a proposition. Through advocacy you debate the pros and cons of that proposition. Examples of inquiry in practice would include fact-finding boards, investigating committees, and grand juries. Examples of advocacy would include courtroom cases, debate on the senate floor, or a political candidate trying to persuade an audience to vote for him.

REFLECTIVE THINKING AND INTENTIONAL REASONING

Reflective thinking seeks to discover a solution to a problem and/or resolve a difficulty through unbiased thinking and reasoning. It employs inquiry at every level of the thought process. The opposite process is intentional reasoning, designed to secure, justify, or defend a predetermined proposition. When you present your need for clothes and money to your parents, it is usually done through the method of intentional reasoning. On the other hand your parents usually use reflective thinking by saying, "Now let's think this through and see if your needs are as great as you think they are."

CRITICISM AND PROPAGANDA

The critical analyst attempts to examine a problem impartially and objectively by obtaining all the data he can. He does not have a preconceived notion which he tries to support. Critical analysis is ideally the method of the researcher, and the pollster. On the other hand the propagandist is paid by an interest group and his job is to influence public opinion on behalf of his backers. He learns the facts only to be able to maneuver his opposition and he is a master at slanting, card stacking, and propagandistic tricks.

COOPERATION AND COMPETITION

Cooperation and competition are difficult concepts to understand in a philosophy for discussion. Cooperation is preferred above competition and yet in every discussion there may be competition. In fact, some competition may even add spice to the discussion. Cooperation cannot be defined as a "wishy-washy" attitude which reflects an individual's lack of character. Proper inquiry cannot take place under this pseudocooperation. True cooperation involves the merging of individual goals into those of the group. However, competition is a real force which must be faced in the conference room or the committee meeting. If it becomes the predominate factor then the group will not be a thinking unit, but a collection of individuals working independently. All of the above elements are present in group discussion but the difference lies in the degree and emphasis of each factor. For the most part discussion utilizes inquiry, constructive thinking, criticism, and cooperative thinking rather than advocacy, intentional reasoning, propaganda, or competition.

A philosophy for discussion is essential for its understanding and implementation. The best tools of discussion are not tools normally used. For instance, natural tendencies often lean towards advocacy rather than inquiry. Consequently, self-discipline is needed to make discussion worthwhile.

DISCUSSION DEFINED

Most definitions of discussion stress cooperation and deliberation of a problem in a face-to-face situation under the guidance of a leader for the purpose of understanding and action. These definitions suggest a rather narrow field of operation, so it seems clearer to define discussion as a mental and verbal discipline for the purpose of problem solving and/or information. In the latter definition a greater emphasis is placed on individual preparation as the discussant develops both mental and verbal disciplines to equip himself for the discussion. Discussion may maintain several different purposes. All discussions are not for the purpose of problem solving. It is also a little unrealistic to say when the discussion is practiced to disseminate information that a lack of information is the problem you are trying to solve. Discussion is an excellent means of disseminating information. Most classroom discussions are not designed to solve a problem, but rather to impart information to members of the class.

There are many forms of discussion but some basic characteristics can help you understand them. Three basic forms of discussion are the panel, the symposium, and the forum. The *panel* is a discussion in which all the members of the group are prepared on all phases of the problem and meet together to discuss it spontaneously. In the *symposium,* members of the group come prepared on a particular phase of the problem and are allowed a definite period of time to present their ideas and information. This can be accomplished by dividing the problem into subareas, and letting each member discuss one area, or by having different members talk about the problem from their individual points of view. If the main purpose of the discussion is to impart information, then the symposium is the most expedient method. Whenever an audience is allowed to participate, the discussion is termed a *forum.* The most successful public discussion combines all three elements by starting with the symposium, then letting members of the group discuss the ideas presented, and finally asking for questions from the audience.

Regardless of which form is used, discussion aims to analyze and solve a problem and/or present information, occurs in a group situation and primarily is group activity, stresses reflective thinking rather than emotional activity, and is initiated for the purpose of action. These features are inherent in discussion regardless of the form employed or makeup of the group.

RESEARCH IN DISCUSSION

Considerable research has been conducted with small groups and sources are cited at the end of this chapter for those who want to study small-group activity in greater detail. However, a word of caution should be included because some of this research has been conducted with psychology students in rather artificial groups, until often there has not been a group-discussion situation, but rather a role-playing situation. Of course, this does not mean that you cannot learn some things from the experimental studies; it just means that you must exercise some common sense in interpreting the findings.

The research in discussion has provided at least five general conclusions that appear reliable:

1. Attitudes towards social problems do change because of discussion. Discussion must be kept on a level of ideas and should always generate more light than heat.

2. People tend to become closer on an interpersonal level because of discussion. The more persons associate with one another in a group, the more they begin to share values and norms, and come to understand one another.

3. As a result of discussion people tend to develop more sound and acceptable ideas. The very nature of reflective thinking aids discussants in validating and adjusting their ideas. Human behavior is both learned and enforced in the small group.

4. The greatest influence in discussion is exerted by the person with the greatest competency and ability. The higher the rank of the member within the group, the more central he will be in the group's interaction and the more influence he will have.

5. The makeup of the group is very important in its success. One member can impede or enhance a group far beyond his numerical weight. Whenever possible be very selective in the makeup of the group. The more objective the individual members of a group are the better the group will be.

Other experiments in task forces, problem-solving groups, leadership qualities, and the like have been conducted and are available for the interested individual. Some experimentation has been conducted with various intragroup communication networks and their resultant structures. Research by A. Paul Hare, Robert F. Bales, Dorwin Cartwright, Kurt Lewin, George C. Homans, and others reinforces the fact that there is much to be learned, explored, and practiced in the area of group interaction.

CLASSROOM DISCUSSION

The techniques and methods of classroom discussion are quite different from those used to solve problems. Though certain similarities will be evident the steps involved are different. The most obvious difference is the goal of the discussion. In the classroom the general goal is informing, clarification of ideas, or inquiry. In the problem-solving discussion the goal is to arrive at workable solutions in order to eliminate or dissipate the existing problem. Another reason for differences between the two forms of discussion is the social structure of the groups. In the classroom there is usually a more authoritarian setting than in a problem-solving group. Although he may strive to be democratic, the teacher still holds certain ethical qualities which make his status different from other members of the class. Consequently, group interaction is affected to some extent. In the problem-solving group there may be some members with more ethical credibility than others, but in general, there is less social difference among the group members. A third difference is in terms of group size. Studies have shown that when groups reach a certain size the characteristics of interaction and leadership are greatly altered.[1] Classroom settings generally include much larger groups than the small groups involved in problem solving.

DEWEY'S PATTERN OF REFLECTIVE THINKING

Although spontaneity is an important element in effective group discussion, preplanning and organization are necessary. Every member of the group should be aware of the steps involved in solving problems so that some important phase of the problem solution process is not neglected. One such set of steps for systematic problem solving was proposed by John Dewey. Though experimentation with variations of these steps has been conducted in many universities the contemporary plan used in

---

[1] For a description of studies concerning group size see A. Paul Hare, Edgar F. Borgatta, and Robert F. Bales (eds.), *Small Groups: Studies in Social Interaction* (New York: Alfred A. Knopf, 1965). Chapter 9, "Group Size," pp. 495–525.

problem-solving conferences is basically the same as that proposed by Dewey over a half-century ago. The steps include:

1. A felt difficulty
2. Its location and definition
3. Suggestion of possible solution
4. Development by reasoning of the bearings of the suggestion
5. Further observation and experiment leading to its acceptance or rejection; that is, the conclusion of belief or disbelief.[2]

The major addition to Dewey's steps has been a result of investigations relating to creative thinking and problem solving. The primary technique added to the above steps is the principle of deferred judgment.

CREATIVE PROBLEM SOLVING

Most of the recent interest in creative thinking stems from Alex Osborn's delightful book, *Applied Imagination.* Mr. Osborn might well be termed the father of creative problem solving. Of particular interest to students of discussion are Osborn's rules for the brainstorming session. These sessions are, in essence, group ideation. They are frequently used in business and industry to foster new ideas, products, and sales techniques. Osborn's rules for brainstorming include:

1. Criticism is ruled out.
2. Freewheeling is welcomed.
3. Quantity is wanted.
4. Combination and improvement are sought.[3]

Thus the brainstorming session is a kind of verbal free-for-all. Criticism is ruled out, and any and all ideas may be presented without fear of condemnation or ridicule. Social fear of this type is one of the greatest obstacles to creativity. Experiments have shown that when no censorship is placed upon the suggestions of group members, more useful ideas evolve than when

---

[2] John Dewey, *How We Think* (Boston: Heath and Company, 1910), p. 71.
[3] Alex F. Osborn, *Applied Imagination* (New York: Charles Scribner's Sons, 1962).

each idea is carefully criticized and analyzed as it is presented. Since combinations of old ideas often lead to brand-new ideas, the creative-thinking experts encourage the "piggy-backing" technique, which is adding to or slightly changing someone else's idea.

DISCUSSION IMPLEMENTED

By combining the Dewey steps with some of the principles of creative thinking you can approach the problem-solving discussion systematically and creatively. The following steps are designed to guide the group from problem to solution in an orderly manner: (1) define the problem, (2) limit the topic, (3) analyze the problem, (4) establish criteria, (5) suggest possible solutions, (6) check solutions against criteria, (7) implement the solution, and (8) evaluate the success of the solution. In some instances certain steps may be eliminated. In others all of the steps will be followed to completion. Remember that the steps should serve as a guide, not a straitjacket to the efforts of the group. They should help rather than hinder group interaction and group goals.

AGENDA FOR PROBLEM SOLVING

Define the Problem

Begin by stating the topic in such a way that it cannot be answered by "yes" or "no." If a topic is stated so that it may be answered by a single affirmative or negative answer, the discussion can end before it ever begins. For example, one group stated their problem in the following manner: "Should the United States Recognize Red China?" When the leader stated the topic one discussant simply said "no," and the discussion could have been completed at that point. Had the topic been stated: "What Should Be the United States' Role in the United Nations Concerning Admittance of Communist Countries?" the discussants would not have been required to take an initial stand and ideas could have been expressed more freely.

If there are terms in the topic which are ambiguous or unclear they should be defined. Sometimes a dictionary can help with the definition, but in most cases an operational definition is best. This type of definition is one which describes in a practical sense the meaning to be attached to the term. You define the term by what it does rather than what a dictionary says it should do. Once terms are defined in agreement with the majority of the group the topic must be limited.

Limit the Topic

There are several considerations which must be made in limiting the topic. These are:

1. Relevance to the group
2. Importance of the specific issue
3. Amount of time allowed for discussion.

Obviously a topic such as, "What Should Be the Role of the Federal Government in Censorship of the Mass Media?" would be too broad for a 40-minute discussion. If such a topic were attempted in that short length of time only the surface information could be treated adequately. If a phase of the problem to be solved is immediate and pressing, this important element should be considered first in limiting the topic. Likewise if a group holds a common interest or purpose, any topic discussed should be limited to coincide with or complement the group goals and ideals.

Analyze the Problem

Analysis of the issues involved in the discussion problem is generally one of the more important steps. In this phase of discussion a complete survey of those causes which contribute to the problem and the effects produced by the causes is conducted. At this point evidence and examples should be presented which relate to the background of the problem. Relevant illustrations and evidence must be sorted out and the rest should be discarded. A thorough job of analysis will save time later in suggesting proposed solutions which are workable and meaningful.

Establish Criteria

Since the possibility exists that some solutions proposed will exceed the limits of good judgment, it is advisable to establish criteria for solutions in advance. The first step is to determine what is expected of the proposed solutions. It may be more expedient to have all members of the group propose possible criteria without making judgments concerning the acceptability of each one until all have been presented. By deferring judgment at this point more meaningful criteria may be suggested. Once all criteria have been proposed, the group should decide upon those criteria which appeal to the majority of group members. Two general criteria which are almost always included are (1) the proposed solution should be workable and feasible; (2) the solution should not protect the majority at the expense of the minority, or *vice versa*.

Suggest Possible Solutions

Begin by investigating the general types of solutions which may solve the problem. Then move to specific solutions which may be utilized. Again the principle of deferred judgment should be used. Criticism should be withheld by the group until all possible solutions have been offered. At this point quantity rather than quality is stressed. Even seemingly ridiculous ideas are welcomed because these may suggest more workable solutions to someone else in the group. Members should seek to improve on ideas that other members suggest. When all possible solutions have been set before the group they must be checked against the established criteria.

Check Solutions against Criteria

If time permits, each specific solution should be checked against all of the established criteria. Each solution should be evaluated as to the degree to which it meets the requirements of the criteria. Those solutions which do not satisfy basic criteria should be discarded and the remaining solutions evaluated in light of the needs of the problem. Finally, it should be decided which solution (s) appear to be best for the particular problem under discussion. If several solutions appear equally to satisfy the established criteria then final selections must be made on the basis of such factors as (1) cost of implementation, (2) relative ease of implementation, (3) short- versus long-range effects of the solution, and (4) predicted adequacy of solution to eliminate or dissolve the problem. The final solution may be a combination of several of the suggested solutions.

Implement the Solution

If the problem-solving discussion is completed within the classroom it may be impossible to implement the solutions. However, thinking through possible means of implementation can be a valuable exercise, since a solution is of no value until it is put into action. The group must discover all possible means of carrying out the proposed solution. At this point the criteria must again be considered. If economics are a factor, then the implementation must not exceed the amount of funds available. Taking all such factors into consideration the group must decide what means of those available are most efficient and effective in initiating the proposed solutions. It is advisable at this time to consider all persons or groups who might aid in the actual implementation of the solution.

Evaluate the Success of the Solution

After the solution has been implemented and given the test of time, it should be studied to determine if it has accomplished its designed purpose. Has it satisfied the need for which it was designed? Can improvements or alterations be made in the solution that would aid its effectiveness? In other words if the solution has been successful it should be kept in force. If it has not, it should either be repaired, replaced, or altered in order to make it meet the need for which it was established. Remember that just because a solution is implemented there is no guarantee it will work. Only after evaluation can the worth of a solution be determined.

LEADERSHIP IN DISCUSSION

Perhaps the most important member of a group is the leader. Yet leadership may be shared among all of the group members. Leadership is defined as "Interpersonal influence exercised in situation and directed through the communication process, toward the attainment of a specified goal or goals." [4] Essentially the leader is a persuader in the sense that his skill in oral or written communication will determine to a great extent the direction of the group. An effective leader will generally direct or influence his group without the members being aware of any concentrated effort on his part. In other words, the leader who does the best job usually makes the members feel that he is the servant rather than master of the group. Both authoritarian and democratic leaders have a place in discussion. Establishing the degree of leader control necessary within a group is first a function of the expectations of the group and second of the urgency of the task to be performed. What the group expects of a leader is a function of the group's norms, social climate, and degree of maturity.

In competitive groups such as the senate or political groups a strong authoritarian leader must obviously control the process of the group. A weak leader in this setting would cause chaos and confusion. The job of the leader in a highly competitive group is one of a referee or "traffic cop." He must maintain a neutral position in order to prevent one side from overpowering the other in the discussion.

Immature groups such as children's clubs or newly formed adult organizations also expect strong leader control. Even though they may actually deny desiring such control, immature groups (especially children) prefer clear, fair, and strictly enforced rules over permissive environment. The leader of an immature adult group must not only conform to the expectations of the group but must also be able to exert strong leadership when required.

The second determinant of leader control is the perceived urgency of a task or problem by the group. Berkowitz found that people seem to feel that the leader should assume strong control (be authoritarian) when the pressures to complete the assigned task (or solve the problem) are not urgent. When group mem-

---

[4] Robert Tannenbaum, Irving R. Weschler, and Fred Massarik, *Leadership and Organization: A Behavioral Science Approach* (New York: McGraw-Hill, Inc., 1961), p. 24.

bers perceive a problem to be urgent they worry less about how the leader should act. The reason for this decreased concern about leadership is the high motivation to solve the problem in the most efficient manner. Unless a leader strongly hampers the group in their solution of the problem his actions will probably go largely unnoticed. In some urgent situations groups have given extraordinary power to the leader (such as the power of the President to assume control of public utilities during times of national crisis). In other situations they have all but disregarded the position or function of the leader.[5] A group functions best when the members are not unduly concerned about the mechanics of leadership. Consequently, as a leader if you can help the group perceive the importance of the problem under discussion the members will be more concerned about solving the problem than about reacting to your role as a leader.

Other factors which can help determine the control of leadership necessary in a group are group purpose, group size, and leader skills. If the group is discussing personal issues, less structure is necessary than when the group is discussing an international problem. In general, the larger the group the greater the need for structure. As a rule of thumb, if a group exceeds 12 to 15 members it ceases to function as a discussion group because of the increased role of the leader. The leader's skill will also affect the kind of control he will exert. If he is inexperienced he will probably attempt to exert less control on the group than if he is an experienced leader.

STIMULATING INDIVIDUAL INVOLVEMENT IN DISCUSSION

Unfortunately many participants in group discussion are unaware of their obligation to contribute to the group effort. They are content to sit for long periods without opening their mouths either to offer a suggestion or discuss comments made by other group members. Obviously if all of the members of the group neglected their responsibilities to contribute to the discussion

---

[5] Leonard Berkowitz, "Sharing Leadership in Small, Decision-Making Groups," in A. Paul Hare, Edgar F. Borgetta, and Robert F. Bales, (eds.), *op. cit.*, pp. 543–555.

there would be dead silence and no problem would ever be solved. Often members lack confidence or are hesitant to contribute because of lack of knowledge or experience. It is the responsibility of the leader in such instances to stimulate the member to become involved in the discussion. The following suggestions may help stimulate involvement in the group process: [6]

1. Make sure that members have a reason for being present at each group meeting or discussion. The group should have a definite purpose, function, or need. All members should have some responsibility in the group so that their presence at the meeting is meaningful. Members who feel no part of the group often begin to miss meetings and eventually stop participating altogether.

2. Make sure each member has an equal chance to participate. If the group is large it may be necessary to divide it into committees, or utilize the "buzz session." If the group is relatively small make sure that one person is not allowed to dominate the discussion. A balanced group is one which produces workable solutions through equal interaction of group members. Explain the importance of balanced interaction to the group so that each member will assume this responsibility.

3. Relate individual goals to the goals of the group. This often first involves examining the goals of the group. Once these are specified and agreed upon, help members understand how their own needs and goals will be furthered through helping the group to attain its goals. Do not hesitate to suggest specific applications of the achievement of personal goals through the group; often members fail to make such applications on their own.

4. Listen carefully and attempt to understand everything that is said. Unless you are aware of what has been said it is impossible to make intelligent remarks about the subject or help the group to understand it. Show each member that you care about what he says and ask questions when you do not under-

---

[6] The suggestions are derived with some adaptation from Victor Harnack and Thorrel Fest, *Group Discussion: Theory and Technique* (New York: Appleton-Century-Crofts, 1964), pp. 318–327.

stand something. As a leader you must help clarify vague points for the group but you should try to understand each concept initially through careful listening.

5. Utilize the principle of deferred judgment. You will recall that the practice of withholding evaluation is a vital step in stimulating an environment for creative thinking and problem solving. This concept is even more important for the leader because any criticism he might make would not only tend to inhibit the free flow of ideas but to associate him with one side of a controversy. This association would indicate he is no longer an impartial observer and could cause serious conflict within the group. Utilize this principle as a leader and encourage other members to do likewise.

6. As a leader evidence strong interest in the discussion. It stands to reason that if the leader acts disinterested in the group discussion the members may follow his example. Since the leader sets the "mood" of the group he must exhibit interest himself before he can expect others to maintain it. This process of self-motivation should not be faked. Pseudointerest can be spotted by many sensitive members of the group and can backfire. Look for aspects about the discussion that have intrinsic interest for you and point these out as the group process evolves.

REGULATING THE DISCUSSION

Once all members understand the need to contribute to the group process it may become necessary to regulate the degree of individual participation. The key to regulating discussion is sensitivity. You must be sensitive to attempts of certain members to enter into the discussion, sensitive to growing hostilities that may arise, sensitive to personal conflicts and personality clashes that evolve, and sensitive to the feelings and attitudes of the group as a whole. This sensitivity may evolve more naturally in some leaders than others. If you find yourself lacking in interpersonal sensitivity it might be wise to decline the leadership role or transfer it to another until this trait can be developed. Once the problem areas are noticed by the leader he must act to resolve them. Perhaps the most recurring problem is the suppressing of an overtalkative or overaggressive member. A reprimand, if used, should be handled tactfully, yet firmly. Rudely curbing a talkative member cannot only cause embarrassment but can hamper group *esprit de corps*. Below are a few techniques which have been used to handle a "bulldozer" or "monopolizer" in discussion:

1. Isolate him by refusing to acknowledge him.

2. Embarrass him by pointing out an obvious fallacy in his evidence or reasoning.

3. Ask leading questions which lead to contradictions.

4. Ask him questions which are above his level of knowledge.

5. Agree with everything he says verbally so he has nothing to disagree about.

6. Have a conference with group members outside of the group meeting and agree to disregard his contributions.

Notice that some of these techniques may cause repercussions which are more harmful than letting the loquacious member continue. Again the leader's sensitivity must help him decide what action is needed at a given moment and the degree of severity or the consequences upon the group. As a leader increases in proficiency he will encourage the group to share the leadership role. When the group operates smoothly the leader's job is greatly simplified.

MECHANICS OF DISCUSSION

Having discussed the nature and types of discussion it is necessary to relate some specific suggestions regarding the practical problems in discussion. These considerations should be noted by the person in charge of the group or by the appointed leader of the discussion:

1. Arrange the chairs around a table, in a circle, or in a semicircle, so that everyone can easily be seen.

2. Limit the number of people in the group to from 12 to 15. The optimum number of participants is generally from 6 to 12.

3. Limit the discussion period to 2 hours if possible. The preferable length of most discussions is 1½ hours. If a longer period of discussion is called for, take frequent breaks.

4. Make sure that the members of the group are introduced to each other before beginning a discussion. Name tags often prove helpful.

5. Try to insure that no interruptions will occur during the discussion period.

KEYS TO EFFECTIVE DISCUSSION

The following five recommendations will serve as a summary of the concepts presented in this chapter. If these suggestions are followed by each group member the discussion process should be more productive and enjoyable for everyone.

1. Speak up! Speak clearly and loudly enough for everyone in the group to hear you. Contribute to the group by offering new ideas and reflecting on the ideas of others.

2. Be courteous! Respect others in the group. Avoid interrupting others or arguing minor points.

3. Pay attention! Listen closely and carefully. Try to follow the thread of thought and ask for clarification when you have a question about what has been stated.

4. Be brief! Do not monopolize the conversation. Make your comments brief and to the point. This allows time for everyone to participate in the discussion.

5. Withhold judgment! Initially it is better to hear all of the ideas from the group before they are evaluated or criticized. This withholding of criticism fosters creativity among the group.

QUESTIONS FOR DISCUSSION

1. In what occupations is discussion an important form of communication?

2. How can an overtalkative member in a group be regulated without destroying the rapport within the group?

3. What techniques can be used to draw a "shy" member into a discussion?

EXERCISES

[Forms for completing the exercises marked with an asterisk will be found in the *Worksheets for Speech—Interpersonal Communication* (San Francisco: Chandler Publishing Company, 1967).]

1. Observe at least one example of each of the following types of discussion on your campus: (1) symposium, (2) panel, (3) forum, (4) buzz session. Write a paragraph on the characteristics of each type and note the main differences among the various types.*

2. Observe the leader or chairman of a dormitory, fraternity, or club meeting. Classify him according to the degree of control he maintains over the group. Discuss whether his concept of leadership appears to be most effective with his particular group.*

3. Watch a discussion on television. What differences do you find between a televised discussion and one not televised? Does the medium demand certain requirements of participants not needed under normal conditions?

4. Using the discussion evaluation forms in the worksheets or others provided by your instructor, evaluate a panel discussion presented in class. If possible have the participants in the discussion group evaluate their own discussion on a similar form and compare the results.

5. Keep a frequency count of the number of times each person talks in a panel discussion. Is there any relationship between number of contributions made by each member and ability as a discussant? If so, attempt to formulate a general rule for participating in discussion.

6. In an informal discussion without an assigned leader what problems arise that do not occur when a leader is present?

7. Some authors indicate that certain discussants play definite roles in discussions. For example, one person might play the role of the "devil's advocate" while another might play the role of "the compromiser." Observe several discussions and keep a record of the different roles you find discussants playing in their respective groups. Do the roles usually correspond with the person's personality outside of the group situation?

8. Divide the class into two separate groups. Have one section arrive at as many "good" solutions as possible to the question: "How can a fisherman catch more fish?" Make sure that that section only reports solutions which they feel are of the highest quality. Secondly, have the other section of the class discuss the same problem but have them report all possible solutions, whether they are ridiculous, funny, or practical. Compare the total number of usable solutions arrived at by each group. Were the results surprising? What principle discussed in this chapter is utilized in this demonstration?

9. Make a list of the qualities that an effective leader should possess.

10. Make a similar list of the qualities of an effective discussant.

11. Criteria are an important element in problem solving. Formulate

your own definition of "criteria." Then make a list of criteria that might be appropriate to most solutions. These are, of course, general criteria. Next, pick a topic for discussion such as "What Role Does the Federal Government Play in Regulating the Mass Media?" Suggest a list of specific criteria which might apply to solutions on this topic.

SUGGESTED READINGS

Barnlund, Dean C., and Franklyn S. Haiman, *The Dynamics of Discussion*. Boston: Houghton Mifflin Company, 1960.

Cartwright, Dorwin, and Alvin Zander, *Group Dynamics—Research and Theory*. New York: Harper and Row Publishers, 1960.

Crowell, Laura, *Discussion: Method of Democracy*. Chicago: Scott, Foresman and Company, 1963.

Hare, A. Paul, *Handbook of Small Group Research*. New York: Free Press of Glencoe, 1962.

Harnack, Victor, and Thorrel B. Fest, *Group Discussion: Theory and Technique*. New York: Appleton-Century-Crofts, 1964.

Osborn, Alex F., *Applied Imagination*. New York: Charles Scribner's Sons, 1957.

Parnes, Sidney J., and Harold F. Harding, *A Source Book for Creative Thinking*. New York: Charles Scribner's Sons, 1962.

Wagner, Russell H., and Carroll C. Arnold, *Handbook of Group Discussion*. Boston: Houghton Mifflin Company, 1965.

Communication without Words | 10

In Chapter 2 you learned that several distinct types of messages are transmitted simultaneously by the communicator. You will recall that the primary stimulus message is transmitted through the most appropriate channel. In most instances this channel is the oral one, utilizing sound waves. However, there are several occasions when the visual channel is needed to transmit the primary stimulus message. It is the purpose of this chapter to describe the different channels through which messages can be transmitted and to illustrate the advantages and disadvantages of each. The main emphasis will be on nonverbal communication since verbal communication is emphasized in most of the other chapters.

VERBAL VERSUS NONVERBAL COMMUNICATION

In the broadest sense *communication* includes all the processes by which one individual may affect another. Communication involves not only written and oral speech, but music, the pictorial arts, the theatre, the ballet, and all forms of human behavior. *Verbal communication* is, therefore, a specific form of message transmission which uses word symbols to represent real objects and ideas. The counterpart of verbal communication is *nonverbal communication*. This mode of sending messages includes all forms of transmission not represented by word symbols and includes sign language, action or movement language, and object or pictorial language.[1]

---

[1] See Jurgen Ruesch and Weldon Kees, *Nonverbal Communication* (Los Angeles: University of California Press, 1956), p. 1.

It is appropriate to begin the study of communication without words by making a detailed comparison of differences between verbal and nonverbal communication. Some of these differences are important in determining which channel (s) of transmission you will select for your communication. Some of the differences are true in generalized applications but may not always hold true in specific instances.

GENERAL CHARACTERISTICS

1. Nonverbal denotation units may be subdivided further than verbal denotation units. For example, portions of a person's face may be seen without perceiving the entire face and identification can still be made with some degree of accuracy. However, monosyllabic words such as "I" and "a" cannot be divided into subclassifications of letters, words, or sounds.

2. Nonverbal communication is continuous whereas verbal communication is based on disconnected units. The facial expression will keep changing as long as the person is alive but sounds and words have a definite beginning and end. Similarly human movements continue to transmit a variety of messages, whereas verbal communication occurs in discrete units.

SPATIOTEMPORAL CHARACTERISTICS

1. Nonverbal denotation can indicate two or more events simultaneously, whereas verbal denotation must indicate events successively in an ordered sequence. A traffic cop can tell the pedestrians to walk while he signals the cars to stop. This is accomplished through gestures with his hands or toots of his whistle. Were he dependent upon verbal cues alone, he would have first to tell cars to stop and then tell the pedestrians to walk.

2. Nonverbal communication is temporally flexible, while verbal communication is temporally inflexible. For example, bodily movements can be carried out slowly or quickly without their meaning becoming distorted. When spoken too rapidly or too slowly language can become distorted to the extent that it is unintelligible.

3. Nonverbal communication is spatially inflexible, while verbal denotation is spatially flexible. All classes of nonverbal com-

munication require a finite amount of space. A person occupies space in a communication setting but his words require no finite space. Even printing in books and magazines may be large or small depending on the preference of the designer.

PERCEPTUAL, EVALUATIVE, AND TRANSMISSION CHARACTERISTICS

1. Nonverbal language expression may be skilled or unskilled, but is usually understandable by the responding communicator. On the other hand the verbal expression of language must be skilled or it risks becoming distorted. This characteristic is a direct result of the sequence in which verbal and nonverbal language is learned, as will be discussed later in this chapter.

2. Understanding of nonverbal expressions is based on empathy, whereas understanding of verbal expressions is based on prior verbal agreement. For example, no explanation is necessary to understand what happens when you run into a brick wall. Conversely, the word *wall* is an arbitrary symbol and is subject to prior verbal agreements between the originating and responding communicator.

DEVELOPMENTAL CHARACTERISTICS

1. Nonverbal language systems are learned much earlier in life than verbal denotation. This results in a physical and psychological need to continue nonverbal forms of expression long after verbal symbols have been mastered. Current theories of therapy for treating psychoses are based on the assumption that even adults need to express themselves through nonverbal channels.

2. Nonverbal communication involves complicated networks whereas verbal codification involves only the central nervous system. Baseball pitchers warm up before each game in order to make fine coordinated physical movements. On the other hand the brain does not need a warm-up period to recall a memorized telephone number.

SEMANTIC CHARACTERISTICS

1. In nonverbal codification, action and objects exist in their own right and generally fulfill practical as well as symbolic functions. In verbal codification, however, words do not exist in their

own right; they are only symbols. For example, that object upon which you sit serves a practical function in addition to a symbolic one. The word *chair,* on the other hand, serves only to represent the object. This concept can be proven by attempting to sit down on the word *chair* itself. Another vivid illustration of this semantic difference between verbal and nonverbal codification can be made by putting side by side an apple and a piece of paper with the word *apple* written on it and taking a bite of each. The object serves a more practical purpose than the word symbol it represents.

2. Nonverbal codification permits redundancies whereas verbal codification produces fatigue when redundant. Think how tiring it would be if you had to repeat the word *good-bye* every time you waved to someone who was leaving. In lengthy good-byes you could repeat the word 20 or 30 times. Or imagine how hoarse the hitchhiker would be if, instead of raising his thumb to each passing car, he had to yell "Would you please give me a ride?" This allowance for redundancies is an important difference between nonverbal and verbal language.

3. Nonverbal codifications are generally much more succinct than verbal codifications. This principle is best demonstrated by the gestures of the head which indicate agreement or disagreement. A simple head nod can mean anything from "Yes" to "I think that the plan you just suggested is worthwhile and it is my opinion that you should present the suggestion to the board of directors for their decision."

4. Nonverbal codifications have emotional appeal whereas verbal codifications exert an intellectual appeal. The word *cat* in isolation generally will arouse little emotion in the average listener. However, the actual observance of a mother cat with two tiny kittens at her side peering in a screen door during a heavy thunderstorm can arouse emotions in even the most hardened individual. Objects and actions generate more emotion than words because they are less abstract and are, in essence, closer to structural reality.

5. Nonverbal codifications are suitable for understanding, whereas verbal codifications are best for reaching agreements. Word symbols by their very nature are abstracted from the structural level. It is possible to communicate ideas which have

no objective referent through verbal language which would be impossible to communicate through the nonverbal channel.

6. Nonverbal codifications represent an intimate language, while verbal codification represents a more distinct language. Politicians have long been aware of this semantic difference between the verbal and nonverbal modes. A handshake is much more effective in securing votes than simply stating, "How do you do?" Similarly, a smile can often achieve more rapport than the words "I like you" or "I'm feeling great today."

The preceding discussion has emphasized the distinctions between verbal and nonverbal communication. The relationship between the two becomes apparent if the natural progression from nonverbal to verbal communication is examined in the development of children. Ruesch relates this progression in the following passage:

> In language development, the gradual shift from nonverbal to verbal codifications occurs in three distinct steps: The earliest forms of codification involve action signals, mediated predominantly through contraction of the smooth muscles, which appear in changes in the color and temperature of the skin, the consistency of bowel movements, the rate of breathing, and other movements, such as sucking, which are subordinated to these autonomic functions. Although such statements as can be made in early infancy usually are unintentional, they are language in the sense that the signals are understandable to both mother and child. Later on, when the child is learning to move, such somatic language is supplemented by action signals mediated through bodily manifestations of the intestinal, respiratory, and vascular systems and is replaced by movements of the face and the extremities. Finally, when social action has been learned, verbal, gestural, and other symbolic forms of denotation replace some of the previously employed methods of action codification.[2]

No one type of communication is inherently more important than another, for the situation determines which mode is most effective. Frank A. Geldard suggests that verbal communication is generally used under the following circumstances:

---

[2] Jurgen Ruesch, "The Infantile Personality: The Core Problem of Psychosomatic Medicine," *Psychosomatic Medicine,* (1948), Vol. 10, pp. 134–144.

1. If rapidly successive data are to be resolved audition is more useful than vision as a means of making temporal discriminations. Also auditory reaction times are typically faster.

2. Where the recipient is preoccupied with other tasks or in a condition of reduced alertness and we wish to "break in" with unexpected messages or warnings.

3. Listening habits being what they are, where relatively brief, easy, highly meaningful materials are to be apprehended and remembered.

4. Where flexibility of message transmission is important the voice spontaneously gives inflectional shadings and emphasis.

5. Where, out of a larger mass of data, we wish to present information germane to an issue at hand—where we can, in advance of message transmission, be highly selective. The trouble with books, maps, and tables (all of them visual devices) is that you have to find what you are looking for.

6. Where visual reception is less available, whether by reasons of environmental conditions that interfere with visibility, unfavorable orientation of the observer (a common visual difficulty), overloading of the visual channel, or outright sensory defect.

Visual nonverbal communication seems to be indicated:

1. Where messages involve spatial orientation or guidance. Vision is the great spatial sense, just as audition is the great temporal one. Pictorial representation is often a boon.

2. Where fine discrimination is needed. Vernier visual acuity is the best sense organs have to offer; we put our trust in needles on scales whenever we can arrange to do so in making precise measurements.

3. Where complex, unfamiliar material is to be comprehended; the material is there, to be looked at again and again if need be.

4. Where reference data have to be immediately available or where simultaneous (or nearly simultaneous) relational comparisons have to be made.

5. Where a recipient of information has to make relatively prompt selection of data from larger stocks of information.

6. Where auditory reception is hampered by unfavorable environmental conditions, overloading of the auditory channel, actual auditory defect, or previously acquired attentional habits favoring vision.[3]

---

[3] Frank A. Geldard, "Some Neglected Possibilities of Communication," *Science*, Vol. 131, (May 27, 1960), pp. 1581–1587. Copyright 1960 by the American Association for the Advancement of Science.

Although certain specific circumstances lend themselves more readily to the verbal mode of communication, an equal number of circumstances favor the nonverbal mode. In most communication situations a combination of these two communication types is desirable in order to obtain maximum effectiveness in the transmission and the reception of messages.

HOW MEANING IS TRANSMITTED

To understand completely the varied types and uses of nonverbal communication, you must first comprehend the principles of how symbols acquire meaning for human beings. It is important to remember that an individual's response to any situation is dependent upon his life orientation (see Chapter 3). Since no two individuals have exactly the same life orientation, no two people perceive the same situation in exactly the same manner. Thus, a word or gesture will have different meanings to two persons, even though the symbol they both perceive is the same. From this line of reasoning the general semanticists, such as Korzybski, Chase, Lee, and Hayakawa, state the theory that the meanings of words are not in the words themselves but are in us as individuals. However, it is easy to forget that objects and gestures do not contain intrinsic meaning. In most cases it is safe to assume that because a car has a brake pedal, the car will stop when you push the pedal to the floor. The exceptions to this general case can cause disaster. Similarly when you step into an elevator and push the button marked "up" you expect to go in that direction. You will unless some practical joker has switched the buttons, the contractor has incorrectly installed the controls, the electricity is off, or one of the many special cases has occurred which prevents the intended meaning of your action from coinciding with the reality of the situation. The point is, even though nonverbal expressions such as objects and pictures are less abstract than verbal expressions, the meaning attached to them is still a function of your life orientation. If you can remember that you designate meaning to the objects and actions you perceive, which may or may not correspond to structural reality, you may improve not only your intrapersonal, but your interpersonal communication.

In verbal communication a large portion of meaning is derived from nonverbal cues. Thus, nonverbal communication is an integral part of the verbal mode. This relationship becomes clearer if the determinants of word meanings are examined. The first determinant is the *referent*. To be able to determine the meaning of a word you must be able to define its referent—the particular action, object, relation between actions or objects, or characteristic of those actions, objects, or relations for which a word stands. In other words, the referent is that object which a word represents.

To be meaningful in communication the referent must provide a *common reference*. The words must have their meaning, not only for the originating communicator but also for the responding comunicator. To be of use in communication words must have common meanings for the members of the group.

Verbal context is also necessary in determining meaning. What any one word means is determined in part by its relationship to the other words with which it occurs. Take for example the word *hood*. Out of context this word has a number of meanings. It could refer to a portion of an automobile, to clothing worn by monks, or even to a juvenile delinquent. In context, however, the specific meaning becomes clear to the hearer.

The *manner of utterance* is the fourth determinant of verbal meaning. In most instances, the way in which a word is spoken determines the meaning it transmits to the auditor. Inflectional changes, change in intensity, the rate of utterance, all may considerably affect the meaning of the word. The word "no" spoken with a certain inflection might be used to connote "yes." The same could hold true with the word "yes." The manner in which words are spoken can completely alter their meaning either in or out of context.

A final determinant of meaning is *personal attitude*. If a speaker shouts in an angry tone or turns red as he speaks, you derive different meaning from his words than if he speaks softly with little emotion. Meaning is a function of signs and their interpretation. Thus, you must utilize all the cues of the moment and interpret them along with the words you hear to derive full meaning from a verbal message.

KINESICS

The last two of these determinants of meaning are directly related to nonverbal communication. Consequently, various levels of this nonverbal mode should now be explored. The science or systematic study of nonverbal interpersonal communication is termed *kinesics*. There are, according to Birdwhistell, three levels of kinesics: prekinesics, microkinesics, and social kinesics. Prekinesics deals with general physiological, precommunicational aspects of body motion:

> Research in microkinesics and social kinesics is preceding upon the assumption that visually perceptible body shifts, whose variations have been repetitively observed and which are subject to systematization, are learned rather than somatogenic.[4]

Birdwhistell has pioneered much of the research in the area of kinesics. He contends that people do most of their communicating with bodily movements rather than with their voices. Though according to one study the average person talks for a total of about 10 to 11 minutes daily, he continually communicates through body movements such as eyes and eyebrows, facial expressions, hands, and even by silence. Birdwhistell reported that the standard spoken sentence takes only 2½ seconds.[5] Consequently, you do not communicate simply by sound. If you do not pay attention to the way a communicator uses his eyes, hands, voice, and other clues, words can confuse you. You should recognize that communication is a continuous, multichannel process. Only at times do you engage in verbalization. Birdwhistell also found that people have discernible dialects of facial expression in different parts of the country. He discovered that each language has its own "body accent" and this can lead to communication breakdowns and misunderstandings. Much of Birdwhistell's research has been based upon studies in microkinesics.

---

[4] Ray L. Birdwhistell, "Background to Kinesics," *ETC.*, (Autumn, 1955), p. 12.

[5] Ray Birdwhistell, "Communication through Body Movements" (unpublished paper presented at the American Psychological Association Convention, Chicago, Illinois, 1965).

"Microkinesics is concerned with the derivation of *kines* (least particles of isolatable body-emotion) into manageable morphological classes." [6] Research in microkinesics is providing a general framework for the study of communication by compiling a dictionary of body movements and their common meanings.

Social kinesics deals with body motion units in their contextual meaning. The context may be provided by the social situation of the moment or the environment in which the message is transmitted. The term *gesture* is most often used when describing this bodily movement, but Birdwhistell restricts the use of the term in the area of kinesics.

Gesture is restricted to those acts or actions which can be immediately interpreted by actor or viewer. Gestures have no more objective meaning than other acts. The vocalized meaning attached to the gesture does not necessarily supply us with the insight into either the differential or the contextual meaning of the action of which the gesture is an interdependent, but deceptively visible aspect.[7]

At certain times the meaning of a word uttered is contradicted by the inflection or intonation of the voice-qualifiers used with it. Such a situation Birdwhistell terms a "kinesic slip." For example, a person may be asked to sample a certain type of foreign food. He might tell his host that the food is delicious, but his facial expression could contradict his words.

CLASSES OF NONVERBAL COMMUNICATION

Having discovered the levels of interpersonal nonverbal communication it is important to consider the different forms this type of communication takes. The first class of nonverbal communication includes objects and pictures. This includes pictographs, comic strips, paintings, sculpture, dancing, and acting, in addition to the ordinary objects which surround you. All of these pictorial forms of communication transmit messages which are nonverbal in nature but very necessary to the understanding of human beings and their needs.

Actions form another class of nonverbal communication. This

---

[6] Birdwhistell, "Background to Kinesics," *loc. cit.*
[7] *Ibid.*, p. 16.

class of communication is sometimes used as a substitution for verbal language and sometimes as an auxiliary device for speech. Muscular movement, facial expression, and posture are all examples of the action class of communication.

The third class of nonverbal communication is sign language. "This includes all those forms of codification in which words, numbers, and punctuation signs have been supplanted by gestures; these vary from the monosyllable gesture of the hitchhiker, to such complete systems as the language of the deaf." [8]

A final class of nonverbal communication, which is often neglected, is cutaneous communication or receiving impulses through the skin. Geldard states: "This skin can make both temporal and spatial discriminations, albeit not superlatively good ones. In either case it is a good 'break in' sense; cutaneous sensations, especially if aroused in unusual patterns, are highly attention getting." [9] Cutaneous communication is being investigated for possible use in the space program for communication between the control center and the astronauts.

In the semistructured communication you gain much information from the action and sign-language classes of nonverbal communication. These forms of nonverbal messages must be received and recognized by the responding communicator along with the verbal messages or else he will be receiving only a fraction of the information being transmitted. In the words of Ruesch and Kees, "to emphasize the nonverbal thus fulfills only one function: to bring our knowledge and skills up to the level of our verbal knowledge and skills. Then—we hope—verbal and nonverbal communication will be treated as a total and inseparable unit." [10]

VISUAL REINFORCEMENT

Nonverbal message forms are frequently called visual aids when included as a part of a speech. Visual aids include, in a general sense, all forms of material which add support to the communication through visual rather than verbal presentation. Among the most common forms of visual aids are objects, models,

---

[8] Ruesch and Kees, *op. cit.,* p. 189.
[9] Geldard, *op. cit.,* p. 158.
[10] Ruesch and Kees, *Nonverbal Communication, op. cit.,* p. 41.

charts, graphs, motion pictures, slides, blackboards, and physical demonstrations. When their size permits, objects are excellent attention getters in addition to explanation givers. For example, a student's demonstration speech on golf would be very weak without a golf club to demonstrate the proper swing. When objects are too large to be carried easily to class, models or pictures may be brought in their place. Graphs and charts can help clarify complicated statistics as well as show relationships which may be missed otherwise. The blackboard is the most common visual aid available in the classroom. The following suggestions are designed to help you make the most effective use of the blackboard in your presentation:

1. Draw quickly during your presentation. If the material is placed on the board before the class hour, it should be covered until the appropriate time.

2. Keep talking as you draw. Do not draw for long periods with your back to the responding communicators.

3. Draw large enough diagrams or words to be seen by all in the room.

4. Do not block the board with your body while referring to your drawings. If necessary, step aside after pointing to your diagram so all can see clearly.

5. When you are finished with each list or diagram on the board erase it. By so doing the drawing will not be an interference message for you or those speakers who follow you.

When using objects and pictures as visual aids, you must consider these additional points. First, does the picture or object explain your message more efficiently and effectively than could mere words? If so, the visual aids are not only helpful but necessary. If they simply clarify or add interest to the words they are also useful, but take the form of complementary stimulus messages. There may be instances when a visual aid detracts from the primary stimulus message by directing attention away from what the communicator is saying. If this is the case the visual aid should be eliminated from the presentation.

A second consideration in the use of visual aids is their size. Is the object or picture of sufficient size to be seen by all present?

If not, your presentation may be hampered. Your audience's attention will be focused on trying to see, rather than trying to understand what message is being transmitted through the visual aid. It is a good idea to have someone hold up the visual aid during a practice session so that you may see it as your audience would during your actual presentation. This preview will give you warning of any defects or distractions inherent in your visual aid. From this experience you may learn that the visual aid is too small, too shaky, or that the colors are not distinguishable at a distance thus making you alter it to suit your presentation.

Thirdly, in handling objects and pictures practice thoroughly beforehand to avoid appearing clumsy. A faulty demonstration of a product has frustrated many salesmen. Similarly, a demonstration by a speaker which does not go smoothly can be detrimental to the achievement of his purpose. When handling pictures make sure they are backed with a stiff cardboard to prevent their falling or bending.

PHYSICAL REINFORCEMENT

One area often neglected by the beginning student of communication is physical reinforcement. Just as there are various ways of presenting ideas, there are also many different modes of physical reinforcement. There are many implicit rules about how to stand and when and where to move, but such rules frequently hamper communication more than they help. As you study the suggestions for physical reinforcement remember two basic concepts. First, the ideas presented here are to be adapted, not adopted; that is, they must feel natural to you if they are to be effective. Secondly, physical reinforcement should evolve from a feeling within and should not be utilized for show. Most people reinforce their communication physically in semistructured conversations, but fail to provide this reinforcement in prestructured communication. The suggestions discussed below may help you transfer your natural physical expression to the prestructured situation. Remember that physical reinforcement usually takes the form of complementary stimulus messages and can have both positive and negative effects upon the responding communicator. The following types of physical reinforcement can add additional meaning to your verbal messages: bodily movement, facial expression, eye contact, and gestures.

BODILY MOVEMENT

Bodily movement serves several purposes in the communicative act. It is a means of holding the attention of the responding communicators as well as releasing tension. A little movement away from the speaker's stand as you begin to speak can steady your knees and help you relax. A rigid stance can generate tension throughout the body and even cause your knees to tremble. A casual step to the right or left of the speaker's stand can help avoid the "at attention" stance. Movement at particular times during the communication can also give your auditors a break because they are able to shift their eyes from one place to another. Some speech teachers even suggest that walking in front of the speaker's stand makes you feel closer to your audience.

A shift of movement at a transitional point may emphasize the transition, but avoid making such movements at each transitional point. Freedom of bodily movement is desirable but it should always be a means to an end and not the end itself. For example, speakers who pace back and forth without meaning are usually ineffective communicators. Bodily movement can become a nervous gesture and, consequently, become a negative complementary stimulus message. Try to avoid the extremes; do not stay in one place or keep on the move at all times. Make your movements natural and purposeful as you let them reduce muscular tension and add emphasis to your ideas.

FACIAL EXPRESSION

Facial expression can add meaning to verbal messages without words as well as communicate by itself. If you say "I love you" with a completely deadpan facial expression, what response do you get? Similarly, an inexperienced reader can render a very exciting bit of prose meaningless by a complete lack of facial expression. Your facial expression is one means of setting the mood of your communication. In normal conversation facial expressions help indicate the difference between a joke and a critical remark. Facial expression in the form of animation can add spice to a message. If the originating communicator is alive and alert, if his eyes sparkle with enthusiasm, his chances of generating enthusiasm in the audience are enhanced. The size of the audience will determine how overt or pronounced your facial expression must be to communicate to your auditors. Your audience must see your facial expression before it can reinforce your message, so be willing to adapt to the immediate audience.

EYE CONTACT

Eye contact accompanies facial expression and helps establish interpersonal contact with the audience. Unfortunately beginning speakers look almost every place but directly at their audience. It is not always easy to look people in the eye because some may not respond favorably to your ideas but even negative responses are important to recognize. Try to free yourself from your notes so you do not have to read your material. Then you can establish eye contact with persons in all sections of your audience. Just as you do not constantly stare at the responding communicator in semistructured conversation, let your eye contact move casually to various parts of the room in prestructured communication settings. If you really have difficulty looking at people, first pick out one person who you feel will be responsive and then move your gaze from that person to the rest of your auditors. Eye contact is a skillful means of showing your auditors that you are interested in them, confident about your message, and aware of their responses.

GESTURES

Gestures must be natural in appearance in order to be effective. Unless gestures evolve from a feeling within, they can be meaningless and become negative complementary stimulus messages. Most individuals utilize gestures in normal conversation; in fact, some could hardly talk if you tied their hands behind them. Yet in prestructured communication their hands become dead weights and they do not know what to do with them. A first step is to free your hands for movement. Keep them out of your pockets, off the speaker's stand, or out from behind your back. A spontaneous gesture is not a separate entity but a part of complete physical reinforcement. Effective gestures have ease, flexibility, proper timing, and never draw attention to themselves. Ineffective gestures, such as the "pump handle" or the monotonous movement of one hand, become only a means of releasing nervous energy. Similarly, such movements as arranging your notecards or playing with a pencil or a ring usually hinder communication. Effective gestures must be a purposeful part of the communicative act and should help to express your feelings. Although gestures are uniquely individual there are certain universal gestures which can work in harmony with oral symbols to increase understanding and interaction.

Six basic movements fit into this universal category. They are pointing, giving or receiving, rejecting, clenching the fist, cautioning, and dividing. The index finger is a natural for pointing to an object, or for signifying a single idea you want to emphasize. The open palm of the hand facing upwards is used often to indicate giving or receiving and can be integrated with ideas in a variety of ways. Rejecting an idea can be reinforced with the palm of the hand down in a sweeping motion away from you. Strong feelings are often reinforced with a clenched fist. The extended palm facing outward, which traffic policemen use to caution motorists, can also be used effectively in speaking. By moving the hand from side to side with the palm held vertically, you can indicate separation of ideas. Each of these conventional gestures must incorporate your own "touch" if they are to be meaningful. No amount of verbal explanation can make you appear natural with your gestures. Skill comes through concentration and practice. The practice should consist of curtailing extraneous gestures by being cognizant of their presence. By avoiding meaningless and repetitious gestures the natural meaningful ones will become prominent.

There may be situations when gestures should be practiced in advance in order to add interest or vitality to the primary stimulus message. When these situations arise it is usually best to concentrate on letting those gestures which come naturally operate and simply work to emphasize or strengthen these. Rarely is it a good idea to practice specific gestures which are not natural.

VOCAL REINFORCEMENT

Verbal communication depends heavily upon the voice for message transmission. Nonverbal communication, at times, is also dependent on the voice as a means of message delivery. The voice transmits information to responding communicators about personality, prejudices, and beliefs. It also helps provide accurate meaning for the words spoken in verbal communication. When voice and message are not in concert, kinesic slips may occur, such as those mentioned previously in this chapter. A well-modulated and effective voice can reinforce both nonverbal and verbal communication. A brief discussion of the characteristics of voice transmission should emphasize desirable and undesirable elements of voice in your communication.

PITCH

You probably have listened to a monotone speaker at some time. Chances are his lack of variety in pitch made his words appear uninteresting. Technically speaking, pitch is the frequency of sound waves which determine the highness or lowness of the voice. In human voice production, pitch is determined by such factors as length of vocal folds, thickness of vocal folds, and tension of muscles in the larynx. You probably have experienced a change in the pitch of your voice as a result of tension or fatigue. Your voice may have a much lower pitch when you first rise in the morning than during the remainder of the day. These differences in pitch are a result of muscle tensions, contractions, and expansions within the larynx. As a communicator you should strive to keep your voice muscles relaxed so your pitch will not be negatively affected.

It is often difficult to determine what pitch is best suited for your message and your personality. Voice scientists suggest that your "optimum pitch" may be roughly determined by singing the scale from the lowest note to the highest note you can reach without straining, and then counting down one third of the scale from the highest note. This should be approximately the pitch you use for your everyday speaking voice and, similarly, the pitch which is natural for your physical vocal mechanism and personality.

Variety in pitch is often stressed in prestructured communication situations. In general, variety is a positive vocal reinforcer. However, variety in pitch without corresponding meaning is not only useless but humorous. Rather than concentrating on developing variety in your pitch for variety's sake, work to make your pitch emphasize important words and phrases and add extra meaning to your entire message. Somewhere between the monotone and the communicator with multivaried vocal frequencies lies the optimum pitch for meaningful effective communication.

QUALITY

The primary difference between a Stradivarius violin and a dimestore violin is tonal quality. Both may have the same range of pitch and the same capacity for loudness but the quality of sound produced from each will be significantly different. Similarly, most human beings have approximately equal capacities for range of pitch and volume but voice qualities are quite different. In fact, it is voice quality which individualizes a person more than any other factor. Quality changes as a result of resonators in the throat and nasal cavities. Because no two human beings are built in exactly the same form, resonators and vocal qualities differ.

Undesirable types of voice quality include fuzziness, nasality, breathiness, shrillness, huskiness, and hoarseness. Among the pleasant characteristics of voice quality are clarity, resonance, richness, and vibrancy. Since quality differences are a result of combinations of overtones with various amounts of energy (breath) directed through the resonators, quality may be improved by learning how to form the most favorable combinations of overtones. Vocal quality improvement involves such fundamental processes as breathing, resonating, and forming words. It is a function of the physical and emotional state of the communicator.

INTENSITY

The intensity of a communicator's voice determines the strength of the verbal stimulus as it approaches the responding communicator's aural receptors. Intensity, often called volume or loudness, refers to the magnitude (or amplitude) of the sound wave rather than the frequency which determines pitch. Loudness in voice production varies with the amount of energy supporting the breath, which flows from the abdominal cavity through the larynx past the resonators.

The communicator must be aware of his capacity to attain specific levels of intensity. He must be able to adjust loudness levels from audience to audience, and from room to room. Since words which are not heard cannot be understood it is usually better to talk too loudly than too softly. A good practice when communicating to a large audience is to project your voice to the people in the last row. If you mentally adjust your projection to that level it is certain that the people in the front rows will be able to hear you.

Apart from assuring message reception vocal intensity plays a vital role in reinforcing verbal messages. No other characteristic of voice can be used with such dramatic and contrasting effect as loudness. Variations in vocal intensity can provide interest, emphasis, and added meaning to your communication.

RATE AND RHYTHM

Though rate and rhythm are different characteristics of voice production, they are considered together because of their intrinsic interrelationship. Rate, of course, refers to the speed of speaking, and rhythm refers to the pattern of pauses and hesitations between words and phrases. Frequently rate and rhythm are detrimental to communication because they serve as negative complementary stimulus messages. For example, if a communicator speaks so slowly that you forget the first part of a sentence by the time it ends, his rate can interfere with your message comprehension. Conversely, an extremely rapid rate of speech can render the message almost unintelligible. Communicators with definite patterns of phrasing often develop a "sing-song" characteristic which interferes with the verbal message. Such a phrasing pattern can even change the meanings of words completely.

In order to make rate and rhythm work positively to reinforce communication you must empathize with the responding communicator. If you make your verbal pattern vary with the needs of your audience rather than according to your own preferences, your rate and rhythm will positively reinforce in your communication. Both rate and rhythm can create specific emotional moods in your message and can help you achieve your specific, general, and personal purposes in communication.

INTERPRETING NONVERBAL CUES

In the face-to-face communication situation the listener has the opportunity to learn a great deal about the communicator from simple observation. A person being interviewed may have certain characteristics that tell more about him than all the words he says. He may wear a certain type of clothes or clinch his fist in a peculiar way when speaking about his father. Often when stress or conflict is present in the mind of the communicator, he will reveal certain symptoms to the listener. The presence of nervous tension is by no means abnormal. When it is recognized by the listener, however, he may more accurately interpret the meaning being transmitted through both verbal and nonverbal cues.

One tension indicator is dryness of the mouth. If a speaker is constantly licking his lips this might be a cue that nervous tension is present. Exaggerated mannerisms or hyperactivity also might suggest apprehension. Nervousness may produce such symptoms as palmar sweat, perspiration on the forehead, dilation of the eyes, or the most obvious symptom, the shaking of the limbs. The old joke about people's knees knocking when they have stage fright is not farfetched. A tremor of the lip or fingers also indicates the presence of tension. Closely allied to this tension indicator is the compulsory nervous hand gesture. A nervous laugh or smile can be meaningful to an alert listener. However, these are often difficult to detect. Rising pitch as a result of tension in the vocal folds is another giveaway to the presence of tension. Similarly, a speaker's pacing back and forth across the floor or doodling on a piece of paper often signals that anxiety is present.

The frequency with which tension signs occur often betrays the intensity of the tension. However, some people try to cover up their tension by appearing overrelaxed. This type of person will talk very slowly and deliberately using few gestures. The presence of conflict, however, is not detected exclusively by means of cues indicating people's alarm. Stress is often diagnosed not by the presence but by the absence of certain cues that, if they were present, would tend to reassure people. A common example is the icy silence that occurs among a mixed group when an off-color remark is made. Also, you may have noticed that the angry man who is trying to pick a fight gets more angry if his opponent remains cool and calm.

Needless to say, not all nonverbal signs in the speaking or interview situation signal the presence of stress or conflict. Some of the signs can simply help the listener tell more about the character of the speaker. Physical appearance may reveal aspects of a person's character. A person's clothing often indicates his perception of self in relation to environment. A person who is meticulous in his dress might also project a propensity for neatness in other areas.

There are those who judge individuals on matters of personal grooming and would go so far, for example, as to conclude that hair styles communicate information to the responding communicator. A girl who bleaches, tints, or dyes her hair might express in this action a dissatisfaction with herself, or a desire to conform socially. A very tight hairdo might indicate high standards of personal conduct. Conversely, women who maintain hairdos which are easy to change may indicate flexibility in personal conduct.

Extreme drowsiness, fatigue, or emotional arousal may at times produce similar slovenly speaking characteristics. Drugs and alcohol also produce defective speech. These conditions when present in the speaker tend to inhibit his ability to organize his thoughts and/or express his ideas.

As was previously noted, the speaker's voice quality is also important to the listener. A harsh voice conveys an impression of a hard, cold individual. A pleasant voice suggests warmth and friendliness. The well-modulated voice with precise grammar may indicate a desire for position or status. You can see the need for recognizing nonverbal cues along with the words which are spoken:

By mentally adding the meaning of what he hears to the meaning that he gets from what he doesn't hear, the listener can learn much about the proficiency, integrity, and motives of the talker. Also a degree of comprehension can be attained that will never be reached when the listener hears only the literal content of the words that enter his ears.[11]

It would be impossible to list or interpret all possible forms of nonverbal communication which might be present in the semi-structured speaking or interview situation. It has rather been the purpose of this section to illustrate the types of cues to look for and to show their importance in obtaining the maximum amount of information from the communicator.

NONVERBAL CUES IN THE INTERVIEW

The interviewer must be especially aware of the importance of nonverbal communication. Words provide only partial clues to meanings which may underlie them. The attitudes surrounding words must also be perceived in order to accurately interpret the intended meaning in the interviewee's message.

There are three considerations regarding nonverbal communication to remember in an interview. Some of these have been briefly mentioned earlier in this chapter.

1. *Nonverbal communication is necessary for the complete understanding of messages.* This statement may be easily proven by listening to a ball game on the radio while watching the same game on television. The oral description by the radio announcer cannot possibly give as much information as the picture on the television screen plus the oral commentary. The same principle holds true in the interview. Simply listening to the interviewee gives you only part of the total picture. Observing his gestures, bodily movement, facial expression, dress, inflectional change, pitch change, and the tension indicators mentioned earlier in

---

[11] Ralph G. Nichols and Leonard A. Stevens, *Are You Listening?* (New York: McGraw-Hill Book Company, 1957), p. 88.

this chapter can add additional meaning to what is said. These nonverbal cues can indicate attitudes and feelings which are much more important than mere facts. However this does not imply that nonverbal communication is more important than verbal communication.

2. *Nonverbal and verbal communication must be received and analyzed simultaneously.* Which form yields the most information to the interviewer depends on the interviewee and the interview situation. It is imperative that nonverbal cues should complement verbal cues in deriving meaning from the interviewee's communication. An example from the guidance counseling situation might help clarify this point.

Johnny had been very restless during his interview with the counselor. Interpreting this behavior as indicative of serious personal problems, the counselor tried to get Johnny to talk about those things which were bothering him. As the interview progressed Johnny became more and more anxious and yet gave no indication of any serious problems which might be confronting him. If the counselor had been conscious of nonverbal cues he might have averted this fruitless session. Had he noticed that Johnny kept glancing at the clock on the wall and had he heard the shouts of Johnny's classmates outside the window, he might have discovered the reason for the boy's unusual behavior. Johnny simply wanted to get outside in time to play ball. Thus you can see that nonverbal cues analyzed in concert with verbal cues can often alter the meaning of messages. This is especially true in the perception of signs of anxiety on the part of the interviewee.

3. *Interpreting nonverbal messages involves inference and subjective evaluation.* Verbal communication also involves inferences in interpretation, of course, but nonverbal messages can be even more ambiguous than verbal ones. The interviewer must recognize that his observations are subjective. He must further realize that his interpretations of these observations involve only degrees of probability. The degree of probability that the interviewer's inferences are correct is dependent upon his life orientation, his knowledge of the interviewee, other nonverbal cues, and the interviewee's spoken message. The more

messages he receives from the interviewee through verbal and nonverbal channels, the greater the probability that the inferences will be accurate.

Reflecting nonverbal messages to the interviewee can help eliminate possible errors in interpretation. This "feedback" to the interviewee can help him achieve greater self-understanding as well as achieve more rapport in the interview situation.

These three considerations apply not only to the interview but to everyday communication as well. If these concepts are fully understood and utilized in all interpersonal communication settings the process of transmitting and receiving messages will be more efficient and effective.

Remember that as a communicator you have access to both verbal and nonverbal channels of communication. Learn to discern when to use one in place of the other and when to use them in concert. It should be obvious that in most instances a combination of the verbal and nonverbal modes will be helpful in effecting your communication. The question, then, is not which to use in a given instance but rather which should receive the primary emphasis and which should be complementary.

QUESTIONS FOR DISCUSSION

1. What special problems exist in nonverbal communication which are not present in verbal communication?

2. What dangers are inherent in the interpretation of nonverbal communication?

3. What special forms of nonverbal communication are utilized by the blind and the deaf?

EXERCISES

[Forms for completing the exercises marked with an asterisk will be found in the *Worksheets for Speech—Interpersonal Communication* (San Francisco: Chandler Publishing Company, 1967).]

1. Attend a speech in which the communicator employs visual aids. Prepare a critical report on the presentation.*

2. Observe the nonverbal cues in a conversation or interview. How

did these cues affect the meaning of words spoken in the communication situation?*

3. Analyze a news report by some prominent television commentator to discover the forms of visual support used.

4. In an attempt to learn more about gestures and how to execute them, observe the gestures of a speaker noting facial and body expression. Write a report on your observations telling whether gestures were natural, over used, under used, and how you would improve, add to or subtract from the movements used.

5. Write five to ten sentences in which gestures of the hand would be needed to execute their meaning and demonstrate in class.

6. List four subjects which would be best explained through visual rather than verbal support.

7. Include the following exercises into a speech given in class.

a. Prepare a visual aid which would have to be distributed to the class to be used properly.

b. Design a phrase or an idea to regain audience's complete attention after you are through with the visual aid mentioned above.

8. Take a famous speech and present it to the class giving the proper gestures to relay the meaning of the original speaker.

9. Repeat the same speech but deliver it without any gestures or visual reinforcement and see what happens to the meaning of the message.

10. List visual aids or supporting materials which are employed in the profession you plan to enter.

11. List five different occupations in which nonverbal communication is an integral form of communication (for example, the whistle or gesture of a policeman).

12. Observe a game of charades and determine why some players are more effective in conveying nonverbal meaning than others.

SUGGESTED READINGS

Birdwhistell, Ray L., "Background to Kinesics." *ETC.*, XIII (Autumn, 1955), pp. 10–18.

Extan, William, Jr., "Human Communication: Nonverbal and Supraverbal." *General Semantics Bulletin,* Nos. 6 and 7, (Spring-Summer, 1951), pp. 16–24.

Hayakawa, S. I., *"Review of Nonverbal Communications: Notes on the Visual Perception of Human Relations,"* by Jurgen Ruesch and Weldon Kees." *ETC.*, XIV (Autumn, 1956), pp. 57–59.

Larson, Orvin, *When It's Your Turn to Speak*. New York: Harper and Brothers, 1962. Chapter 8, "Your Way of Speaking," pp. 82–90.

Mudd, Charles S., and Malcolm O. Sillars, *Speech: Content and Communication*. San Francisco: Chandler Publishing Company, 1962. Chapter 15, "Delivery: Visual Elements," pp. 295–309.

Weinberg, Henry, "Some Functional Patterns on the Nonverbal Level." *ETC.*, IV (Spring, 1947), pp. 192–212.

Wendt, Paul R., "The Language of Pictures." *ETC.*, XIII (Summer, 1956), pp. 281–288.

The Responding Communicator | *11*

The term interpersonal communication implies an interaction between an originating and a responding communicator in the communicative act. The responding communicator is more than just a listener for he must react to the originator's message in order to complete the communication cycle. Listening, however, is a primary function of the responding communicator. Before he can properly evaluate and react to the originator's message he must hear, understand, and remember the concepts being presented. It is in the areas of receiving and correctly evaluating messages that listening becomes of prime importance.

AN INSTRUCTIONAL PROGRAM ON LISTENING

Before the functions of the responding communicator are described in more detail a special section on listening will be presented. This section is programed for increased comprehension and understanding. The information about listening will be presented a bit at a time. Each bit or frame, unless otherwise indicated, requires you to write down one or more answers on the material presented.[1] After you write your response to the frame, you will receive immediate feedback regarding the correctness of your answer. Thus, as you proceed through the program, the material on listening will be presented and, at the same time,

---

[1] Answer sheets may be found in your workbook: Gordon Wiseman and Larry Barker, *Worksheets for Speech—Interpersonal Communication* (San Francisco: Chandler Publishing Company, 1967). If no workbook is used write answers on blank sheets of paper.

you will receive feedback indicating your understanding of the terms, principles, and concepts. It is hoped that you will find it easy to learn about listening through completing this program.

PROCEDURE

A frame is the space between the two dividing lines in the programed section. It consists of a unit of information, some questions which relate to the information presented in the same frame or a preceding frame, and the correct answers to the questions. Each frame is divided into two sections. The material in the upper portion of the frame contains the explanatory material and questions to be answered. In the lower section of each frame the answers to the questions are provided. The frames begin at the top of each page and go vertically down to the bottom of the page. The first frame is followed by the second, third, and so on.

Use a sheet of paper to cover the answer in the bottom of each frame until you have responded to the question. Read the frame carefully and then write your answer(s) on your answer sheet. Make sure that the number of the frame on the answer sheet corresponds with your answer so you can go back and check any questions you might have missed. After you have responded to the frame, slide a sheet of paper down the page to expose the correct answer in the bottom of the frame. If your answer is incorrect mark an "x" beside it and reread the frame. If your answer is correct continue to the next frame.

CONVENTIONS USED IN THE PROGRAM.

a. One blank (——) indicates that one word is missing and must be supplied on your answer sheet; two blanks (—— ——) indicate two words; three blanks (—— —— ——) indicate that three words are missing and must be supplied, and so on.

b. The bracketed note [*phrase*] indicates that several words or a sentence are missing and must be supplied.

c. Clues or hints are sometimes supplied. For example, (a——) means that the answer begins with a letter "a." (a—— b——) means that the first word begins with "a" and the second word with "b."

Try to keep in mind, while going through this program, that you are not taking a test but you are learning about listening. If at times it seems as though the material is repetitious this is only true because the program is attempting to reinforce terms, principles, or concepts. Finally, when responding to the blanks in the frames, try not to look back at your other answers on the answer sheet.

Now you are ready to begin.

PART I: LISTENING AND COMMUNICATING

1. How much time do you spend communicating each day? One study revealed that approximately *70 percent* (or 2/3) of an adult's waking day is spent in *verbal communication*. **Copy down the italicized words on your answer sheet before you go to the next frame.**

ANSWER

70 percent (2/3)   verbal communication

2. During the time you are awake you spend about 70 percent of your time in —— ——. Verbal communication includes reading, writing, speaking, and listening. According to the same study, you spend about *45 percent* of your time *listening*.

ANSWER

verbal communication

3. Of the —— —— of your waking day spent in verbal communication, about —— —— of this time is spent listening.

ANSWER

70 percent (2/3)   45 percent (1/2)

4. Since about 45 percent of your time spent in communication is spent ——, it is not surprising that a survey among hospital administrators revealed that almost 2/3 of them rated *listening* as the form of communication most important to their jobs.

ANSWER

listening

5. —— is probably the most important form of verbal communication in which you engage every day. Some studies have even found that people are influenced more by what they *hear* than by what they *read*.

ANSWER

Listening

6. The importance of l—— should not be underestimated. There is some evidence to show that people are more influenced by what they —— than by what they read.

ANSWER

listening   hear

7. Even though about —— —— of your time spent in verbal communication is spent *listening*, you have had much more training in the other communication forms of reading, writing, and speaking. The training you have received in these areas is not proportional to the degree you use them. From the standpoint of time spent using each of the communication forms, you should receive the most training in listening.

ANSWER

45 percent

8. The amount of training you receive in learning to l—— is not proportional to the time you spend using this form of communication. In your formative years you received the most training in communication forms such as r——, w——, and s——.

ANSWER

listen   reading   writing   speaking

9. Contrary to what you may think, you can learn how to be a more effective listener. The first thing you should understand is that *listening is a combination of what you hear, what you understand, and what you remember.* Listening is more than just hearing, understanding, or remembering; it is a c—— of these elements.

ANSWER

combination

10. *Hearing, understanding, and remembering*—listening is a combination of all of these. Thus, in understanding how to listen more effectively you must keep in mind that listening is a combination of what you ——, ——, and ——.

ANSWER

hear   understand   remember

Review Frame

11. **The purpose of this review frame is to help you find out how much you have learned up to this point. Read and answer each question carefully. Do not check your answers until you have completed the frame.**

a. Approximately what percentage of time do adults spend in verbal communication each day? —— ——
b. Of this, about how much time is spent in listening? —— ——
c. What form of verbal communication did hospital administrators consider most important to their job? ——
d. Are people influenced more (according to several studies) by what they hear or what they read? —— —— ——
e. The training you receive in learning to listen **is/is not** proportional to the time you spend using this form of communication.
f. What is listening a combination of? —— —, ——, ——

ANSWER

a. 70 percent (2/3)   b. 45 percent (1/2)
c. listening   d. what they hear
e. is not   f. hearing, understanding, remembering

PART II: WHY LISTEN?

12. There are many different reasons why you listen. Some of these reasons are: (1) to *pass examinations,* (2) to *improve personality,* (3) to *gain financial benefits,* (4) to *improve self-confidence,* (5) to *aid in developing language facilities,* and (6) to *gain a shortcut to knowledge.* Each of these reasons will be discussed separately. **Go on to the next frame.**

13. From a practical point of view you often listen, as a student, in order to *pass examinations.* When you listen carefully, you will usually receive resultant dividends when examination time comes around. A very practical reason for listening, then, is to help yourself p—— e——.

ANSWER

pass examinations

14. Aside from helping you to —— ——, listening can also *improve personality,* by making people better conversationalists. Being a good listener is the first step toward being a good friend. Taking time to listen to others can make them feel more kindly disposed toward you and, in turn, i—— p——.

ANSWER

pass examinations   improve personality

||||||||||||||||||||||||||||||||||||||||||||||||||||||||||||||||||||||||||||||||||||||||||||||||||||||||||||||||||||||||||||||||

15. As a student, you listen in order to — —; you listen to become a better conversationalist and to — —. Another reason you listen is to *gain financial benefits.* Listening to your teachers, the radio, television, speeches, your friends, and others can be profitable at times because of ideas you acquire and skills you learn. You often listen, then, in order to — — —.

ANSWER

pass examinations   improve personality
gain financial benefits

||||||||||||||||||||||||||||||||||||||||||||||||||||||||||||||||||||||||||||||||||||||||||||||||||||||||||||||||||||||||||||||||

16. Passing examinations, improving personality, and gaining financial benefits give you excellent reasons for listening. There are still other reasons. One of these is to *gain self-confidence.* If you listen carefully in class, you will be more likely to answer questions intelligently when asked. If you are paying attention, you stand less chance of being caught "asleep" in class. Thus, when you listen carefully you are alert and prepared, and you — — —.

ANSWER

gain self-confidence

||||||||||||||||||||||||||||||||||||||||||||||||||||||||||||||||||||||||||||||||||||||||||||||||||||||||||||||||||||||||||||||||

17. An important reason for listening is to gain self-confidence. You also listen to help further *develop language facilities.* Since you listen more than you read it stands to reason that you learn more words through listening than through reading. By listening, you also learn correct pronunciation (nearly impossible to learn by reading). Listening therefore helps to d— l— f— further.

ANSWER

develop language facility

||||||||||||||||||||||||||||||||||||||||||||||||||||||||||||||||||||||||||||||||||||||||||||||||||||||||||||||||||||||||||||||||

18. The reasons for listening thus far discussed are to pass examinations, to improve personality, to gain financial benefits, to gain s——c——, and to develop l—— f——. A final reason, one of the most important, is to *gain a shortcut to knowledge.* When you listen you can learn vast amounts of material much more quickly than if you had to find it in a book and read it. By listening to directions, you can proceed more effectively and efficiently than if you had to find your way by trial and error. Listening, then provides a s—— t—— k——.

ANSWER

self-confidence   language facilities   shortcut to knowledge

Review Frame

19. **Read and answer each question carefully. Do not check your answers until you have completed the frame.**

a. By listening carefully in class you are more likely to p—— e——.
b. By being a better conversationalist through listening you can i—— p——.
c. From a practical standpoint, listening can help you gain f—— b——.
d. By staying alert through listening you can gain more s—— c——.
e. By listening to others speak, you are helped in the development of your own l—— f——.
f. When you need to know information quickly, listening can be a s—— t—— k——.

ANSWER

a. pass examinations
b. improve personality
c. financial benefits
d. self-confidence
e. language facility
f. shortcut to knowledge

PART III: TYPES OF LISTENING

||||||||||||||||||||||||||||||||||||||||||||||||||||||||||||||||||||||||||||||||||||||||||||||||||||||||||||||||||||||||||||||||||||||||||||||||||||||||||||||||||

20. Knowing the importance of listening and some of the reasons why you listen, consider the three different types of listening: appreciative listening, critical listening, and discriminative listening. *Appreciative listening* is listening to any sound which *pleases you.* Stated in somewhat more technical terms, appreciative listening is listening to any kind of stimulus which is gratifying to the hearer. In this type of listening it is not the content of the message which is important but rather the way the words or music sound. Listening which is gratifying to you as a hearer is called a— l—.

ANSWER

appreciative listening

||||||||||||||||||||||||||||||||||||||||||||||||||||||||||||||||||||||||||||||||||||||||||||||||||||||||||||||||||||||||||||||||||||||||||||||||||||||||||||||||||

21. —— —— is listening which is gratifying to the hearer. A second type of listening is termed *critical listening.* Critical listening is listening for the purpose of *evaluating speakers' arguments and evidence.* As a critical listener, you weigh the evidence presented, decide upon the validity of statements, question sources of materials, and so on. This listening for the purpose of evaluating speakers' arguments and evidence is called c— l—.

ANSWER

Appreciative listening   critical listening

||||||||||||||||||||||||||||||||||||||||||||||||||||||||||||||||||||||||||||||||||||||||||||||||||||||||||||||||||||||||||||||||||||||||||||||||||||||||||||||||||

|||||||||||||||||||||||||||||||||||||||||||||||||||||||||||||||||||||||||||||||||||||||||||||||||||||||||||||||||||||||||||||||||||||||

22. Appreciative listening is listening to sounds which —— ——
while critical listening is for the purpose of —— speakers'
evidence and arguments. A third type of listening is called *discriminative listening*. Discriminative listening is listening for the
purpose of *comprehending ideas and information presented*. If
you are a discriminative listener in the classroom you listen for
the content of the instructor's lecture. Listening for the purpose
of comprehending ideas and information is called d—— l——.

ANSWER

please you (are pleasant)   evaluating
discriminative listening

|||||||||||||||||||||||||||||||||||||||||||||||||||||||||||||||||||||||||||||||||||||||||||||||||||||||||||||||||||||||||||||||||||||||

Review Frame

23. **The purpose of this review frame is to see if you understand
the three types of listening which have been discussed. Do not
check your answers until you answer all three questions.**

a. Appreciative listening is listening which [*phrase*].
b. Listening for the purpose of comprehending ideas and information is called —— ——.
c. Define critical listening.

ANSWER

a. pleases the hearer *or* is gratifying to the hearer
b. discriminative listening
c. listening for the purpose of evaluating speakers' arguments
   and evidence

|||||||||||||||||||||||||||||||||||||||||||||||||||||||||||||||||||||||||||||||||||||||||||||||||||||||||||||||||||||||||||||||||||||||

PART IV: SOME MISCONCEPTIONS ABOUT LISTENING

24. People often have several misconceptions about listening. Some of these are that: (1) *a poor listener is lacking in intelligence,* (2) *listening is directly related to hearing acuity,* (3) *listening cannot be improved through practice,* and (4) *learning to read will automatically teach you to listen.* It will be the purpose of this section to dispel these false notions. **Go on to the next frame.**

25. Contrary to what some people would believe, listening and intelligence are not directly related. A poor listener is *not necessarily lacking in intelligence.* People often appear stupid because they do not listen and, therefore, do not know answers to certain questions. This is not due to lack of intelligence but, rather due to the fact that they did not listen. Thus a poor listener is not necessarily l—— i—— i——.

ANSWER

lacking in intelligence

26. Besides realizing that a *poor listener* is not necessarily —— —— ——, you should also be aware that listening is *not directly related to hearing acuity.* Certainly, if a person cannot hear he cannot listen. A person with normal hearing, however, may be a poor listener and not perceive some of the words which are spoken to him. There is no basis for the assumption therefore, that there is a direct relationship between l—— and h—— a——.

ANSWER

lacking in intelligence   listening   hearing acuity

27. Thus far you have learned that a —— —— is not necessarily lacking in intelligence, and that listening is not directly related to —— ——. You next should realize that listening can be *improved through practice.* The only qualification of this statement is that you need to *practice good listening habits.* It is possible to improve listening if you p—— g—— l—— h——.

ANSWER

poor listener   hearing acuity   practice good listening habits

28. You should —— —— —— —— if you want to improve your listening ability. It is important that you work very hard to improve your ability to listen because when you learned to read *you did not automatically learn to listen.* Learning to read will not automatically teach you to listen for two main reasons: (1) *listening is a social activity* while reading is done alone, and (2) *a listener must adjust to the rate of the speaker* while the reader can set his own rate for maximum comprehension. It must be realized then that learning to read will not automatically teach you to ——.

ANSWER

practice good listening habits   listen

29. The process involved in learning to read is not the same as that of learning to ——. This is basically because (1) reading is done alone while listening is a —— —— and (2) while a reader can set his own rate a listener must [*phrase*]

ANSWER

listen   social activity   adjust to the rate of the speaker

Review Frame

30. **Before going on to the next few frames review the misconceptions about listening:**

a. Is there a direct relationship between listening and hearing acuity?
b. Is a poor listener necessarily lacking in intelligence?
c. Listening **can/cannot** be improved.
d. Listening can be improved *only* through practicing good habits. [True *or* False]
e. Give two reasons why learning to read will not automatically teach you to listen.

ANSWER

a. No.
b. No.
c. can
d. True.
e. (1) Listening is a social activity; reading is done alone.
   (2) A reader can set his own rate while a listener must adjust to the rate of the speaker.

PART V: BAD LISTENING HABITS

31. In order to improve your listening habits, it is first necessary to be aware of some bad habits which should be avoided. Some of these habits which interfere with listening are: (1) *faking attention*, (2) *memorizing what the speaker says*, (3) *avoiding difficult listening*, (4) *dismissing a subject prematurely as uninteresting*, (5) *criticizing physical appearance and delivery*, and (6) *yielding easily to distractions*. Recognizing and avoiding these bad habits can greatly improve your listening abilities. **Go on to the next frame.**

‖‖‖

32. Some people only pretend to listen to the speaker when, in actuality, their minds are millions of miles away. They may occasionally nod in agreement with the speaker, but they have no idea what he is talking about. These people are guilty of the bad listening habit *faking attention*. You cannot hope to receive value from a speech unless you listen to it. You receive little value if you f—— a——.

ANSWER

fake attention

‖‖‖

33. Other people have a habit of *memorizing what the speaker says*. They begin to remember facts and statistics and forget to continue listening to the remainder of the speech. By listening for general ideas rather than specific facts, there is little need to memorize the facts presented by the speaker. Thus, you should not pretend to listen or f—— a—— nor should you go to the opposite extreme and try to [*phrase*].

ANSWER

fake attention   memorize what the speaker says

‖‖‖

34. Another dangerous listening habit is to *avoid difficult listening*. At times, if the subject matter is strange, new, or difficult you may tend to stop listening completely. This habit could be dangerous if you should happen to miss important information. In order to be a better listener, you should not a—— d—— l——.

ANSWER

avoid difficult listening

‖‖‖

35. Even though a subject might be technical in nature or seem strange you should not a—— d—— l——. You should also be careful not to *dismiss a subject prematurely as uninteresting.* A subject often might not appear interesting at the onset of the speech; however, you should try to stimulate your own interest in the topic. By forcing yourself to be interested at the beginning you will usually find that there is something interesting in the speech after all. If you dismiss [*phrase*] you will get nothing from the speech and will be practicing a bad listening habit.

ANSWER

avoid difficult listening   a subject prematurely as uninteresting

36. In order to be fair to the speaker you should not dismiss [*phrase*]. You should also try to avoid *criticizing delivery and physical appearance* of the speaker if you want to listen carefully. By not making mental judgments about a speaker's dress or peculiar mannerisms you keep your mind free to gain maximum information from the presentation. In order to get the most out of a speech you can improve your listening by not c—— d——

ANSWER

a subject prematurely as uninteresting   criticizing delivery

37. By keeping from [*phrase*] of the speaker you can gain the most from his presentation. You can also improve your listening by not *yielding to distractions.* Interference is usually present in a communication situation. Although it is the speaker's job to overcome the interference it is also necessary for the listener to do his part. By listening for the content of the message you can help overcome interference by not y—— t—— d——.

ANSWER

criticizing delivery and appearance   yielding to distractions

|||||||||||||||||||||||||||||||||||||||||||||||||||||||||||||||||||||||||||||||||||||||||||||||||||||||||||||||||||||||||||||||||

Review Frame

38. Several listening habits have been discussed which should be avoided. Let's see how many you can remember.

a. If you only pretend to listen to the speaker you are —— ——.
b. If you try to remember specific details you are [*phrase*].
c. If you stop listening when the subject is new or strange you are —— —— ——.
d. If you decide that you do not want to hear the speech on the basis of the title you are [*phrase*].
e. If you look for faults in the speaker's presentation you are [*phrase*].
f. If you let interference overcome the message you are —— —— ——.

Remember that these six bad listening habits should be avoided.

ANSWER

a. faking attention
b. memorizing what the speaker says
c. avoiding difficult listening
d. dismissing a subject prematurely as uninteresting
e. criticizing delivery and physical appearance
f. yielding to distractions

|||||||||||||||||||||||||||||||||||||||||||||||||||||||||||||||||||||||||||||||||||||||||||||||||||||||||||||||||||||||||||||||||

PART VI: RULES FOR EFFECTIVE LISTENING

|||||||||||||||||||||||||||||||||||||||||||||||||||||||||||||||||||||||||||||||||||||||||||||||||||||||||||||||||||||||||||||||||

39. Having discovered some of the habits which are not conducive to effective listening you are now ready to learn some rules which will help improve your listening ability. Five of the best rules to improve listening are: (1) *adjust to abnormal listening conditions,* (2) *adjust to emotion-rousing words and ideas,* (3) *recognize central ideas,* (4) *utilize notes properly,* (5) *reconcile thought rate with speech speed.* **Go on to the next frame.**

|||||||||||||||||||||||||||||||||||||||||||||||||||||||||||||||||||||||||||||||||||||||||||||||||||||||||||||||||||||||||||||||||

40. Many conditions may be present in the communication situation which are not conducive to effective listening. A first rule for good listening is to *adjust to abnormal listening conditions*. Such distractions as noisy neighbors or classmates, poor rapport in the classroom, or bad physical conditions in the room can all hinder listening. In order to be an effective listener you should adjust to these a—— l—— c——.

ANSWER

abnormal listening conditions

41. Adjustment to —— —— —— such as a very hot room, lack of seating space, or loud talking in the corridor can aid you in becoming a better listener. A second suggestion to improve listening is to *adjust to emotion-rousing words and ideas*. There are certain words which may arouse strong emotions in you. These emotions can be favorable or unfavorable but they nevertheless can tend to make your mind wander from what the speaker is saying. They occasionally might even cause you to misunderstand what the speaker is trying to say. One author calls these words "dynamite words" because of the explosion they create in your mind. In order to improve listening you should learn to adjust to these [*phrase*].

ANSWER

abnormal listening conditions
emotion-rousing words and ideas

42. When words create an emotional impact you should —— to them if you hope to be a better listener. You can adjust by (1) *withholding evaluation* of what the speaker says, (2) *hunting for negative arguments to refute your own predispositions,* and (3) *rationalizing the impact of these words on your behavior.* These are three ways in which you can help [*phrase*].

ANSWER

adjust   adjust to emotion-rousing words and ideas

43. In order to adjust to emotion-rousing words and ideas you should first w—— e—— about what the speaker says. This delaying of evaluation will help to keep your mind free for listening as well as help to minimize emotional reactions which might occur. —— —— is one means of adjusting to emotion-rousing words and ideas.

ANSWER

withhold evaluation   Withholding evaluation

44. Another technique for adjusting to emotion-rousing words and ideas besides —— —— is to *hunt for negative arguments* to refute your own predetermined views toward the speaker's words or ideas. By looking for other views besides your own you can help minimize emotional involvements' which might be present. A second technique for [*phrase*] is to hunt for —— —— to refute your own predispositions.

ANSWER

withholding evaluation
adjusting to emotion-rousing words and ideas
negative arguments

||||||||||||||||||||||||||||||||||||||||||||||||||||||||||||||||||||||||||||||||||||||||||||||||||||||||||||||||||||||||||||||

45. Hunting for —— —— to overcome your own biases can aid listening through helping you adjust to [*phrase*]. Another suggestion to help adjust is to *rationalize the impact* of these emotionally laden words. By realizing that words are not the things they stand for, but only symbols, you can easily rationalize their importance. Although words do not affect you emotionally at times you should try to r—— t—— i—— in order to improve your listening skills.

ANSWER

negative arguments   emotion-rousing words and ideas
rationalize their impact

||||||||||||||||||||||||||||||||||||||||||||||||||||||||||||||||||||||||||||||||||||||||||||||||||||||||||||||||||||||||||||||

46. Adjusting to abnormal physical conditions and emotionally laden words are two devices for improving listening. A third technique is to *recognize central ideas* in the speaker's presentation. The problem of memorizing specific facts from speeches was discussed earlier. By skimming over the subpoints and central ideas you can make the presentation much more meaningful. If you r—— c—— i—— you can grasp the important concepts of the speaker's presentation.

ANSWER

recognize central ideas

||||||||||||||||||||||||||||||||||||||||||||||||||||||||||||||||||||||||||||||||||||||||||||||||||||||||||||||||||||||||||||||

47. If you search for —— —— rather than specific facts and examples you can aid your listening ability. Another method for improvement is to *utilize notes properly*. By taking good notes (not too brief, not too long, but just right) you can keep your mind alert and follow the central ideas of the speaker. You should u—— n—— p—— in order to gain maximum benefit from the presentation.

ANSWER

central ideas   utilize notes properly

||||||||||||||||||||||||||||||||||||||||||||||||||||||||||||||||||||||||||||||||||||||||||||||||||||||||||||||||||||||||||||||

48. Proper —— of —— can help you to be a better listener, by keeping your mind alert. A final suggestion for improving listening is to *reconcile thought rate and speech speed*. You can think much faster than you can speak. A normal speaker talks at a rate of about 130 words per minute. You can listen and comprehend at a rate of about 400 words per minute. Because of this difference in thought rate and speech speed you may often race ahead of the speaker when he is talking and let your mind begin to wander. You must control this tendency and try to reconcile your t—— r—— with the —— of the speaker.

ANSWER

utilization   notes   thought rate   speed *or* rate

Review Frame

49. Let's see if you remember the rules for effective listening.
a. What two adjustments should you make in order to improve your listening abilities?
b. You **should/should not** look for central ideas in the speaker's presentation.
c. Proper note taking **can/cannot** help to improve listening.
d. Thought rate **is/is not** the same as normal speech speed.
e. In what ways can you adjust to emotion-rousing points and ideas?

ANSWER

a. adjust to abnormal listening conditions   adjust to emotion-rousing words and ideas
b. should
c. can
d. is not
e. withhold evaluation   hunt for negative argument rationalize the impact of emotionally laden words

Go back and review those items which you missed.

OTHER FUNCTIONS OF THE RESPONDING COMMUNICATOR

Having completed the special material on listening you are now aware of one of the most important functions of the responding communicator. There are other functions he must perform, however, which are also important. One of these is providing appropriate feedback to the originating communicator.

RESPONDING MESSAGES

You will remember the three types of response messages which you may send to the originating communicator:

1. Primary response messages
2. Complementary response messages
3. Auxiliary messages

If necessary, review Chapter 2 for discussion of these different types of messages you send as a responding communicator. Review also the types of feedback which these messages may indicate. It is your responsibility to insure that your feedback is clear in its meaning and is appropriate to the message being transmitted.

Some of the most common forms of response messages are nods of the head, gestures of approval or disapproval, applause or boos, silence, or words of reply. If you are in a group you may use only nonverbal expressions as feedback. In a face-to-face situation you may reply with words as well as gestures.

In order to avoid having your response messages misunderstood by the originator several suggestions might prove helpful:

1. If there is a question in your mind whether the originator perceived your response message, send it again. Redundancy in communication can become boring but some is needed to insure clarity and proper understanding.

2. If nonverbal expressions such as nods or gestures are used in response to messages, make sure they are clear in their meaning. Make nods of approval definite so they won't be misinterpreted.

If a gesture means to go ahead repeat it so the message is clear to the originator. Do not be afraid to exaggerate gestures for clarity.

3. Beware of delayed response. If you need a period of incubation before responding to a communication indicate this to the originator. A period of silence before a response may be misinterpreted by the originator as negative or ambiguous feedback.

4. Make sure that you understand the message before you respond. Much needless deliberation has occurred because a response was made to a message that was not completely understood. Do not hesitate to ask for clarification or definitions before you respond. This clarification will add to the importance of your feedback.

5. Avoid extremes in responding. This suggestion may seem contradictory to one of those above, but it actually is not. It means that you should time your responses at appropriate intervals (for example, respond at the end of a paragraph or phrase). Continual nodding during a communicator's message may be distracting and may serve to interfere with his transmission. In addition it might suggest that you are simply agreeing to be nice and are not actually utilizing the ideation process in evaluating the ideas being presented.

In summary, remember that you have a responsibility as a responding communicator to be an effective and critical listener. In addition your responses must be made clear to the originating communicator so that the cycle of communication may be completed.

QUESTIONS FOR DISCUSSION

1. How can listening affect grades in college?

2. What are the functions of the memory, the learning process, and the hearing mechanism in effective listening?

3. How much responsibility lies upon the speaker in helping the responding communicator listen? How much responsibility rests upon the responding communicator?

EXERCISES

[Forms for completing the exercises marked with an asterisk will be found in the *Worksheets for Speech—Interpersonal Communication* (San Francisco: Chandler Publishing Company, 1967).]

1. Keep a day-by-day checklist over a period of 1 week and note each time you find yourself practicing a bad listening habit. Each time you find yourself failing to listen properly concentrate on avoiding this habit and see if your list gets shorter as the week progresses.*

2. Observe carefully the listening habits of:

a. the members of a class during a lecture.

b. the congregation at a church during a sermon.

c. the members of an organization during a meeting.

Make a list of bad listening habits that you observe. Try to suggest ways which the speaker might have helped the listeners avoid these habits.*

3. Select a partner from your class and attend together a speech given on campus. Have your partner take notes while you just sit and listen. After the speech, compare what you remember without notes with what your partner remembers from the notes he took. Report the differences to the class.

4. Plan to attend a speech you do not think you will understand and expect to be uninteresting. Before attending the speech, read some material concerning the topic or learn something about the speaker's background and see if this makes the speech understandable and interesting to you.

5. In a brief report to the class explain the different types of listening needed for the following situations:

a. a football game on the radio.

b. a classroom lecture on biochemistry.

c. a conversation between a boy and girlfriend.

d. a Beethoven sonata.

6. Consult the suggested readings at the end of the chapter and read other views on listening. Compile a list of suggestions to improve listening. Note differences among the suggestions given by different authors.

7. Prepare a report on the psychological and physiological processes involved in listening. These include the hearing mechanism, the process of learning, and the functions of memory. Show how each function contributes to the listening process.

8. Conduct a brief survey to determine the importance of listening

in different occupations. If significant differences occur between occupations attempt to explain the causes for such differences.

9. During the period of an entire day keep a log of the amount of time you spend:

(a) reading.
(b) writing.
(c) speaking.
(d) listening.

Compare your results with those cited earlier in this chapter.

10. Pick two speakers in class and alter your pattern of responding to each. During the first speaker's presentation give him no feedback at all. During the second speaker's presentation provide total feedback to his speech. Note differences these changes in response methods made in the speaker's effectiveness.

SUGGESTED READINGS

Barbara, Dominick A., *The Art of Listening*. Springfield, Ill.: Charles C. Thomas, Inc., 1958.

_____, "Listening with a Modest Ear." *Today's Speech*, IX (February, 1961), pp. 1–3.

Education, LXXV (January, 1955). (Complete issue deals with listening and listener behavior.)

Johnson, Wendell, *Your Most Enchanted Listener*. New York: Harper and Brothers, 1956. (A very readable account of listening techniques and breakdowns).

Kelly, Charles M., "Mental Ability and Personality Factors in Listening." *The Quarterly Journal of Speech*, XLIX (April, 1963), pp. 152–156.

Lieb, Barbara, "How To Be Influenced Discriminatingly." *Today's Speech*, VIII (April, 1960), pp. 24–26.

Nichols, Ralph G., "Do We Know How to Listen? Practical Helps in a Modern Age." *The Speech Teacher*, X (March, 1961), pp. 118–124.

Nichols, Ralph G., and Leonard A. Stevens, *Are You Listening?* New York: McGraw-Hill Company, 1957. (The entire book relates to problems and techniques of effective listening.)

APPENDICES

A. Criteria for Communicative Evaluation

B. Agenda for Problem-Solving Discussion

C. Guide for Oral Practice

D. Sample Speech Outlines

E. Suggested Topics for Informative and Persuasive Speeches

F. Suggested Topics for Impromptu Speeches

G. Suggested Topics for Informative Lectures on Communication

H. Suggested Topics for Group Discussions

Criteria for Communication Evaluation | A

I. FLOW OF THE COMMUNICATION

A. How well did the communicator use transitional phrases and sentences to connect ideas?
B. Did the communication move continuously toward the direction of the specific purpose?
C. Was the movement of words and ideas smooth or jerky?

II. SELECTION OF APPROPRIATE WORD SYMBOLS

A. Did the communicator make the symbols work for him? Were the symbols accurate and vivid?
B. Was the style of the communication befitting the occasion, the audience, and the topic?
C. Did the communicator use correct grammar?
D. Were sentence structures in proper form?
E. Were the symbols sufficiently concrete (depending on the topic) for maximum understanding by the audience?

III. USE OF COMPLEMENTARY STIMULUS MESSAGES

A. To what extent did the communicator reinforce his communication with facial expressions, gestures, or bodily reinforcement?
B. Were visual aids used to support the primary stimulus message?
C. Were aids used correctly and effectively?

Consensus—Over-all Transmission of the Message

IV. COHESIVENESS OF THE MESSAGE

A. To what extent did the communicator unify his communication through:
   1. arrangement of materials?
   2. thought units?
   3. language?
B. Was the whole communication integrated or a composite of separate ideas?

V. USE OF DEVELOPMENTAL DEVICES

A. Did the communicator exhibit a knowledge of the developmental devices?
B. Were the examples, analogies, statistics, illustrations, and the like meaningful in terms of the audience's life orientation?
C. Did the developmental devices appeal to all of the five senses?
D. Was a variety of developmental devices used?

Consensus—Over-all Content of the Message

VI. ANALYSIS AND ADAPTATION TO AUDIENCE

A. How well did the communicator know his own life orientation?
B. How well did the communicator analyze the audience's life orientation?
C. Did the communicator adapt to these orientations in his presentation?

VII. FULFILLMENT OF SPECIFIC ASSIGNMENT

A. How well did the communicator observe the time limit and other rules set forth by those in charge of the communication setting?
B. Was the communication the type specified in the assignment?
C. Did the communication add to your body of knowledge?
D. Did the communicator indicate that he had probed his subject in sufficient depth?

E. Did the communication appear to have had a sufficient incubation period?

F. Was the communication of sufficient maturity for the audience?

VIII. GENERAL EFFECTIVENESS OF COMMUNICATION

A. To what extent was the primary stimulus message clear?

B. Was the central theme predominant throughout the communication?

C. Did the communicator make an effort to help you know his primary stimulus message?

D. Did the communicator use the most effective medium of transmission available for his primary stimulus message?

E. Did the communicator eliminate items which might detract from his communication?

F. Did the communicator handle effectively any other interference that arose during his communication?

G. Was the communicator in control of the communication situation at all times?

Agenda for Problem-Solving Discussion | B

The following steps should be followed in a systematic order:

I. DEFINE THE PROBLEM.

A. State the topic in a way that may not be answered by "yes" or "no."
B. Define the important terms in the topic.

II. LIMIT THE TOPIC ON THE BASIS OF:

A. Relevance to the group,
B. Importance of specific issues,
C. Amount of time reserved for discussion.

III. ANALYZE THE PROBLEM.

A. Study the causes and effects of the problem.
B. Sort out the relevant evidence, illustrations, and the like and discard the rest.

IV. ESTABLISH CRITERIA FOR THE POSSIBLE SOLUTIONS.

A. Determine what is expected of the proposed solutions.
B. Defer judgment on which criteria should be accepted until all of the possible ones have been suggested.
C. Select those criteria from the many suggested that are accepted by the majority of the group.

V. SUGGEST POSSIBLE SOLUTIONS.

A. Decide on the general approaches to the problem.
B. List all of the proposed specific solutions but defer judgment on any of them until they have all been suggested.
   1. At this point quantity rather than quality is wanted.
   2. Even seemingly ridiculous ideas are welcomed—these may suggest to someone else in the group more workable solutions.
   3. Members should seek to improve on ideas that other members suggest.

VI. CHECK THE INDIVIDUAL SOLUTIONS AGAINST THE ESTABLISHED CRITERIA.

A. Check each solution against all of the proposed criteria.
B. Compare the degree to which the solutions satisfy the requirements of the criteria.
C. Discard those solutions which do not satisfy basic criteria.
D. Evaluate the remaining solutions in light of the needs of the problem.
E. Decide which solution(s) appear to be the best ones for the particular problem.

VII. IMPLEMENT THE SOLUTION.

A. Through what ways and means may the solution be carried out?
B. Of the available solutions, which are most efficient and effective?

VIII. EVALUATE THE EFFECT OF THE SOLUTION UPON THE PROBLEM.

A. After the solution has been tested has it accomplished its purpose?
B. Has it satisfied the need?
C. Can improvements or alterations be made in the solution that would aid its effectiveness?

Guide for Oral Practice | C

Speech is both a science and an art. The artistic element necessitates much oral practice. In fact without oral practice a written speech can rarely accomplish its ultimate goal efficiently or effectively. Consequently, after a speech has been organized and prepared, a definite sequence of oral practice [1] can help polish it for maximum effectiveness. The guide for oral practice suggested here should be adapted to each person and each particular speech.

SESSION I

Sit down and think through the speech as a unit. Start with your specific purpose and what you hope to accomplish. Work to insure the interrelatedness of main points. If main points do not seem to form an integrated unit, then change them. This first step should precede oral practice.

SESSION II

A. Practice giving main ideas and subpoints from outline and ad-libbing transitions while seated (two times).
B. Practice giving main ideas, subpoints, and supporting material from outline and ad-libbing transitions while standing (two times).

---

[1] Successive practice sessions should take place at least a day apart, but avoid waiting too long between sessions. If your speech is 5 minutes long, the entire practice time using this schedule will be only 60 minutes. A speech worth giving certainly deserves an hour's oral preparation.

SESSION III

A. Practice giving main ideas, subpoints, and supporting material from outline and ad-libbing transitions while standing. Work on trouble spots and phrasing problems as they occur until they are corrected.
B. Transfer main points from outline onto note card(s). (Use only one side of each card.)
C. Practice giving the communication solely from note cards, consulting the outline only when necessary.

SESSION IV

A. Practice giving the communication solely from note cards, consulting outline when necessary. Are you reinforcing your ideas physically?
B. Practice giving the communication with the note cards (two times). Do not consult the outline.

SESSION V

A. Practice the communication in front of an audience (roommate, friends, or the like) with note cards. Work on eye contact and gestures.
B. Go over rough phrasing spots or portions that you forgot in your earlier practice (this session should take place the night before final performance). Then get a good night's rest.
C. Think through entire communication to make sure you have it well in mind.

SESSION VI

Present final communication.

Sample Speech Outlines | D

DREAMS[1]

General Purpose: To inform
Specific Purpose: To explain several new discoveries in the science of dreams.

I. *Introduction:* When we are awake we have one common world, but when we are asleep each turns to a world of his own.

    A. Our world of dreams—Heraclitus spoke of the object of speculation.

    B. Dreams foretold future

        1. Abe Lincoln—assassination

        2. Dream events in your life

II. *Body:* Only within the last 5 or 6 years have superstitious views on dreaming been upset by fascinating discoveries which have led to a new science of dreams.

    A. Did you dream last night? Science has shown that all of us dream every night.

        1. Not 1, but 4–7 dreams

        2. (20 percent of sleep time in dreamland) 1½ hours

        3. Ability to detect dreaming—accidental 1952.

            a. Prof. N. Klietman—U. of Chicago—sleep cycles.

            b. Eye movements (under lids).

---

[1] Sample outline of speech to inform, submitted by Sharon Mechling, student at Ohio University.

    c. Gathered adult volunteers.

    d. Put electrodes on eye sockets.

    e. Observed—every sleeper has eye movements in clusters each night.

    f. Put electrodes on scalp.

    g. Found Brain Wave Pattern.

    h. Further support for theory

        (1) When sleeper awakened immediately after eye movement, he remembered dreams

        (2) When awakened other times did not recall dreams

  4. Can't monitor everyone, but evidence is strong.

B. If we dream so often why can't we remember our dreams?

  1. *Old* idea—ashamed, repress them.

  2. New idea—low grade mental activity similar to brain mechanism of a drunk. Like drunk, dreamer can't remember.

  3. Lab work confirms—delay wakening dreamer 5 minutes after eye movement stops, poor recall. After 5-10 more minutes, no recall.

  4. Some scientists believe people who claim never sleep actually sleep without knowing it, dream they're awake.

C. If we dream so much is there a reason for it?

  1. To find reason—Dr. William Dement.

    a. Put volunteers through "torture test."

    b. Men awakened as soon as started dreaming, then allowed to go to sleep immediately.

    c. During day, men irritable, had difficulty concentrating.

    d. Sleepers stated more dreams—successive nights

        (1) 1 man (7-10-17-21-24) dreams

        (2) making up for interrupted dreams

  3. Experiment over, dreamed more—until regained emotional composure.

  4. Dement said ". . . If I had kept it up, they would have gone nuts . . ."

III. *Conclusion:* Each one of us spends 20 per cent of our sleep-time in dreamland.

    A. With 2½-3 billion people, 4-7 dreams each night, no wonder there is a chance of dreaming an incident which actually occurs.

    B. Remember you recall only dreams which occur shortly before waking.

    C. Keep in mind dreams are valuable possessions. We have anxiety without them.

BIBLIOGRAPHY

Galton, Lawrence, "How Dreams Help Keep Us Sane." *Popular Science,* Vol. CLXXVIII (May, 1961) , pp. 83-86 ff.

"Minimum of Dreaming Found To Be Required." *Science News Letter,* Vol. LXXI (March 17, 1962) , p. 169.

CRUELTY TO CHILDREN [2]

General Purpose: To stimulate
Specific Purpose: To make audience aware of the amount of cruelty children receive.

  I. *Attention*

    A. Story

        1. Two boys age 12 and 10

        2. Beaten for:

          a. Saying same prayer twice

          b. Wearing boots instead of slippers in the house

          c. Breathing through mouth instead of nose—pliers used on nose

          d. Spending too much money—beaten with vacuum cleaner cord

        3. Bodies covered with scars, bruises, and sores

        4. Appearance: thin and pale

---

[2] Sample outline of speech to stimulate, submitted by Frances Kreitzer, student at Ohio University.

B. Statistics
   1. Yes, this is an actual case, one out of thousands that have happened in the last few years.
   2. In 1962, 662 cases were reported in the newspapers. Of these, 25 per cent died. Goodness knows how many cases were not discovered.
   3. Estimated over 100,000 children are mistreated every year—cruelty causes more deaths than auto accidents, leukemia, or muscular dystrophy.
   4. This means that one out of every hundred are mistreated by either neglect, ill-treatment, or assault.
   5. The rate is increasing each year.

II. *Problem*

A. Can we, as normal, comfortable human beings just sit here complacently?
   1. 99 out of every 100 seems to be happy, well-treated, and normal
   2. Why worry about the rest?
B. Cruelty is a course of action causing unnecessary suffering of mind or body to another.
   1. Usually inflicted by kicks, punches, twisting of arms, beating with hammers, belts, burns with cigarettes, irons, or scalding water.
   2. Most common are fractures of arms and legs.
   3. Also common is permanent brain damage.
      a. Report of 71 hospitals
      b. 302 maltreated, 33 died, 85 suffered permanent brain damage
C. Four main reasons why cruelty used
   1. Parent primarily concerned with own needs and pleasures—selfish.
      a. Feel threatened, fatigued, and frustrated by the child's demands.
      b. Inability to love and protect child.
      c. Disappointment—mother wanted lovely daughter

because she was unattractive, but daughter unattractive also.

d. Rejection—see self in child.

e. Jealousy—compete with child for mate's attention
and love.

2. Environmental influences

a. Things not going well.

b. Parents do not get along well.

c. Not enough money for necessities.

d. Drinking.

e. Above cause stress and tension—nearest target is
child.

3. Deep-seated feelings

a. Always angry

b. Bad childhood

4. Child unwanted—highest percentage

a. Stunted children—confined to small playroom or
bedroom for $10\frac{1}{2}$ years

b. Had nice clothes and toys, also pets and a television

c. Now teenagers but not matured—have physiques
and emotions of 9-, 7-, and 5-year-old (now are 18,
15, and 13 chronologically).

d. Little chance of becoming fully mature.

e. From the account all the above reasons had a part
in the cruelty.

III. *Solution*

A. Criteria for solution

1. Acts of cruelty must not be overlooked

2. Innocent child must be protected

B. Plan of action

1. Must recognize problem and then educate each person so he can become a responsible parent.

2. Demand laws requiring doctors to report suspicious
cases to social agencies while protecting doctors.

a. Hesitates because difficult to find proof.

b. His word against parents.

c. Does not want to be sued by parents for slander.

d. At present only 13 states have any kind of laws.
3. Story
   a. Four children missed too much school.
   b. Filthy home
   c. Parents warned
   d. 11 days later cleaned up by help and advice
   e. Happy family was result
   f. Shows that warning and education plays big part in ending cruelty

IV. *Best Solutions*

   A. Education
   B. Rehabilitation

V. *Action*

   A. Awareness of problem—be on guard
   B. Support NSPCC and Childrens Bureau
   C. When children are made to suffer it is not the offending parent alone who is guilty. We are all guilty.

BIBLIOGRAPHY

"Battered Child Syndrome—Child Beating." *Time,* LXXX (July 20, 1962), p. 60.
"Child Battering." *Time,* LXXXV (January 8, 1965), p. 43.
"Mystery of the Stunted Children." *Life,* LIII (August 29, 1962), pp. 63-64.
"Shocking Price of Parental Anger." *Reader's Digest,* LXXXV September, 1964), pp. 181-183.
"Terror Struck Children." *New Republic,* CL (May 30, 1964), pp. 11-13.
"When They're Angry." *Newsweek,* LIX (April 16, 1962), p. 72.

RESOLVED: THAT THE UNITED STATES SHOULD ABOLISH ALL FOREIGN AID [3]

General Purpose: To convince
Specific Purpose: To convince students that the United States should abolish its foreign aid programs

---

[3] Sample outline of speech to convince, submitted by William H. Ford, student at Ohio University.

I. *Attention*

   A. How many of you actually realize what large sums of money are leaving the United States each year?
   B. The following figures are what Congress was asked to appropriate for foreign aid for the fiscal year, 1966.
      1. $1,170 million for military assistance
      2. Economic assistance of $2,210
      3. $1.7 billion for loans
      4. $155 million for international organizations
   C. How can we ever hope to escape a large deficit in our national budget as long as billions of dollars are leaving the United States each year?

II. *Problem*

   A. How many of you ever stopped to examine the countries to which foreign aid is sent? After analyzing our foreign aid program, I resolve that all foreign aid by the United States should be abolished.
   B. To reach this conclusion it is necessary to examine several countries which receive our foreign aid.
      1. The United States is pouring more money into Latin America now than ever before.
      2. Governments receiving our aid are using the money to seize the ownership of private businesses.
      3. Week-by-week losses by government owned businesses in Argentina, Bolivia, Brazil, Columbia, and Venezuela exist.
   C. United States taxpayers are actually paying for losses caused by deficits in nationalized industries or socialism. Is this what you as Americans want? To help finance socialism in foreign countries?
   D. After $2 billion in aid, trouble has arisen for the United States from 4 dictators in 4 countries
      1. Egypt
      2. Algeria
      3. Cambodia
      4. Indonesia

E. The voting record in the United Nations of the countries that we have helped clearly shows that on important issues they have sided with Russia. Are you satisfied to help these countries with aid and then have them side with Russia?

III. *Solution*

A. Because of the gratitude that has been shown for United States foreign aid immediate action must be taken to halt our foreign aid payments.
B. Congressional action to curb this drain on the American money supply must be taken now.
C. If any foreign aid is still to exist, the requirements to obtain it should be made very stiff.

IV. *Best Solution*

A. If immediate action is taken, enormous losses to our money supply could be prevented.
B. Our national debt could decrease.
C. There would be extra money for ending
   1. Slum areas
   2. Water pollution
D. We would all benefit from this extra money saved by abolishing foreign aid.

V. *Action*

A. I say that this action will not be possible unless we all fight.
B. Send petitions to your congressmen.
C. If the proper pressure is applied severely enough, it is possible to abolish foreign aid and prevent the ridicule of the U.S. by foreign countries.

BIBLIOGRAPHY

"Trouble for the U.S. from Four Dictators." *U.S. News and World Report* (January 11, 1965), p. 16 and 59.
Tower, John G., "Let's Stop Financing Socialism in Latin America." *Reader's Digest* (January, 1964), pp. 121-124.

"Foreign Aid Program for 1966." *The Department of State Bulletin* (March 8, 1965), pp. 343-345.

"How Nations Aided by U.S. Vote in the United Nations." *U.S. News and World Report* (August 24, 1964), p. 12.

Suggested Topics for Informative and Persuasive Speeches

E

Thrill Pills
Juvenile Delinquency
What To Do after College
Enlist—Don't Be Drafted
Appreciation of Parents
Police Power
Water Pollution
How to Look for a Summer Job
Animal Talk
Volcanoes and Fissures
Developments in Tire Safety
How to Deceive with Statistics
Computer Dating
St. Patrick (the man)
Mystery of Dreams
Traffic Safety
Communism in the U.S.A.
Population Explosion
Pet Thieves
Cheating in College
Crime and Apathy
Palmistry
Extrasensory Perception
Origin of the Solar System
The Naturalization Process
Mental Illness

Unidentified Flying Objects
Development of Slang Expressions
Graphology
How to Purchase a Car
The Image of the American Abroad
The Decline of Patriotism
The Space Race
The Obsolescence of War
Essential Qualities of a Teacher
Authoritarian vs. Democratic Government
Commercialization of College Athletics
Unethical Advertising Practices
Effect of Credit Cards on American Life
Do We Have a Real Two-Party System in the
    United States?
Vices and Virtues of Medicare
The Balance-of-Payments Deficit
The Role of the College Newspaper
Contemporary Prose and/or Poetry
Commercialization in the Music Industry
Should Everyone Go to College?
The Significance of a National Holiday
Ethics in Big Business
The Greatest Living American
Drugs on the College Campus
Slick Magazines and Declining Morals
Government Regulation of Radio and Television
Frauds in Medicine
Modern Weather-Forecasting Techniques
Several Needed Inventions
Planning Meals Economically

Suggested Topics for Impromptu Speeches | F

I'll Never Do It Again
Deer or Dear Hunting
My Favorite Children's Story
Modern Art
It Pays To Be Honest
Three Ways to Waste Time
If I Made the World
My Feelings about New Year's Resolutions
Three of the Most Important Things I Have Learned about
   People
The Most Important Part of One's Personality
The Joy in Having Lots of Relatives
And Then I Became a Man (Woman)
Three Simple Ideas about a Car That Everyone Should Know
Why Every Man Should (Should Not) Get Married
Three Ways Not to Influence People
Joining the Boy Scouts
God's Gift to Mankind
What I Admire in Women
A Man's Duty to His Country
Why I Like (Do Not Like) to Live in My Town
The Richest Gift My Parents Gave Me
My Prediction for the World Series
My First Love
My Favorite Person
Why I Dislike Yakking Women
Why I Feel a Faith is Important

As a Man Thinketh
What Not To Do in an Emergency
Patience Is a Virtue
My Mother's Best Cooking
Fishing for Fun
I Knew Better
Why Everyone Should Have a Pet
To Drink or Not To Drink
My Most Embarrassing Moment
My Feelings about Cheating on Exams
Students Should (Should Not) Be Allowed To Have Cars on
    Campus
Three Things Not To Do if You Want a Successful Marriage
Three Ways to Relax
Women's Clothes that Disturb Me
The Trials of a Father (Mother)
Three Traits I Admire in a Man
The Joy of Being a Boy (Girl)
I Can't Stand His Type
My Favorite Book
The Best Movie I Ever Saw
Morals on the College Campus
How to Live To Be 100
The Best Teacher I Ever Had
How Not to Get a Job

Suggested Topics for Informative Lectures on Communication | G

Gestures
Visual Aids
Evidence
Types of Reasoning
Speech Mechanism
Ethics of Speaking
Perception
Feedback
Style
Delivery

Persuasion
Memory
Brainstorming
Conference Leadership
Role Playing
Group Dynamics
Group Discussion
Thinking Process
Sociometry
Nonverbal Communication

Suggested Topics for Group Discussions | H

What Is the Relationship between Parent Education and the Curbing of Juvenile Delinquency?

To What Extent Does the R.O.T.C. Program Prepare Adolescents for Military Service?

What Are the Elements To Be Considered in Utilizing Population Control as an International Policy?

To What Extent Does Greek Affiliation Affect the College Student?

What Should the United States Do in Regard to the European Economic Community?

What Should Be the Role of the United States in South American Diplomatic Relations?

How Can the Government Best Control the Increase in Defense Spending?

What Should Be the Role of Student Government as a Control Body on Campus?

How Should the United States Continue its Foreign Policy in the Panama Canal Zone?

To What Extent Should Consumer Credit Be Regulated by Government and Business?

What Is the Effect on the Pupils of Homogeneous Grouping in the Classroom?

How Can the Home Help To Prepare Us for Living in Our Present-day Society?

How Could the Federal Government Transfer Some Executive Responsibilities from the President and Vice-President to Lesser Officials?

How Can We Educate People To Make Better Use of Their Leisure Time?

What Should Be the Role of the United States in Promoting International Government and Peace?

How Can the Loss of Talented Youth between High School and College Be Curbed?

How Can the Present System of Education in the United States Be Improved?

What Are the Factors To Be Considered in the Public Power Versus Private Power Issue?

What Are the Factors To Be Considered in the Economic and Educational Development of Southeast Asia?

What Measures Can Be Taken To Reduce the Accident Rate on Our Nation's Highways?

What Should Be the Future Policy of the United States on Nuclear Test Bans?

What Considerations Should Be Given in Educating the Masses as Opposed to Concentrating Our Education on the Superior or "Gifted" Student?

What Are the Possibilities of a Country Attaining a True Democratic Government?

To What Extent Should Government Farm Subsidies Be Used To Maintain Adequate Food Supply and Prices?

What Action Should the United States Take To Control Illegal Gambling?

What Policies Should the United States Take Toward the Propaganda of the U.S.S.R.?

What Should Be the Federal Government's Policy towards Legalized Abortions?

What Are the Implications in the Sino-Soviet Split?

INDEX